All the Mothers Are One

All the Mothers Are One

Hindu India and the Cultural Reshaping of Psychoanalysis

Stanley N. Kurtz

Foreword by S. J. Tambiah

Columbia University Press   New York

CHRPB IN AUGKMINE

Columbia University Press
New York   Oxford

Copyright © 1992 Columbia University Press
All rights reserved

This book is dedicated to my mother,
Fonda Kurtz,
and to the memory of my father,
Bernard Kurtz.

Contents

List of Illustrations

Foreword
S. J. Tambiah

Psychoanalytic theory has some brilliant contemporary practitioners, but none of them have yet fully tackled the theoretical task that awaits them: to recast and apply those features of classical Freudian theory, especially regarding the dynamics of early childhood experience—which they accept as having *general* import—in terms that are context sensitive to the primary family structures, sociocentric networks, and cultural valuations of different societies. This form of cultural reshaping of the psychoanalytic framework holds the possibility of uncovering childhood development patterns predicated on norms and practices profoundly different from those on which classical psychoanalytic theory was based.

Stanley Kurtz's book is an imaginative, bold, tightly argued attempt that qualifies as an innovative implementation of that program. He demonstrates that current psychoanalytic work on Hindu (and South Asian) societies is still hobbled by a commitment to an underlying account of socialization beholden to the dominance of concepts of individualism, individuation, and primacy of a single mother and child dyad. He demonstrates, among other things, that the systematic exploration of the fact that in the Hindu joint family a multiplicity of women, not a single 'natural' mother, collectively rear children leads to the appreciation that the impetus and goal of development in Hindu society is not individuation but an integration into the collective groups that structure the social order. This key principle also enables him to place Santoshi Ma as a momentary refraction of a larger group of other Hindu goddesses.

Standing on the shoulders of others, Kurtz may be one of the first to break through a theoretical and comparative barrier. His advocacy of a reshaped psychoanalytic anthropology, liberated from the juridical sentence of failed individuation, should inspire other investigators of non-Western societies.

S. J. Tambiah
Professor of Social Anthropology
Harvard University

Acknowledgments

I owe a great deal to Komal Kothari and his family. Komal Kothari introduced me to India and gave me both his hospitality and the benefit of his deep knowledge of the people and culture of Rajasthan. Many thanks also to Vijay Dan Detha and his family, particularly Mahendra Dan Detha. My association with the entire staff of the Rajasthan Institute of Folklore (Rupayan Sansthan), established by Komal Kothari and Vijay Dan Detha, provided me with an extraordinary glimpse into the heart of Indian life. Rupayan Sansthan's diligent efforts to understand and preserve the culture and folklore of Rajasthan have been, and will continue to be, much appreciated by scholars of India everywhere.

I am also grateful to Minu Singh for her expert work transcribing and translating tapes of my field interviews. I thank her as well for the benefit of her deep knowledge of Indian life generally, and of Santoshi Ma's worship in particular. Thanks to Govind Shahi for further help with the transcription and translation of interviews and to Peggy Harrison for typing out transcripts of English translations.

Above all, I express my gratitude to the many devotees of Santoshi Ma—those who ventured occasionally to her temples as well as those regularly blessed by her visitations—who took the time to help me understand the meaning of this goddess and, more important, the meaning of the larger Goddess.

Numerous friends and colleagues in America have supported me and given me the benefit of their response to this work. I am grateful to Eric Feigelson, David Spain, Suzanne Kirschner, Peter Wood, David Hansell, Christopher Atwood, Robert Gorham Davis, Richard Parker, Arthur Kleinman, Robert Goldman, Pauline Kolenda, and Judith Rosenthal, all of whom read and commented upon portions of this book or early versions of it. My sincerest thanks also go to Gioia Stevens of Columbia University Press for her kind and careful assistance and for her faith in this project.

I am particularly indebted to the many teachers who have nurtured my interest in this project over the long term. Wyatt Mac-Gaffey of Haverford College first taught me anthropology and helped inspire me to enter the discipline. Professor Alan Dundes of UC Berkeley gave me crucial training in the application of psychoanalysis to anthropology and has long encouraged my interest in that field. Usha Jain, Karine Schomer, and Bruce Pray taught me Hindi at UC Berkeley and made the difficult process of learning a language into a genuine pleasure. Professor John Hawley gave me the opportunity to present the results of my initial research on Santoshi Ma to a larger audience.

I will always be in debt to professors David Maybury-Lewis and Nur Yalman, who brought me into the Harvard Department of Anthropology and provided me with the training that fundamentally shaped all my subsequent work. Charles Lindholm has also been an invaluable influence and support over the years. I am particularly grateful for his intelligent guidance of my efforts to unite psychology and anthropology. Robert LeVine's thoughtful and enthusiastic support for this work has been of enormous value to me. The interest in my project shown by both Gilbert Herdt and Bertram Cohler of the University of Chicago has been particularly gratifying. Above all, I am grateful to Professor Stanley Tambiah, whose training for, patience with, and generous support of this enterprise have been the condition of its success.

I also wish to thank G. Morris Carstairs, Sudhir Kakar, Alan Roland, Gananath Obeyesekere, and Melford Spiro. Throughout this book I attempt to critique and reshape their psychoanalyses of culture in India and in other parts of the world. However critical of their work I may seem, I acknowledge here my overwhelming debt to their efforts. It is no exaggeration to say that my work would have been impossible without theirs. I hope this book will be seen as a tribute to the extraordinary progress these thinkers have already made in developing a psychoanalysis of culture.

Thank you to Susan Seymour, professor of anthropology at Pitzer College, for allowing me to quote passages from her dissertation, *Patterns of Child-Rearing in a Changing Indian Town*, and to SUNY Press for granting permission to reproduce a passage from "Rapist or Bodyguard, Demon or Devotee?" by Kathleen M. Erndl in Alf Hiltebeitel, ed., *Criminal Gods and Demon Devotees: Essays on the Guardians of Popular Hinduism* (Albany: State University of New York Press, 1989). I am thankful as well to the anonymous reader for Columbia University Press, whose critique of this book prompted a significant expansion of its argument.

I owe a very special debt of gratitude to Gwendolyn Atwood, whose understanding of psychoanalysis and whose facility with the English language were given to me as gifts in the form of frank, thoughtful criticism and enthusiastic encouragement.

Finally, I thank my parents, Bernard Kurtz and Fonda Kurtz, to whom I dedicate this work. In the fullest sense, they educated me. Their love for me and faith in me have made this work possible.

Note on Transliteration

I have tried to keep this book accessible to non-Indologists. Thus, I have used Anglicized spellings for deity names, place names, caste names, and other widely known Hindi terms. Other words in Hindi are italicized and presented according to the conventional system of transliteration. I pluralize Hindi words by adding the English *s*.

Like all deity names, Santoshi Ma's name is presented in Anglicized form. Properly marked it looks like this: *Santoṣī Mā*.

All the Mothers Are One

Chapter 1

Introduction: God in a Stone

In the course of my research on the Hindu goddess Santoshi Ma, I was sometimes told the following story: There was once a simple farmer, who one day observed a priest worshiping an image of god. After watching the worship for some time and with a growing sense of devotion, the farmer asked the priest to give him an image so that he too might worship. The priest, however, seeing no sense in entrusting a divine image to an ignorant farmer, put the man off. Although day after day the priest promised to provide an image, he never fulfilled his pledge. At last, however, the farmer was insistent enough, and the exasperated priest bent down, picked up an ordinary rock, and gave it to the simpleton saying, "This is God."

The happy farmer carried the stone home on his head. After bathing it, he offered it food and milk. The farmer was disappointed, however, that the food he offered never seemed to diminish. His god, he thought, was refusing his gifts. Things went on like this for some time. The farmer fed and cared for the rock, but the rock never ate. Even when the farmer went into town, he took care to see that his children fed the stone. Still, the stone failed to eat. This continued for six days.

Finally, on the seventh day, the farmer decided that if his god was refusing his worship, there was nothing left but to kill himself. So when the stone once again failed to eat, the farmer drew his knife and prepared to take his own life. At just that moment, however, god emerged from the stone and ate the offerings. Thus the farmer was saved by god and by the depth of his own devotion.[1]

This story is interesting not just for its content but for when and why it was told to me. I was researching a goddess I considered "new." Thirty years before, the idea of Santoshi Ma did not exist (Kurtz 1990:37–102).[2] Many older Indians realize that this now-popular goddess was unknown in their childhood. In fact, the chief agent of Santoshi Ma's popularization was a spectacularly successful Hindi-language film based on this goddess's myth. This film was released in 1975, well within the memory of the vast majority of devotees I encountered. Yet when asked about Santoshi Ma's novelty, informants rebelled at the question's implication that a new goddess is also an artificial or humanly created goddess. In response, my informants told me the story of the farmer and the stone.

Hindus use this story to get across the point that God is omnipresent and eternal. Because God is thus, to speak of a particular form of the divine, like Santoshi Ma, as something new makes no sense. Santoshi Ma is simply a part of the everpresent Deity. Similarly, to think that a human being can manufacture an artificial god is also mistaken. This is because everything actually *is* God already. Thus, even when the priest tried to appease the foolish farmer with a simple stone, he actually *was* giving him God. It required only the farmer's naive faith for this truth to be made manifest.[3]

It was quite some time before I came around to this point of view. Santoshi Ma was interesting to me precisely because I thought she was new. I felt certain that her spectacular rise to popularity could reveal something important about the changing nature of Hinduism and thus about the social changes that must lie behind such a shift in ideology. I was wrong.

The trouble began on the airplane, even before I had begun work in the field. I was sitting next to a Hindu woman who had performed Santoshi Ma's fast, or *vrat*. After some talk of Santoshi Ma, she told me that I really ought to go on a pilgrimage to Santoshi Ma's main shrine in Jammu. She described this pilgrimage site in some detail, including the famous cave one had to crawl through to see the divine image of Santoshi Ma. I was delighted to have discovered news of a great Santoshi Ma shrine of which I had not heard in my earlier research. Shortly after landing, however, I was disappointed to find that the shrine this woman had described was actually the chief pilgrimage site of another goddess, Vaishno Devi.

At first I wrote off this incident as a case of misinterpretation or confusion of language. I was sure that the woman had used the name Santoshi Ma in describing this shrine to Vaishno Devi, but I assumed she had either made a mistake or had gone out of her way to please me by using a name for the goddess with which I was familiar.

Time and again, however, experiences such as this were repeated. People would respond to my insistent questioning about Santoshi Ma by mixing up talk of her with a discussion of other goddesses (Brand 1984:9–10; Erndl 1984:11–14; Kurtz 1984:1–2). They would speak about all of these goddesses as if they were named Santoshi Ma. Once I got wind of this pattern, I tried my best to set my informants right. I would stop them and say, "No, you don't understand, I'm asking about Santoshi Ma, specifically Santoshi Ma, only Santoshi Ma and no other." Sometimes, even then, it was difficult for my informants to follow me. When they finally realized what I was getting at, however, they revealed a puzzling sense of incomprehension mixed with what appeared to be an air of gentle mocking. They seemed to be telling me in as kindly a manner as possible that it was absurd to be interested only in Santoshi Ma as if she were not one and the same as all the other goddesses.

More rarely, this sort of exchange provoked another kind of reaction in my informants. When they finally became aware of my peculiar insistence on speaking of the form of the Goddess named Santoshi Ma and no other, their respect for me appeared to rise considerably. "You are a very great man," I was told on one such occasion, seemingly without irony.

Looking back on all this, I can see that the simple farmer was me. Hinduism had casually tossed this naive, earnest graduate student, begging for a divinity on which to do a dissertation, a rock.

"This is God," I was told, and I dutifully began to worship. Something was wrong. I didn't understand. This was only a rock.

I was terribly pleased with my very own special deity, but informants seemed unable to share my exclusive preoccupation with her. Nor did my elaborate attentions seem to be squeezing very much in the way of a response out of my stone. That is to say, all of my attempts to delineate the unique features of this goddess were frustrated. The more I tried to differentiate either her characteristics or her devotees from the theological conception or social location of other deities, the less distinctive her identity came to seem. Santoshi Ma was not taking shape, and her lack of response was driving me into a desperate state of yet more obsessive focus on Santoshi Ma and Santoshi Ma alone.

Shall I be believed if I tell the reader that my sincere but wrongheaded devotion to this stone eventually yielded an epiphany? The retelling of my vision is the task of this book. I shall do my best to rouse a sense of conviction in the reader, and the best strategy for this is a straightforward accounting of how I came to see what I believe I have seen.

Did I see God? Yes and no. I am not a Hindu. I do not "believe" in Santoshi Ma, or any of the other Hindu deities. On the other hand, I do not believe that I was the simple farmer in merely a metaphorical sense. That is, I think our story tells a literal truth about the Hindu *idea* of God. This idea works in precisely the manner Hindus say it does. Their notion of the divine knows neither borders of time, place, substance, nor identity, and this, I think, has consequences for our interpretation of data from the field.

The reason I could not distinguish a specific social or ideological identity for Santoshi Ma is that she is not in fact a separate and distinct divine being. Although she has a particular name and form, these things are of limited significance and do not correspond—as Western thought usually takes them to—to a unique and stable identity. When Hindus freely "mixed" her name with those of "other" deities, they were neither erring nor merely trying to please me (although my level of interest and understanding *were* affecting their choice of name). They were simply operating on the complex notion of a multiformed great Goddess in their accustomed manner.

It was only my insistent naïveté that permitted me to grasp this.

Had I moved too quickly into the knowing, Western, scholarly terminology of identification of one goddess with another, I would never have been able to abandon my underlying individualist assumptions. That is, I would have retained the conviction that novel social forces explain the rise of Santoshi Ma, simply presuming, in the face of evidence to the contrary, that such forces were disguised or absorbed by the tendency to identify distinctly new goddesses with old ones. Such unsubstantiated suppositions have for too long been operative in scholarly encounters with the Goddess's many forms (Kurtz 1990:37–102). Only by taking the simpler path of the farmer was I able to realize that the traditional scholarly tools for the explanation of a seemingly new deity's rise were flawed in the case of Hinduism—Santoshi Ma, properly understood, is neither a new goddess nor even a goddess separate from any other. My refusal and/or inability to get too smart too fast helped me in the end to see God. It worked for me for the same reason that it worked for the farmer. Precisely because the Hindu notion of deity, in the deepest sense, really is everywhere, sincere and concentrated attention to any small piece of reality, no matter how misconceived initially, is bound to lead to the larger truth behind it. The moment I finally saw Santoshi Ma was also the moment she dissolved back into the larger notion of Goddess from which she came. I finally understood why my informants had seemed to confuse her so with her fellow deities. These informants, as we have seen, understood from the start both the foolishness and the potential for wisdom in my own puzzling way of approaching the greater Goddess.

It was only after having seen and thus dissolved Santoshi Ma back into her source that I was able to make sense of her. Only then was I able to "classify" her in relation to her fellow divine beings. Indeed, once she had been dissolved, I realized that my real problem was the classification of all goddesses—or rather, the classification of the everchanging manifestations of the single great Goddess. It is this larger problem to which my attention was ultimately turned. The results, however, were very different for having come from my epiphany of diversity in unity.

There is another sense in which I think my method works, like the farmer's, by not understanding too quickly. In this study, I employ both structuralist and psychoanalytic theory. My use of these methodologies, so notorious for their Western origins and biases, is related, paradoxically, to my persistent refusal to lapse into the individualist terminology of deity identification when something that was incomprehensible in my frame of reference was going on in front of me. This is because the very awareness of cultural difference, which makes it possible to take seriously the Hindu idea that individuality is an illusion, blocks an unquestioning and uncurious acceptance of this alien point of view. It is not sufficient, therefore, to take a strictly hermeneutical route, restricting oneself to mere interpretation and explication from "the native point of view." For this would be to deny or disguise the fact that the assumptions at the base of the native point of view are neither fully shared by me nor, initially at least, comprehensible to me.

It is no longer fashionable to ask "Why?" "Why do they think and act that way?" This is so because such questions seem always to lead us to reduce the phenomena in question to another order of reality, our reality. The truth is, however, that we do secretly still ask ourselves "Why?" Our very insistence, in fact, on dealing with the substance of an alien ideology on its own terms contains the admission that these terms are not our own. How then, unless we face the gulf between points of view honestly, can we hope for anything other than a contrived tolerance?

I maintain that a truer sort of understanding comes from acknowledging and playing out the genuine tensions and contradictions between the points of view of observer and observed. Only by fighting ideas that strike us as absurd and alien can we ultimately grasp them. Only by initially forcing the theoretical systems that encapsulate our culture's view of reality onto alien material can we hope to reform those very theories so that they may do justice to what we know of the "other" while still being true to the beliefs we must confess we continue to hold.

Thus, I attempt to move in this book toward a new sort of structuralist psychoanalysis, a theoretical synthesis that blends these two Western points of view with each other while also transforming them into something new in light of what we are about to learn of another culture's outlook. The product of this synthesis should be a new psychology of Hinduism.

I argue, then, that a solution to the riddle of Santoshi Ma's apparent rise to popularity is coterminous with a solution to several larger questions. Santoshi Ma is, ultimately, a single stone out of which we may draw an understanding of Hindu divinity at large. As we come to understand Santoshi Ma, we comprehend more deeply that she is of a piece with the larger Goddess and that she reveals the pattern and meaning of the Goddess's capacity for diverse manifestation.

Insight into the precise nature of the Goddess's unified diversity in turn gives us a crux around which to build a combination and transformation of structuralist and psychoanalytic approaches to Hindu life. Structuralist studies of India as well as my Hindu informants stress the primacy of a divine or human being's relationship to the social whole (Dumont 1970a, 1970b, 1980). Consistent with this, structuralist studies concerning the Hindu context discount the existence of independent, individual essences. If an individualist Western psychoanalysis could be reworked in such a way as to incorporate this perspective, we might produce an explanation of the origins of Hindu divinity that satisfies the disenchanted modern mind while also doing justice to the truths of Hindu life embodied in the kaleidoscopic Hindu system of deity production. From this new perspective, for example, we can come to understand how the complex identity transformation among divine Hindu mothers rests on an equally complex unified diversity obtaining among human mothers in the Hindu family.

In this book, then, I wish to rework our Western psychoanalysis in light of a structuralist interpretation of Hindu divinity. Our analysis begins with the problem of Santoshi Ma's origin, yet it goes beyond this, for Santoshi Ma ultimately dissolves herself into the larger Goddess of which she is but a moment. Our structuralist reworking of psychoanalysis thus solves the riddle of Santoshi Ma, and it also—and necessarily so—suggests a much broader understanding of the Hindu world. Here follows, then, a synopsis of the course of our inquiry.

Chapter 2, "Santoshi Ma Dissolved—The Goddess Constituted," shows the problem of explaining Santoshi Ma's phenomenal "rise" by reference to fundamental historical or sociological changes to be a false one. Santoshi Ma, it is argued, is anomalous neither in respect of her devotees nor her character. The birth of this goddess is simply one example of the ongoing process inherent in the Hindu notion of deity itself, a process whereby various conventional permutations of the traditional Goddess are created out of and absorbed into one another. It is Santoshi Ma's base in the modern medium of film rather than any distinctive quality that accounts for the notably rapid spread of this manifestation of the traditional Goddess. Above all, the reason for this is that while Santoshi Ma's cinematic portrayal is somewhat unorthodox, her day-to-day worship in homes and temples is entirely ordinary.

Thus, the riddle of Santoshi Ma's "rise" is resolved into the question of how and why her film was able to play in an unconventional and yet successful way on Hindu attitudes toward the Goddess. I suggest that the ambiguous nature of film as a medium in India gave the movie about Santoshi Ma license to draw out a core ambiguity in the Hindu image of the Goddess—her diversified unity.

Toward the close of chapter 2, I attempt to establish the traditional nature of Santoshi Ma by constructing a new classification of Hindu goddesses. This scheme of classification serves to fit Santoshi Ma into her proper and unproblematic context. Beyond this, however, the suggested organizational scheme for the permutations within the larger Hindu Goddess illuminates the underlying tension between unity and diversity in her image. This tension, generally disguised in ordinary worship, is what the film about Santoshi Ma so successfully exploits and exposes.

To solve the riddle of Santoshi Ma's popularity and to fully understand her relation to other goddesses, we must gain insight into the tension between unity and diversity within the image of the Goddess. In two chapters on Hindu child-rearing practices, "Psychoanalytic Approaches to Hindu Child Rearing: A Critique" and "Renunciation on the Way to the Group: A New Approach to Early Hindu Childhood" (chapters 3 and 4), I lay the groundwork of a psychological explanation of this tension. I assume that attitudes toward divine mothers, i.e., goddesses, are rooted in childhood attitudes toward human mothers.

This link between human and divine mothering is central to the work of G. Morris Carstairs (1967) and Sudhir Kakar (1978), two of the most important psychoanalytic students of Hindu Indian culture. However, whereas these scholars understand the Hindu orientation toward the group as the dangerous persistence of an early tie to the mother, I argue that Hindu child rearing actually promotes a psychic movement of the child away from exclusive attachment to the natural mother and toward a more mature participation in the life of the family group. Unfortunately, traditional analysts generally miss the distinctive Hindu method of breaking the early tie between mother and child. This is because psychoanalytic observers keep their focus on the failure of Hindu parents to directly refuse requests made by their children. However, the analysts overlook the subtle ways in which the natural mother pushes her child toward a voluntary renunciation of infantile pleasures. They also miss the strategies by which the larger family pulls the child out of its attachment to the mother and into a more mature participation in collective life. I call this complex, unforced movement of the Hindu child away from the natural mother and toward the group *renunciation*. A sense of immersion in a unified group of "mothers" thus provides no evidence of Hindu symbiosis or pathology; instead, it is the outcome of a gradual and culturally distinctive process of maturation for the Hindu child.

It is the attainment of a mature sense of immersion in a group of family women that Hindus emphasize and celebrate when they tell us that "all the goddesses are one." Yet the diversity within the image of the Goddess is built out of the tension between the early, unmodified attachment to the natural mother and the later movement toward what I call the in-law mothers of the family as a whole, that is, toward the other women in the joint family.[4] Santoshi Ma's film gained success because of its ability to probe beneath the mature surface of unity, thereby activating feelings deriving from a period when the exclusive attachment to the natural mother and the antagonism toward her female rivals in the group were still in force.

In chapter 5, entitled "The Ek-Hi Phase," I develop a theory of early Hindu psychology based on the foregoing examination of Hindu child-rearing practices as well as on an analysis of Hindu ritual and myth. The goal of the ek-hi phase is the aforementioned psychic movement away from the natural mother and toward the larger group of mothers in the Hindu joint family. In the chapter on the ek-hi phase, I show in detail how Santoshi Ma's film and myth play on the tensions worked out during this period of development, a period that corresponds to the Western pre-oedipal phase. Also, in building up a model of the Hindu ek-hi phase, I undertake a detailed reshaping of the psychological mechanism known as *splitting*. This reworked understanding of splitting allows us to add particulars to the classification of goddesses presented in rudimentary form in chapter 2.

Treatment of the ek-hi phase is followed by chapter 6, "The Durga Complex." In that chapter the Hindu stage of development corresponding to our Western oedipal period is discussed. While the themes in Santoshi Ma's myth are chiefly suggestive of ek-hi conflicts, the concept of the Durga complex enables us to make sense of central themes in the mythology of many other goddesses. Ultimately, however, the tension between exclusive attachment to the natural mother and attachment to the larger family group (including the natural mother) is identified as the theme that underlies and unites all stages of Hindu child development and all types of Goddess imagery.

In the Durga complex, the tension between the boy's tie to the natural mother and his tie to the collective women of the joint family is played out through images of self-castration. Analysts, such as Carstairs and Kakar, have interpreted such self-castration imagery as evidence of a pathological, unresolved "negative Oedipus complex." I argue, however, that Hindu self-castration imagery actually indicates a movement toward healthy masculinity by way of the culturally distinctive developmental principle I call renunciation. In this view, images of phallic sacrifice in Hindu myth and ritual do not signal defensive retreats from masculinity but voluntary renunciations of the incestuous tie in favor of a mature psychic movement into the life of the larger family group.

A comprehensive solution to the riddle posed by the rise of Santoshi Ma thus requires a broad reorientation toward the psychological theories often used to explain Hindu religious imagery. Just as understanding Santoshi Ma requires a renewed focus on the oneness of the Goddess, so, too, the problem of Santoshi Ma bids us rethink the place of the group in psychological theory. As I set forth a psychological explanation for the diversified unity of the Goddess, then, I rework traditional psychoanalytic theory in an attempt to purge it of the Western individualism that makes its application to

Hindu materials so problematic. By the end of the chapter on the Durga complex, the problem of Santoshi Ma has been resolved and integrated into this larger effort to understand psyche and culture. The conclusion of the chapter on the Durga complex thus serves to round off the systematic developmental psychology of Hinduism offered in this book.

The last three chapters are applications of the psychological system presented in chapters 1 through 6. In chapter 7, "Clinical Psychoanalysis in India: Toward a New Reading," I show how an awareness of the tension between the natural mother and the in-law mothers leads to a new understanding of clinical psychoanalyses with individual Hindu Indian patients. This reinterpretation of clinical case studies by analysts like Sudhir Kakar (1979, 1980, 1989, 1990a, 1990b) and Alan Roland (1988) adds depth and conviction to the critique of traditional psychoanalytic theories of Indian culture presented in chapters 1 through 6.

In chapter 8, "South Asia and Beyond: Obeyesekere and Spiro," I offer a detailed critique of work by two eminent psychoanalysts of culture. The goal here is to bring my systematic interpretation of Hindu psychology into explicit relation to the most general problems in comparative psychoanalysis. This is because, in my view, the final fruit of our investigation of Santoshi Ma is a new general approach to the cross-cultural use of psychoanalytic theory. A careful critique of Obeyesekere and Spiro makes it possible to illustrate the full comparative implications of this approach. In chapter 8, for example, I argue that the notion of a Durga complex permits us to see profound cultural variation in what has previously been treated as a pan-cultural group of oedipal emotions. The idea of a Durga complex reveals the distinctive nature of the Hindu case by clarifying the decisive role played by the group in the life of the Hindu child. A group-oriented analysis of other cultures would therefore allow for a similar reworking of universalist oedipal theory.

In chapter 9, "Toward a Cultural Reshaping of Psychoanalysis," I state positively, rather than through critique, the general principles of a suggested new comparative psychoanalysis. The argument here is presented in clear and simple terms. The chapter sets forth, but does not recapitulate, the position outlined in the book as a whole. We arrive at the same conclusion as that offered in the body of the book but move forward by way of an examination of the comparative problem of love in psychoanalytic theory. In this chapter, there is no detailed examination of Indian ethnographic material. The chapter ends with a brief reflection on what our culturally reshaped psychoanalysis may or may not be able to tell us about the problem of balancing career and motherhood, and about the related issue of group child care, in contemporary America.

Above all, then, this book is about groups—groups of parents and groups of deities. I argue here that the endless generation of seemingly new Hindu deities (a process that ultimately forces one to a recognition of their underlying unity) recapitulates, reinforces, affirms, and celebrates an earlier process in which the Hindu child moves beyond an exclusive attachment to the natural mother and toward a mature sense of immersion in a diverse, yet unified, group of mothers in the Hindu joint family. For us, then, the diversified unity of Hindu deities will act as a window onto the complex, unconscious representation of the parental group in the Hindu mind. In order to gain such insight, however, the pervasive individualism in our theories of deity formation and in our theories of psychology must be recognized and recast in order to accommodate the distinctive conditions of Hindu social life. Taking the lesson of the simple farmer, we put our faith in the Hindu notion of God and use that faith to dissolve the boundaries that only seem to divide one part of the Hindu world from another.

Chapter 2

Santoshi Ma Dissolved— the Goddess Constituted

My fieldwork yielded two "rock bottom" experiences on which I have built my approach to the Hindu Goddess. Each of these experiences has the same root: the frequently stressed idea that all the goddesses are one. In this "all are one" perspective, each "individual" goddess is merely an aspect of the larger Goddess that ultimately encompasses these partial forms. The first of my two crucial field experiences was described above. I am referring to the tendency of informants to "mix up" the identity of Santoshi Ma and "other" goddesses in the course of discussion and worship (Brand 1984:9–10; Erndl 1984:11–14; Kurtz 1984:1–2). The second experience followed on my attempts to delineate the distinctive nature of Santoshi Ma through questions about a cinematic variant of her myth.

Whatever her prehistory may have been, the effective beginning of the worship of Santoshi Ma came with the publication, somewhere around 1962, of small pamphlets in the vernacular containing her basic myth and ritual (Kurtz 1990:37–102). In 1975 this myth became the basis of a film about Santoshi Ma. This film enjoyed enormous commercial success. In the course of its transfer to the screen, however, the myth underwent some important changes. To wit, a story involving a dispute between Santoshi Ma and three revered and traditional Hindu goddesses, Lakshmi, Parvati, and Brahmani, was grafted onto the original myth.

Early scholarly notice of Santoshi Ma focused on the breadth and rapidity of her rise, which was attributed in great part to the popularity of the film (Kurtz 1990:1–143). The spectacular nature of Santoshi Ma's success was almost uniformly taken as *prima facie* evidence of some novelty in her character. The film's dispute theme, moreover, seemed to highlight an opposition to older goddesses.

Following the trend of this early scholarship, I sought to elucidate distinctions between Santoshi Ma and more traditional Hindu goddesses by asking devotees about the film's theme of dispute among the goddesses. I was encouraged in this by the opportunity to see the film with an Indian audience. It was clear from the audience reaction that the scenes of the goddesses' dispute were particularly relished. It seemed obvious that the dispute motif was at the root of the film's success and thus at the root of the popularity of Santoshi Ma herself.

To my surprise, however, ordinary devotees of Santoshi Ma, including many who had seen and cherished the film, criticized, denied, or forgot the upshot of the dispute between the goddesses. Again and again I was told that the scenes of dispute had been added on by the filmmakers for strictly commercial purposes. Such fighting between goddesses could never really take place, devotees of Santoshi Ma assured me, because all of the goddesses are really part of the same larger Goddess: "All of the goddesses are one."

On the one hand, I could not accept my informants' response at face value. The dispute scenes were vital to the plot and success of the film. The film as a whole was uniformly revered, and clearly the spectacular rise to prominence of Santoshi Ma depended in very great measure on the success of the film. Nonetheless, I had to reckon with the intensity and uniformity of my informants' response to close questioning about these scenes in the film.

I had to grant my informants, moreover, that in actual worship the "all are one" theme did seem to win out. In her temples as well as in private homes, worship of Santoshi Ma was part and parcel of the worship of the great Goddess in all her forms. In these contexts, as we have already seen, Santoshi Ma's identity was blended inextricably with that of other goddesses—sometimes, in fact, with the very same goddesses to whom she was opposed in the film.

I finally realized that the notion of the ultimate unity of the Goddess could not simply be dismissed as a truism. I could not put this question on the backburner while devoting my attention to a delineation of Santoshi Ma's distinctive nature. It would be necessary to bring the idea that all the goddesses are one into the center of the analysis. Only after I began taking the idea that all the goddesses are one seriously was I liberated from the futile effort to explain Santoshi Ma's rise according to conventional historical or sociological theories.

The typical historical approach to the problem of Santoshi Ma and to the problem of seemingly new deities generally has been sustained by scholars in the field of history of religions (Kurtz 1990:37–46). In this view, there is a kind of cyclical process of development wherein a deity emerges from worship by common village people, including women and those of low caste, eventually to gain acceptance by men and Brahmans—those, in other words, representing the more literate, urban, and Sanskritic tradition. As a popular deity moves through this process of Sanskritization, its rougher features are said to be softened. It grows less malevolent, for example, and is less likely to accept impure offerings of meat or alcohol. To encourage this process of Sanskritization, the deity is identified with the revered gods and goddesses of the so-called great tradition. Eventually, with success on a broad scale, the deity grows distant from the needs of ordinary people. This, then, initiates a new cycle. To replace a now ossified deity, a new one emerges from the "little" tradition of the villages.

Much of the early scholarship on Santoshi Ma sought to make sense of her rise along the lines of this model (Kurtz 1990:37–46). From my new perspective, however, the data did not fit. More important, there was no *need* for them to fit. The realization that Santoshi Ma was not a *distinct* being meant that she could not be a *novel* being. This is what my informants had been trying to tell me through the story of the simple farmer. Once the lesson began to take, I could see that Santoshi Ma had not gradually gained the features of a Sanskritic deity. Rather, seemingly contradictory features said to characterize deities from either the "great" or the "little" tradition had been present simultaneously and from the beginning in a complex and shifting sort of divine character. From the very start, Santoshi Ma had been created as an aspect of an ongoing larger Goddess whose character of its very nature shifts from moment to moment and context to context.

Far more difficult for me than the abandonment of the historian's approach was the liberation from the point of view of the sociologist. As long as I continued to think of Santoshi Ma as a separate and thus as a new, deity, it seemed necessarily to follow that her rise would have to be traced to some changing social situation. I set about to determine the social location of her devotees, certain that their unique situation would make sense of this goddess's new-found popularity. I was sufficiently sure that such an explanation would emerge to ignore the repeated assurances of informants that Santoshi Ma's devotees were no different than the followers of other deities. Only after the complete frustration of my efforts to define her unique social situation did I begin to pay attention to the devotees who had told me all along that "all the goddesses are one."

All this brought me back to the work of Louis Dumont. I recalled that in an early analysis of a popular South Indian deity, Dumont had argued against explaining the contradictions in a deity's character by reference to historical movement from a "great" to a "little" tradition (Dumont 1970a). Instead, Dumont offered a structural explanation, linking changes in divine character to contextual shifts in a given deity's relationship to other beings. Combining this with Dumont's later work on the absence of the normative individual from Hindu Indian thinking (Dumont 1970b, 1980), I realized that the entire problem of Santoshi Ma's rise was a false one. Santoshi Ma was not a distinct individual, and because of this, she was not new. Her complex character made sense as a variant of the unified yet shifting and complex overall conception of a larger Goddess. She was simply born into the living matrix of this complex larger Goddess, so to speak, and had no need of explanation. The solution was clear, yet doubts remained.

No matter how much I sought to liberate myself from the notion that Santoshi Ma was a distinct and therefore novel being, I was confronted by the historical reality of "her" appearance on the scene in 1962 and her spectacular success since 1975. Even if it was true that her distinct name, myth, and ritual were really of a piece with that of other similar goddesses, why should another nondifferent goddess have been needed, and why should a traditional deity have gained such spectacular popularity under a new form?

The first response to these problems was the realization that our knowledge of Santoshi Ma's recent historical appearance does not change the fact that she functions in the current system as a consistent part of a unified structure. It is a mistake to confuse our notion of history with that of the Hindus. Even when our historians grant that Durga is an ancient goddess, they do not mean "ancient" in the same sense as do Hindus. We do not believe that Durga originated in the infinite past, any more than we believe in similar origins for Santoshi Ma. Each of these goddesses is historically "new" from our scholarly perspective. Yet each is also part of a consistent and unified structure of ideas about time and identity. It would be a mistake to break into this system by analyzing its operations according to our notions of time.

This point, however, while correct and important, continues to leave doubts. The mind rebels. Santoshi Ma, even as a new form for something old, even as part of a unified system of supposedly ancient or eternal deities, is nevertheless *new*. How can this novelty be explained?

The answer to this question brings us back to the circumstances of Santoshi Ma's birth as a child of the modern print and film media. Santoshi Ma, I came to realize, is simply a single instance of a recurrent phenomenon in Hinduism—the birth of seemingly new deities (Kurtz 1990:1–143). This process is an endemic feature of the system and rarely calls for sociological or even historical explanation. The difference in Santoshi Ma's case is simply one of degree. The root of her spectacular success is less any unique feature of her character than the fact that its base in modern media has propelled her across traditional regional boundaries in a relatively short period. In Santoshi Ma we have an example of how modern media are able to raise the ordinary and endemic process of the multiplication of deities to a higher power. The ability of these media to swiftly spread news of Santoshi Ma to a wider public has contributed to the creation of a false sociological problem. Santoshi Ma is not new because the creation of new versions of old deities is itself not new. In Santoshi Ma's case we are simply seeing the traditional process through a magnifying glass, so to speak.

We are back, then, to sociology. There *is* a sociological explanation for the rise of Santoshi Ma. It has to do, however, with the effect of social change on the media in which deities are represented. The sociological attempt to explain the rise of Santoshi Ma as a distinct or novel being is not wrong because sociology is "wrong" but because the constitution of Santoshi Ma as a *distinct being* subject to sociological analysis is itself misconceived.

Still, there are problems. It is true that Santoshi Ma is actually one of a number of deities who have been given broad new popularity because of their connection to the modern media of print and film (Kurtz 1990:103–143). Granting this, however, it must still be admitted that the degree and swiftness of Santoshi Ma's success are unusual. The key to this, moreover, is obviously the film. While it is true that Santoshi Ma in worship and conception is of a piece with the greater Goddess, her portrayal in the film as a goddess disputing with traditional goddesses is both unusual and a clear source of the success of the film. The novel nature of the film spread Santoshi Ma's popularity. Having been thus publicized, however, Santoshi Ma's worship remained entirely conventional and fully integrated in the worship of traditional goddesses. Thus we must come to understand the appeal of the film's unorthodox presentation of deity. Although Santoshi Ma's actual worship is entirely conventional, the initial and unusual spread of her popularity is attributable to the transformation the medium of film was able to work on the more "orthodox" written myth about her.

The particular characteristics of film as a mythic medium, I shall argue, made possible the unique transformation of Santoshi Ma's myth. Film in India is not treated as a profane medium. During showings of Santoshi Ma's film, the theater is transformed into a kind of temple, and the act of seeing the film is often taken to be worship (Dharap 1983:79).[1] On the other hand, in the minds of ordinary Hindus, the fact that film is a commercial medium places it at a lower level of power and purity than other means of worship.[2] The ambiguous nature of film, therefore, permitted the transformation of a conventional goddess myth into a myth that was both more exciting and more controversial than the more ordinary variety. The mode of analysis I shall offer, then, does more than simply treat different versions of a single myth as variants of a common structure (Levi-Strauss 1963:217). Different versions of myth *are* variants of a single structure. Careful attention to medium and context, however, permits one to peer down through tensions and ambiguities in the reactions to different versions of a myth into successively deeper layers of conscious and unconscious conflict.

The problem of the rise of a seemingly new goddess, then, has been transformed into a problem of the transformations worked by different media of presentation on the mythic structure of traditional goddess worship. These transformations do not yield a new being. Rather, they allow us to see, if only for a moment, more deeply into the nature of an old being. But what exactly does this mean? What are we trying to find out?

We need to know the source of the endemic multiplication of Hindu deities as well as the nature and meaning of their ultimate unity. These two problems are inseparable although not usually treated as such. Most efforts to classify Hindu deities, and particularly Hindu goddesses, set aside the problem of their ultimate unity and go about drawing distinctions between diverse types. I shall argue, however, that only by understanding the nature of divine unity can we clarify the process and content of divine diversification. Indeed, understanding the common thread underlying and interrelating all deity production is the problem at hand. For we purchased our sociological solution to the rise of Santoshi Ma only at the price of undertaking to solve yet another puzzle. If Santoshi Ma is a particular instance of the general process of divine multiplication, how and why does that process work, and precisely where does Santoshi Ma fit into it?

This issue of classification has already been raised in the scholarly literature on Santoshi Ma. For example, those who have tried to trace Santoshi Ma's rise to processes of social change have also argued that this goddess's characteristics are novel with respect to accepted categories of the divine. Specifically, it has been claimed that Santoshi Ma, who is both without a husband and predominantly benevolent in character, is an unusual sort of goddess (Das

1980:54). According to the prevailing view, in other words, benevolent goddesses are generally represented as wives, and more ambiguous or malevolent goddesses are represented as unmarried.

I shall argue, however, that Santoshi Ma is the decisive anomaly for a system of divine classification coming under increasingly serious criticism in the field of Indology. Taking off from the problematic of Santoshi Ma's case and making particular use of the special characteristics of the dispute between the goddesses in the film about Santoshi Ma, I shall offer a new system for the classification of Hindu goddesses. More than this, I hope to account for the structure and dynamics of this system by rooting it at one level in the tensions and constraints of the kinship system, and, at a still deeper level, in the structure of the Hindu psyche.

This system of goddess classification and its accompanying explanation will do more than simply order the goddesses with respect to one another and more than simply dissolve Santoshi Ma into her natural and unproblematic context. It will explain, as no one has really attempted to explain before, why informants return again and again to the insight that all the goddesses are one. It will also show how this stress on unity is tied to the specific content of goddess difference. Thus we shall reveal the social and psychological roots of Hinduism's kaleidoscopic yet somehow unified system of deity multiplication.

There are two ways in which Santoshi Ma prompts us to rethink the generally agreed upon classification of Hindu goddesses into benevolent, married and malevolent, unmarried types. First, as noted, Santoshi Ma herself is a predominantly benevolent goddess who is represented without a husband. Second, in the film about her, she is opposed to three married goddesses who are quite explicitly malevolent. It would be tempting, therefore, to see the film as a simple reversal of ordinary goddess roles. There is some truth to this, and I do think the film highlights aspects of the two goddess categories that are generally *somewhat* submerged. What really makes the film risqué, however, is not so much the character of its goddesses as the fact that they are explicitly placed in opposition to one another. The malevolence of married goddesses and the benevolence of single goddesses is, in fact, far more widespread than the traditional system of goddess classification allows. While scholars are increasingly pointing to this lacuna in the current model, no satisfactory new system has been introduced.[3]

The classification of Hindu goddesses into married, benevolent and unmarried, malevolent types is preeminently the work of Lawrence Babb (1970, 1975:215–230). Whatever its difficulties, Babb's classification has held up for so long because it contains a great deal of truth. Goddesses do seem to be divided into married and unmarried types. Moreover, Hinduism does echo with powerful themes of dangerous female sexuality and the need for husbands to "tame" that sexual danger. This is the source of Babb's association between marriage and benevolence and his opposition of these features to unmarried malevolence.

The character of the Goddess in her various manifestations, however, defeats this classificatory scheme with troubling consistency. Returning to Babb's original work, we can see how he finessed these complexities from the outset. When Babb encounters malevolence in married goddesses, for example, he stresses the ways in which this malevolence is ultimately "tamed" (1975:223). Thus Babb moves from an initial acknowledgment of ambiguity in married goddesses to an eventual picture of them as almost completely benevolent.

In the matter of single goddesses, the problem is deeper still. Babb focuses here on Kali, who is particularly ferocious in character, while underplaying the much more mixed characteristics of Durga (1975:219–222). More significant, Babb simply glosses over the fact that Kali is frequently represented standing on the body of her prone husband Shiva. In fact, she is pictured thus in an illustration in Babb's own book (1975:220). Thus, by his own criterion of iconographic representation (1975:222), the preeminent example of the malevolent goddess would seem to be classifiable as a married goddess! Clearly, despite its significant merits, Babb's system needs reconsideration and reformulation.

The key to such a reformulation, to my way of thinking, lies in the work of Lynn Bennett on the status of women within the structure of the Nepali Hindu system of kinship (1983), a system that closely resembles the one found throughout much of Hindu India (Aziz 1985:217; Friedlander 1985:160). The title of Bennett's work, *Dangerous Wives and Sacred Sisters*, encapsulates her thesis. Bennett elaborates two sets of female status set against each other and in tension within the overall system of kinship. On the one hand, women are conceived of according to a dominant, patrifocal model. From this perspective, women are seen as not entirely trustworthy additions to joint families structured by descent through males. Because the interests of the woman marrying into a family are at first more directly connected to those of her husband than to those of her husband's larger household, which is headed by her father-in-law, the wife is perceived as potentially subversive to the solidarity of the family. She always poses the danger, it is feared, of influencing her husband to weaken the joint family by demanding a partition of its holdings.

On the other hand, according to Bennett, women are also perceived from the point of view of a less pronounced but still important filiofocal perspective. In this outlook, women are seen not as wives or in-laws but as daughters and sisters. From this viewpoint, women provide no long-term, concrete benefits to the household although, on this very account, neither do they present a danger. The young daughter produces merit for the father who gives her away to the family of her husband, and as a sister she provides spiritual protection for her brother. The young girl as sister and daughter also provides her father and brothers with a personal relationship to a woman that is relatively free of the restraint demanded by the decorum of married adults within the Hindu joint family.

The symbol of the distinction between these two points of view, we might say, is the difference between the protected, restrained, veiled state of a woman as a wife and daughter-in-law in her husband's household, and her uncovered, relatively unrestrained, affectionate behavior when she returns on periodic visits to her natal household.

For Bennett, these two perspectives on women, the dominant patrifocal model and the subsidiary filiofocal model, are symbolically mediated through the role of the mother. In producing offspring for the continuation of the patriline running through her father-in-law and husband, a daughter-in-law and wife redeems herself and counters her dangerous potential for the solidarity of the joint family. In doing so, she draws farther away from her natal household, while at the same time fulfilling and deepening the merit acquired by the father who gave her away.

The curious thing about Bennett's opposition between dangerous wives and sacred sisters is that it runs quite counter to the traditional classification of goddesses offered by Babb (Paul 1984:1001). For Babb, the married pole is benevolent and the single pole malevolent. For Bennett, the situation is reversed. This contradiction is a significant problem for Bennett herself because she seeks to link her oppositions between female roles to Babb's traditional classification of goddesses (Bennett 1983:261–318). The system falls apart, however, because of the fundamental contradiction between the two points of view.

Although I believe she herself has not seen its full implications for the classification of goddesses, Bennett's work sheds a remarkable light on the problem of Santoshi Ma. The conflict in the film between Santoshi Ma and the three married goddesses is a prototypical representation of the opposition between dangerous wives and sacred sisters. The connection is all the more impressive when we realize that Santoshi Ma in the film is a sister-daughter goddess. She is created on the brother-sister festival of *Rakshā Bandhan* in order that Ganesh's sons may have a sister with whom to celebrate this festival, and she is the daughter of Ganesh.

The reason for the film's popularity, then, is that it taps into the opposition, which is usually more mediated, between the patrifocal and filiofocal models of women. In general, *all* goddesses are mothers, and at the end of the film about Santoshi Ma, it is this quality of motherhood that eventually connects the goddesses and ends their conflict. Specifically, it is emphasized that Parvati is the mother of Santoshi Ma's father, Ganesh. During most of the film, however, all the contradictions between Bennett's two models of Indian women are given an unusual degree of overt expression without the mediating quality of motherhood that brings them together. This gives the film its exciting yet controversial quality.

I am not arguing here that Babb's classification of goddesses ought to be rejected in favor of Bennett's. Bennett's reversal of the poles of benevolence and malevolence goes too far. She underplays, for example, the danger represented by the virgin daughter to her natal household (Yalman 1963). Her work, however, provides the advantage of specifying some of the features of goddesses that constantly emerge to subvert Babb's classic model. With the aid of Bennett's

FIGURE 1

Goddess Classification Scheme

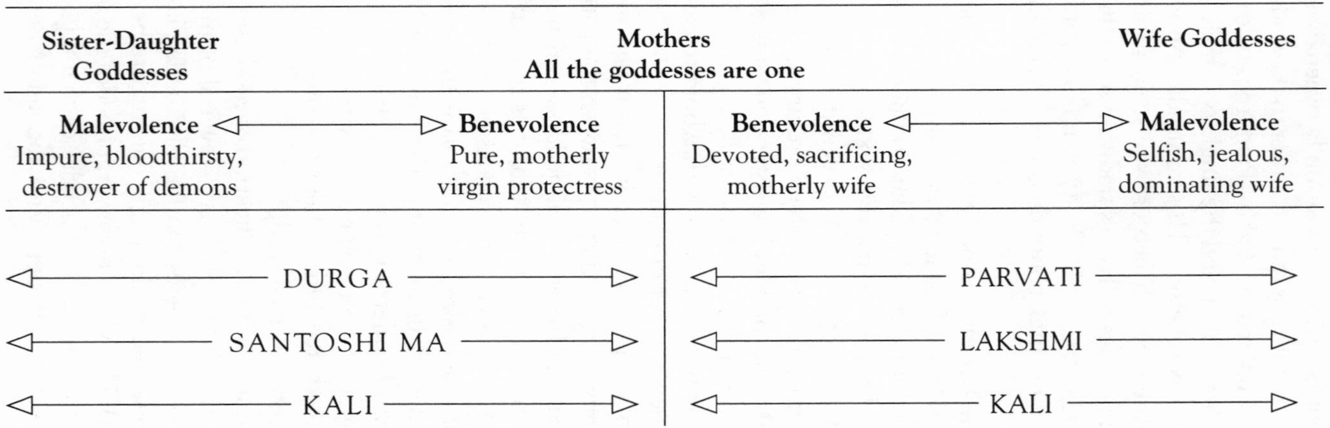

Sister-Daughter Goddesses	Mothers All the goddesses are one		Wife Goddesses
Malevolence Impure, bloodthirsty, destroyer of demons	**Benevolence** Pure, motherly virgin protectress	**Benevolence** Devoted, sacrificing, motherly wife	**Malevolence** Selfish, jealous, dominating wife
DURGA		PARVATI	
SANTOSHI MA		LAKSHMI	
KALI		KALI	

work, it is now possible to construct a new model that is complex enough to incorporate the insights of both Bennett and Babb yet simple enough to usefully order the sometimes chaotic raft of Hinduism's proliferating goddesses. Bennett's contribution to this model is threefold. First, she allows us to see the sources of benevolence on the part of single goddesses and malevolence on the part of married goddesses. Second, she shows that the category of single goddesses is not merely unmarried, but quite specifically a category of sister-daughter goddesses. Finally, she allows us to see that each of the two poles, sister-daughter, and wife–daughter-in-law, is transformed into a central mediating status of mother.

The proposed classification is diagrammed in figure 1. In this model, both poles are able to show both benevolence and malevolence. The particular character of these qualities, however, differs for each type of goddess. Malevolence in the wife–daughter-in-law mother goddesses[4] derives from selfishness and jealousy, the same characteristics that, according to the patrifocal perspective, lead women to endanger the solidarity of the joint family. Benevolence in these goddesses derives, as Babb would have it, from a "taming" of these tendencies under the control of and in full subordination to the interests of a husband and child. Malevolence in the sister-daughter mothers derives from their anger over the sexual advances and/or physical attacks of males, particularly demons. Benevolence in these goddesses derives from a motherly spirit of protectiveness for dependent gods as well as from the purity and freely given affection of the sister and daughter. Along with many other goddesses, Santoshi Ma fits comfortably onto the predominantly benevolent portion of the sister-daughter mother pole.

This scheme allows us to preserve Babb's essential division of married and single goddesses along with his insights into female danger and the need for male control. At the same time, it enables us to account for the complex mixture of benevolence and malevolence occurring at the two poles. These complexities have continued to draw scholarly criticism on Babb's scheme without, however, provoking its definitive rejection. Moreover, the new scheme provides us with a way of understanding the complex unity created among all goddesses under the unifying umbrella of "mother." For example, the traditionally puzzling insistence that virgin goddesses are also mothers is here acknowledged. The nature of this connection between virgin and mother is, in fact, what finally must propel us from a strict accounting for this scheme in terms of kinship to a deeper, psychological level of interpretation.

The sources of benevolence and malevolence as well as the connection to motherhood seem relatively clear at the wife–daughter-in-law pole. As already explained, the two sides of these goddesses' character are versions of the transformation of the dangerous wife, who is subversive to the solidarity of the joint family, into the cooperative and bountiful wife-become-mother.

The link between the pure and kind sister-daughter of the filiofocal perspective and the fierce yet protective mother goddess under sexual and martial attack by demons is less clear. The link is there, however, and the uncovering of its psychological sources will reveal a similar psychological level underlying the already explained pole of the wife–sister-in-law goddesses. These deep psychological processes, in turn, are the source of the constant reminders by devotees that all the goddesses are one.

The meaning of the association between virgins and mother goddesses has already been the subject of scholarly debate. In a classic exchange, E. Kathleen Gough's psychoanalytic interpretation of South Indian puberty rites was followed by an alternative sociological interpretation offered by Nur Yalman (Gough 1955; Yalman 1963).

Gough explains the ritual mock marriages of virgin girls on the Malabar Coast as attempts to neutralize the dangerous powers invested in virgins by virtue of their unconscious association with the powerful, castrating oedipal mother. In support of her argument, Gough highlights the identification of young virgins with the blood-thirsty and demon-slaying goddess Bhagavadi (associated with Durga and Kali).

Yalman responds with both a principled caution and an alternative explanation. Yalman points out the inherent difficulty—or impossibility—of explaining the symbolism of locally and culturally varied ceremonies according to universal psychological phenomena. He goes on to show convincingly that the caste-based interest in the purity of lineages results in a heavily ritualized concern for female purity.

M. R. Allen, in his study of the worship of virgins in Nepal (1976), refers to the work of Gough and Yalman. On the one hand, Allen says that his aim is: "to confirm her [Gough's] empirical finding that amongst the Nayars, and most probably throughout the Hindu world, the virgin goddess is infused with the spirit of a sword-wielding, blood-lusting, and sexually desirable destroyer of male demons" (Allen 1976:298). On the other hand, Allen rejects Gough's psychoanalytic explanations of this symbolism and holds instead with Yalman's connection between the dangerous state of the menstruating virgin and the concern for caste purity. For Allen, the weak link in Gough's argument is her emphasis on the fact that the goddesses Bhagavadi, Durga, and Kali are all both virgins and mothers. According to Allen, whatever the claims of informants, "there is little that I can see of the truly maternal in any of these goddesses" (1976:315).

A resolution of these issues is important, for on it depends our understanding of the link Hindus claim exists between the virginity and the motherhood of certain of their goddesses. Indeed, from my point of view, the issue here is the significance of one side of our classificatory scheme, the sister-daughter (and thus virgin) mother goddesses.

I suggest that any successful approach to these issues must take into account the positions of both Gough and Yalman. Gough, I think, does highlight an important link between the symbolism of the virgin sister-daughter and the symbolism of the mother. We cannot follow Allen in dismissing clear testimony from informants affirming the motherly character of these fierce virgin goddesses, simply because they do not fit our notion of the "truly maternal." Moreover, although Yalman's link between concern for caste purity and the ritualization of female puberty cannot and must not be denied, neither can it fully account for the symbolic or theological complexities of the gentle yet fierce virgin mother goddess. I think that we can make sense of these complexities in psychological terms.

On the other hand, no progress can be made on these issues without taking into account Yalman's fundamental point about psychological explanations. The symbolism of particular cultures cannot be explained by reference to universal psychological phenomena. Traditional psychological anthropology has consistently failed to confront this difficulty. Typically, a way around it is found by connecting cultural variation to variation in the *intensity*, *quantity*, or *degree of development* of universal psychological processes.

I offer a different approach. I suggest the creation of models that treat psychological variation across cultures as differences in *kind* or *quality*. From this perspective, arrests or advances in development *can* be identified. Yet here they would be arrests or advances within culturally distinct lines of development. In other words, instead of explaining Hindu rituals in terms of a universal Oedipus complex, we would refer them to their psychological roots in the Oedipus myth's Indian cousin, something we might name, the *Durga complex*.

In taking this road, I simply play out within psychology the technique Dumont applied within sociology. Where Dumont refuses to view caste as an extreme form of a familiar and universal social stratification, we too shall refuse to see throughout the Indian material simply an unusually pronounced concern with, or misfiring of, oedipal conflicts (Dumont 1980:247–266). Thus we break from the methodology of Gough.

This approach should enable us to follow Yalman's admonition to keep to the level of social facts and still allow access for the tools of depth psychology. Such an explanatory strategy promises not a combination of distinct sociological and individual-psychological explanations but a unification of various types of sociological explanations, those involving caste, kinship, *and* psychology.

The creation of a qualitatively distinct model of Hindu psychology will require much groundwork. In particular, it will be necessary to take a new look at ethnographic and theoretical accounts of Hindu child-rearing practices, for these accounts serve at present as the foundation of several important psychoanalytic psychologies of Hinduism. This reconsideration of Hindu childhood is the task of the next two chapters. Following this groundwork, we return to the problem of goddess classification with a new perspective.

Chapter 3

Psychoanalytic Approaches to Hindu Child Rearing: A Critique

Here I begin a reshaping of psychoanalysis designed to preserve psychoanalytic insight into links between images human and divine, yet also intended to honor the particularity of the Hindu situation. In return for the reader's patient attention to this reworking process, I shall offer a way of looking at things that plausibly reveals the meaning of both Santoshi Ma and the larger Goddess of which she is a version.

Given what we have learned so far about divine mothers, it is clear that a psychoanalytic study of human mothers must take seriously the ultimate oneness of seemingly independent beings in the Hindu universe. Thus, for example, where traditional psychoanalysis focuses on a child and its mother, we must learn to understand children who live amidst the complex but unified array of caretakers in the Hindu joint family. As currently constituted, however, psychoanalysis is ill suited to such an approach, its intellectual framework having been shaped by our Western individualism. Nonetheless, extant psychoanalytic studies of Hindu child rearing establish a vital starting point for our work.

Recent years have witnessed a resurgence of interest in the psychoanalytic study of Hindu childhood. G. Morris Carstairs' classic early work (1967) has been carried forward in a new form by Sudhir Kakar (1978). More recently, Alan Roland has compared Hindu and Japanese psychology (1988) in a study that builds on and transforms work by Carstairs and Kakar. Increasingly, these psychoanalytic studies influence scholarly treatments of Hindu religion and society. Works by O'Flaherty (1980), Courtright (1985), and Mandelbaum (1988), for example, make considerable use of the psychoanalytic literature on Hindu childhood. Indeed, broader theoretical and comparative studies of culture and personality are beginning to attend to the literature on Hindu development (Obeyesekere 1981, 1984, 1990; Spiro 1982). Hindu society now stands second to none as a generative locus of scholarship in the field of psychological anthropology.

Yet response to the psychoanalysis of early Hindu life remains mixed (Pocock 1961, Kondos 1986). Psychoanalytic studies, however careful to mark the particularities of the Hindu case, are often dismissed as misguided attempts to fit Hindu culture into an alien mold. Critics of the analysts, however, generally limit themselves to a cursory tour of dangers and distortions in the current approach. To date, there are no systematic, alternative theories of Hindu child psychology. Nor is there even a compendium of data on Hindu child-rearing practices from which current or new psychological theories could be fashioned or judged.

This chapter attempts to lay the foundation for a new approach to Hindu child psychology through a critique of the psychoanalysts based on ethnography. Studies by Carstairs, Kakar, and Roland, I argue, are based on a flawed account of Hindu childhood, an account neither modified nor examined since it was first set forth in 1957 by Carstairs. Attention to anthropological reports of Hindu child rearing reveals defects in the psychoanalytic account and suggests an alternative theoretical construction. In the following chapters I offer the fundaments of a new Hindu developmental psychology. Here, I simply suggest the outlines of this approach so as to provide a context for the critique of Carstairs, Kakar, and Roland that follows.

The neglected player in psychoanalytic treatments of Hindu child rearing is the group. Traditionally, psychoanalytic studies focus only on the interaction between the Hindu child and mother although after age five, the father's influence is granted importance. Analysts give caretakers outside the nuclear family (e.g., the mother's mother-in-law and sisters-in-law in the joint family) merely passing attention. When acknowledged by analysts (and this is seldom), members of the broader family group are seen as pale copies of the mother or the father, functioning merely to reinforce, diffuse, or disrupt the care offered by the central figures.

I see the group as a primary player in the psychological growth of the Hindu child. No mere copies of parents, group members, as a group, counter the influence of mother and father, drawing the child out of a baby's loves, fears, and hatreds and immersing the growing child in the group itself. Hindu mothers and fathers, moreover, gently push the child out of the parental orbit into that of the group.

The traditional psychoanalytic focus on relations among individual actors in the nuclear family yields a different view. Analysts give us a Hindu child locked in the mother's embrace. In this traditional account, the mother's indulgent presence surrounds the child until around the age of five the father's discipline intervenes traumatically. This juxtaposition of prolonged indulgence and sudden frustration is said to mark the Hindu adult with a hidden yearning for the idyllic past, a time when child and mother were one. In this psychoanalytic view, the Hindu orientation to the group is not the successful outcome of a characteristically Hindu manner of distancing from the mother but a regressive search for the mother, a quest for a union now lost.

This chapter dissects the evidence on which this viewpoint is based and introduces additional evidence not properly taken into account by psychoanalytic observers. I argue that psychoanalysts have moved too quickly from evidence of physical closeness between the Hindu mother and her child to assumptions about the intimacy of this pair. In fact, the Hindu mother is careful not to load her physical care with the kind of attention or "mirroring" it would carry in the West. I argue that the Hindu mother's careful mixture of care and restraint acts in a culturally distinctive manner to push the child outward, away from her and toward the group, even as it reassures the child of her caring presence. Psychoanalysts rarely catch this mixture of contact and restraint, seeing instead unmitigated closeness between mother and child. Even glimpsing the mother's restraint, however, analysts take it as yet more evidence of her disturbed relation to the child. This is the viewpoint I wish to rework. Again, however, my purpose in this chapter is not to spin out a group-oriented view of Hindu child psychology but to prepare the ground for such work in the following chapters by a careful critique here of Carstairs, Kakar, and Roland. This approach entails no outright rejection of psychoanalysis but rather a radical attempt to adapt it to the conditions of Hindu society.

G. Morris Carstairs' work is not only the earliest important psychoanalytic treatment of Hindu childhood, it is virtually alone in being grounded on an author's personal field observations. Indeed, Carstairs' account of Hindu child rearing remains the foundation for nearly all later psychoanalytic work.[1] Understanding Carstairs' limitations thus provides the basis for a critique of Kakar and Roland.

Carstairs emphasizes the physical closeness between the Hindu mother and her child (1967:63–76,157). In the first two years, child and mother are seldom apart. Commonly, the baby is seen astride the mother's hip. The mother holds her child this way even as she does her chores. Past age two, when the child is somewhat less often by the mother's side, it is common to see a relative, perhaps an older sister, holding the child astride her hip. The child sleeps with the mother, and the breast is kept accessible. No baby is allowed to cry for long since the breast is offered on demand. Citing a Hindu proverb, Carstairs compares the child to the king. What the baby wants it gets. Its needs are indulged. Children, for example, are rarely scolded for soiling in the home. Indeed, informants stress that mothers uncomplainingly clean up a mess. Carstairs says suckling is moderately prolonged, weaning taking place between the age of two and two-and-a-half years. Weaning, Carstairs tells us, is difficult, provoking many days of crying and anger. This is because the Hindu child has never been accustomed to frustration prior to weaning.

In Carstairs' account, one of the few frustrations in early Hindu childhood comes in the presence of the father's mother—the mother's mother-in-law (1967:66,68,71,157). Carstairs' discussion of the mother-in-law's role illustrates the treatment of third-party caretakers in the traditional psychoanalytic model. In Hindu custom, if there is no cry for the breast, a mother ought not to pay attention to her child in her mother-in-law's presence. Often, if the mother-in-law is in attendance, the child will be given over to her by the mother. Thus, says Carstairs, the reliability of a mother's care is compromised by her mother-in-law's presence.

Here, then, is an example of psychoanalytic individualism. Analysis centers on the intimate bond between two individuals—mother and child. Other family members are granted importance only insofar as they interfere with or support this primary relationship. Elsewhere, Carstairs is more sanguine about the effects of group caretaking on the Hindu child (1967:75). He says the care of other family members for the growing child actually reinforces, by contrast, the importance of the uniquely gratifying relation to the mother. In other words, less satisfying care by substitute mothers deepens the attachment to the more giving natural mother. However, from this perspective, too, the group is important only insofar as it affects relations between the primary individuals.

Carstairs' account of Hindu childhood takes an ominous turn when the father enters the picture (1967:67–70,75–76,147,159–167). This does not occur for some time, however, as the child remains close to the mother even after weaning. A Hindu boy[2] does not enter the world of men to any considerable extent until the age of five, and if no younger siblings arrive, he may periodically take the breast up to or even beyond this age. Around age five, however, the Hindu boy is thrust into the orbit of his father and suddenly expected to grow up. Now he must help at home, obeying the rules of caste and kinship. Now he must abandon the mother's embrace. Worse, his father remains a cool and distant authority figure. Again, this is particularly so in joint families, where the grandfather's presence obliges the father to maintain a respectful distance from his child. For Carstairs, movement into the orbit of the father represents a "catastrophic reversal of the infant's early blissful situation" (1967:160). Moreover, for Carstairs, the Hindu mother's early care of her baby is "too good" (1967:157). Carstairs maintains, therefore, that this contrast between excessive early indulgence and dangerously harsh later frustration yields a child prone to regress to early infantile pleasures—a child filled with unresolved fear and anger toward unreliable, disappointing parents (1967:157–169). What Hindu child care lacks, Carstairs tells us, is the gradual training in frustration tolerance that enables a healthy Western child to cope with the demands of maturity (1967:157). In Carstairs' account, then, typical Hindu child rearing emerges as significantly more pathogenic than the child rearing commonly found in the West (1967:158–159).

While the negative implications of this analysis are clear enough, Carstairs is not entirely comfortable with the sense of Hindu pathology that emerges from his work. Toward the conclusion of his analysis, he notes the dangers of taking too dark a view of Hindu life. Carstairs lauds the serenity and calm of the well-adjusted Hindu family. Yet, while bowing to what he calls "a gracious and civilized way of life," Carstairs owns that the calm of Hindu family life is "perhaps a precarious calm, based on the suppressing rather than on the resolving of underlying tensions" (1967:168–169). In the end, then, Carstairs is forced to affirm the pejorative implications of his analysis.

Sudhir Kakar, an Indian psychoanalyst writing some twenty years after Carstairs, works to moderate the harsher implications of Carstairs' approach. The difficulty with Kakar's analysis is that he tries to moderate Carstairs' negative evaluation of Hindu child rearing without significantly modifying either Carstairs' ethnographic account or Carstairs' theoretical approach. Kakar relies on only a very few observational sources for his factual description of Hindu child rearing, and clearly Carstairs' is foremost among these (Kakar 1978:196–197). Most significantly, Kakar makes virtually no use of the most detailed anthropological account of Hindu child rearing to date—Leigh Minturn's study of child rearing among a village Rajput caste (Minturn 1966). As we shall see, Minturn's account calls some of Carstairs' most important conclusions into question.

Like Carstairs, Kakar stresses the Hindu child's prolonged physical contact with the mother, breast-feeding on demand, and the traumatic shift to the demanding orbit of the father at around age five—a period Kakar calls the "second birth" (1978:79–103,126–133). In various ways, however, Kakar works to mitigate the negative implications of Carstairs' analysis (1978:14–36,85–86). For example, Kakar points out that Hindus value group solidarity over individual independence. Thus, while acknowledging that the child's prolonged closeness to the mother leaves him unprepared for independent activity and fearful of isolation, Kakar maintains that our negative evaluation of these characteristics is a cultural artifact. While Hindu parents do not prepare their child for independence, this, Kakar argues, is entirely consonant with the dominant Hindu cultural values.

Kakar's emphasis on cultural reinforcement of psychological traits is problematic. A traditional psychoanalyst would ask about the source of this cultural support. Indeed, for the most part, Kakar himself, like other psychoanalytic observers of culture, claims to ground cultural tendencies in psychology. Yet if Hindu culture reinforces what psychoanalysts call pathology, must not this cultural tendency itself be a product of, and evidence for, the pathology in question? Even if we argue that social structure and child-rearing practices reinforce each other in a kind of circle of causation, mere compatibility between these causal forces does not settle questions of pathology. Psychoanalysis' negative evaluation of Hindu child-rearing practices is built deeply into its theory. Unless Kakar modifies this theory, at least in its application to Hindu India, we can expect that its negative evaluation of "dependent" or group-oriented behavior will emerge.

This is what happens in the body of Kakar's analysis. Kakar's attempt to explain away the negative psychoanalytic evaluation of Hindu character is undermined by the inner logic of the theory upon which he grounds his work. For example, Kakar denies that Hindu fears of independence or isolation represent regression or fixation at the oral-narcissistic stage of development (1978:28,130). Further, Kakar rejects entirely the Freudian notion that an excess of early satisfaction "spoils" a child, leaving him unable to handle diminutions of pleasure (1978:87–88). Yet Kakar surreptitiously restores each of these notions in his discussion of the Hindu second birth—the period after age five when the mother's indulgence ends and demands are placed upon the boy by the father (1978:126–133). Kakar's entire analysis turns on the way this so-called crackdown phase precipitates a "narcissistic injury of the first magnitude" in the Hindu child. According to Kakar:

> The abrupt severance of the four- or five-year-old boy from the intimate company of a single paramount "other" and the radical disruption this entails partly explain the narcissistic vulnerability of the male psyche in India. . . . In spite of the emotional "riches" that a long and intense loving reciprocity with the mother may store up in the individual's inner world, this same intense exclusivity tends to hinder the growth of the son's autonomy, thereby leaving the psychic structure relatively undifferentiated, the boundaries of the self vague, and the inner convictions—"I am perfect" and "You are perfect but I am part of you"—more or less uncompromised in their primitive emotional originality. (Kakar 1978:130)

Kakar lays exclusive responsibility for the narcissistic injury discussed above upon the second birth. Nonetheless, the negative consequences of an "abrupt severance of the four- or five-year-old boy from the intimate company of a single paramount 'other'" must be a product not only of the later separation but also of the earlier prolonged and near-exclusive attachment described. The very existence of an "abrupt severance" depends upon the prior period of unmodified closeness. Thus, despite explicit denials, Kakar has adopted Carstairs' theory of early overindulgence complicated by later traumatic disappointment. The outcome, moreover, seems clearly to be narcissistic fixation. In the following passage, Kakar struggles with this implication of his analysis:

> I would contend that among Indian men the process of integrating these archaic narcissistic configurations developmentally is rarely accomplished in the sense that it is among men in the West. This does not mean that Indians are narcissistic while westerners are not. Adapting one of Freud's metaphors, we might say that westerners have fewer "troops of occupation" remaining at the home base of archaic narcissism, the bulk of the army having marched on—although under great stress they too may retreat. In contrast, Indians tend to maintain more troops at the narcissistic position, with the advance platoons poised to join them whenever threatened or provoked. (Kakar 1978:130)

While Kakar denies narcissistic fixation in the Hindu male, the metaphor he employs is precisely Freud's way of describing the phenomena of fixation and regression (Freud 1966:341). The above passage appears to be a denial, but in fact it is an explicit affirmation in Freudian terms that pathology among Hindus exceeds that found among Westerners. Thus, while Kakar stresses the cultural acceptability of Hindu dependency needs, his theoretical approach, almost against his will, forces us to view such needs as pathological.

In fact, despite the overt attack on Carstairs' spoiling theory, Kakar finds another way of explicitly asserting the pathogenic character of the Hindu mother-child interaction. Kakar argues that the closeness between the Hindu mother and her male child borders dangerously on premature sexual seductiveness (1978:87–103). Kakar notes that the status of the young Hindu mother is tied to the bearing of children, particularly sons. He argues that the importance of a male child to his mother prompts in her an untoward emotional investment—an investment unconsciously communicated to the child through excessive physical ministrations. This seductiveness is heightened, Kakar argues, by the relative coolness of Hindu husband-wife relations. In all too many cases, Kakar asserts, the Hindu child is his mother's chief emotional outlet. Even as Kakar rejects Carstairs' spoiling theory, then, its pattern is restored under the heading of seduction.

Kakar's seduction theory is significant for the emphasis it places on the emotional quality of the mother's physical attentions. Consider, for example, the passage in which Kakar sets forth his view:

> An Indian mother, as we have shown, preconsciously experiences her newborn infant, especially a son, as the means by which her "motherly" identity is crystallized, her role and status in family and society established. She tends to perceive a son as a kind of saviour and to nurture him with gratitude and even reverence as well as with affection and care. For a range of reasons, the balance of nurturing may be so affected that the mother unconsciously demands that the child serve as an object of her own unfulfilled desires and wishes, however antithetical they may be to his own. The child feels compelled then to *act* as her saviour. Faced with her unconscious intimations and demands, he may feel confused, helpless and inadequate, frightened by his mother's overwhelming nearness and yet unable (and partly unwilling) to get away. In his fantasy, her presence acquires the ominous visage of the "bad mother."
>
> (Kakar 1978:88–89)

Kakar here assumes that the mother's "overwhelming nearness" flows from and communicates to the child an intense emotional involvement. I argue, however, that traditional psychoanalytic interpretations of Hindu child rearing err in drawing conclusions about the emotional character of early mother-child relationships from such physical data. While it may be true that a Hindu mother is "grateful" for the birth of a son and even that the son is "revered," it is misleading to characterize the quality of this gratitude and reverence as excessive emotional involvement. Language like "gratitude and even reverence . . . affection and care," as used in the passage above, clearly implies a Western-style intimacy or "love" relationship between mother and child—a relation that I shall argue is not truly present in the Hindu case. Kakar compounds the difficulty when he notes that the seductive "bad mother" theme in India differs from its Western counterpart only in that it is more "pervasive" and "intense." In fact, the emotional tone of the Hindu mother-child relationship is quite different from that found in the West, and I argue that this difference is best conceived of as one of kind rather than degree.[3]

As noted, although Kakar makes only the most cursory reference to it (Kakar 1978:193), he is aware of Leigh Minturn's study of Hindu child rearing (Minturn and Hitchcock 1966). Yet the central thrust of Minturn's study is the assertion that while the Hindu mother and child are physically close, this physical closeness is unaccompanied by the emotional relation it would betoken in the West. Kakar's description of the seductively intimate mother-child bond— a description constructed out of early observations, such as those by Carstairs, and out of Kakar's own analyses of Hindu symbol and fantasy—cannot survive critical examination based on more recent anthropological field studies of Hindu child rearing. Before critiquing the analysts from an ethnographic standpoint, however, consideration of the work of Alan Roland, the most recent psychoanalytic student of Hindu culture, is in order.

While his work resembles Carstairs' and Kakar's in many essentials, Roland makes a more radical effort than Kakar to break free of Carstairs' invidious distinction between Hindu and Western child rearing. Roland is particularly aware of how deeply such judgments are embedded in theory (1988:312–333). Given that Western child-rearing norms are part and parcel of psychoanalytic developmental theory, Roland points out, it is inevitable that cultures raising children differently than we do will appear pathogenic. By making this point clearly and explicitly, Roland prepares us for a revision in psychoanalytic theory itself. Moreover, Roland moves in the direction of such a revision by elaborating the notion of a Hindu "we-self"—a kind of group ego in which a given individual is embedded (1988:242–288). From the perspective of Roland's we-self theory, there is something more than mere cultural support for the Hindu child's so-called dependence or lack of individuation. There are, instead, culturally distinctive psychological structures with their own pattern of normalcy and their own line of development.

The advance represented by Roland's notion of the we-self, however, is compromised by the traditional theoretical context in which he continues to embed it. This theoretical framework, in turn, rests on Roland's acceptance of a factual account of Hindu child rearing that differs very little from that of Carstairs (Roland 1988:230–235). As with Carstairs and Kakar, Roland derives evidence of a strong emotional bond from the physical closeness of the Hindu mother and her child. That is, Roland takes a physical closeness—extreme by Western standards in both quality and length—to indicate that the early symbiotic union between the Hindu mother and her child is carefully prolonged rather than gradually transcended. Thus, despite his stated goal of developing a distinctive Hindu path of psychological development—one with its own norm and structure—Roland is pulled toward a view of Hindu development as giving exaggerated expression to certain trends in its Western counterpart. This is because for Roland the nature of the union between Hindu mother and child is not qualitatively different from that found in the West. Rather, the Hindu mother-child relationship is an extension of patterns familiar to us.

Roland sets forth some of his central ideas in the following passages:

> I sense that this ongoing mirroring in Indian relationships . . . goes way beyond mirroring in adult American relationships. It is from these empathic observations that I conclude that the narcissistic dimension is more pervasive, more intense, and in general of more

paramount importance in Indian . . . psychological and social functioning than in American. . . .

How does this intricate patterning of we-self regard develop? And to what extent does it differ from the predominant mode of child development in America? Self psychology posits the significant emotional investment and empathic resonance that mothers have with their children as being central to an infant's and young child's basic sense of inner esteem; and Indian mothers in particular seem to make an extraordinary investment in their children. . . . Intense, prolonged maternal involvement in the first four or five years with the young child, with adoration of the young child to the extent of treating him or her as godlike . . . develops a central core of heightened narcissistic well-being in the child. Mothers, grandmothers, aunts, servants, older sisters, and cousin-sisters are all involved in the pervasive mirroring that is incorporated into an inner core of extremely high feelings of esteem. But it is clear that the subtle expectations and valuing are not for the increasingly autonomous exploratory behavior of the American toddler, . . . but rather for the child's growing emotional interdependence and sensitivity to others.

(Roland 1988:246, 248–249)

Here Roland locates the source of the we-self in an extremely "intense" narcissistic union between the Hindu mother and her child, a union characterized by powerful "empathic resonance" or emotional "mirroring." Clearly, Roland is arguing that Western patterns of early mothering are taken to extremes in the Hindu case.

Roland does give a role to the family group in these passages, but this role is modeled on that of the mother. Empathic mirroring from both the mother and others is said to train a child in interdependence and emotional sensitivity. In this scheme, then, the group acts not as a counter to the narcissistic union with the mother but helps to extend that union to the social whole.

To be sure, toward the close of his treatment of the Hindu "spiritual self," Roland offers a counterpoint to this vision of Hindu personality as an extreme development of certain Western psychological trends. The bulk of Roland's analysis of what he calls the Hindu spiritual self focuses on continuities between the child's early, intense experience of symbiosis with the mother and themes of unity in Hindu life (1988:289–306). Like others, Roland points to similarities between the Hindu sense of unity with the universe and the early experience of unity with the mother and the larger family. In a final, brief "counterpoint" to this discussion, however, Roland points in another direction (1988:307–310).

He argues that the notion of detachment from immediate emotional connection, a theme central to Hindu spirituality, in some sense marks out the spiritual self as a realm of autonomy within the larger Hindu experience of unity. He cites, for example, stories in which individuals are actually able to fulfill family responsibilities more competently and confidently when they practice a spiritual detachment from emotional bonds. Thus, Roland is able to argue that Hindu narcissism, although extreme by our standards, does not become pathological. This is because an overall symbiosis is balanced by an inner, "spiritual" autonomy that is different from the one found in the West but that nonetheless assures a healthy course of development.

I think Roland is on the right track here. The overall analysis, however, is seriously hampered by his emphasis on narcissism and by his acceptance of the traditional psychoanalytic view of Hindu child rearing. Roland provides no clear grounding in child-rearing practices for the detachment he finds in the spiritual self. Thus, Roland's interest in detachment remains merely a counterpoint to his overwhelming emphasis on narcissism and symbiosis. As we saw in the passage quoted above, this is because Roland implicates a Hindu child's natural mother, along with the many other mothering persons, in a pervasive mirroring process. From this point of view, the attention directed to the child by the family extends the narcissistic union of mother and child to the group as a whole.

The difficulty with this idea of pervasive narcissism in Hindu family life, as I argue below, is that neither the mother nor the other family members are engaged in an intimate exchange or reflection of emotions with the child. Moreover, I maintain that the natural mother's stance toward the child differs significantly from that of the family at large. These differences act to push the child away from the connection to the natural mother and toward connection with the family group. I argue that it is this push away from the mother and toward the group that generates the Hindu emphasis on detachment from emotional bonds. From this perspective, then, the link with the group does not so much extend the child's sense of unity with the mother as it introduces the child to a sense of belonging quite contrary to his selfish desire for exclusive possession of the mother. This, in turn, explains why Hindu spirituality links detachment—an overcoming of selfishness—with the discovery of unity.

In this view, then, the early sense of unbounded unity characteristic of primary narcissism is not simply transferred unbroken from the mother to the family. On the contrary, heretofore neglected complexities in the early Hindu caretaker-child interaction break primary narcissism in a culturally distinctive way. This breaking of primary narcissism explodes the Hindu child's sense that he and the mother exist in an unbounded, symbiotic union. Indeed, the passing of primary narcissism allows the Hindu child to recognize his mother as a distinct self with distinct interests and thus to selfishly seek exclusive possession of her as an object. At this point, a selfishly attached child is left to discover, or rediscover, a complex and highly transformed sense of unity by sacrificing a desire for exclusive possession of the mother and moving toward immersion in the group. The model of the Hindu psyche I elaborate below is built upon this tension between the child's selfish attachment to the mother and his more detached immersion in the group. I argue, therefore, that we must break far more radically with current empirical and theoretical approaches to Hindu psychology than does Roland.[4]

The alternative view of Hindu psychology I elaborate below proceeds from the critique of Carstairs, Kakar, and Roland set forth in this chapter. Thus we turn to several anthropological field studies that provide data needed to transform our understanding of current psychoanalytic accounts. These studies do not so much expose the analysts as mistaken as they reveal the problematic way in which data on Hindu child rearing have heretofore been interpreted.

The most wide-ranging anthropological study of Hindu child rearing is that of Leigh Minturn.[5] Although Minturn's study paints a picture sharply at variance with that of Carstairs, she agrees with the psychoanalysts on many particulars (1966:105–113). The mother is the primary caretaker in the early years: carrying the child frequently, sleeping with it, and nursing on demand. There is little effort to control urination or defecation, and soiling accidents thus go unpunished. Despite these points of agreement, however, Minturn shows the emotional context in which this physical care operates to be entirely different from what a psychoanalytic observer might expect. Consider these extended excerpts from Minturn's account:

> During the day, when the infant is not in need of food or some other attention, it is placed on a cot with a quilt or sheet entirely covering it, to protect it from insects and envious glances. Babies are often so well hidden by piles of quilts that one cannot detect their presence. Generally, unless the baby cries, no one pays any attention to it, and it lies well covered in the midst of the busy courtyard until it expresses its demands in loud and persistent crying. Children, particularly boys, who have been born after several years of barrenness or after the death of several children, may be accorded more attention. . . .
>
> The life of the Rajput baby is, aside from the daily bath, bland and free from stress, but it is also free from deliberate creative stimulation. A person in the village is viewed as a member of a group rather than as an individual. . . .
>
> Whereas a mother who conceives of her child as a unique individual emphasizes how he differs from other children, the Rajput mother, for whom all people are but transient elements in a permanent group structure, insists that "all children are alike."
>
> This attitude is, no doubt, accentuated by the fact that the village mother has had far more experience with children than a mother raised in an isolated nuclear family. She has grown up in a household where the advent of a new baby was a fairly common occurrence. She has seen babies born, seen them nurse, seen them live and grow up, and seen them die. She has probably cared for a younger sibling or cousin herself. Furthermore, she has her own children in the company of older women to whom childbirth is a familiar experience. Therefore, babies are neither the objects of interest nor the objects of anxiety that they are in this country. A mother does not fear that her child is sick every time it cries; she knows better. But, by the same token, she is not as delighted with its smile because she also knows that all babies smile. She therefore continues with her usual routine, attends to her infant's needs but does not hover over it or "drop everything" to rush to its side. . . .
>
> The elderly men who sometimes care for babies may "play" with them, but usually neither the women nor the girls who go about their own activities with a baby on their hips spend much time interacting

with the child. The baby receives attention only when it cries or fusses. When it thus exhibits distress, the mother, another woman, its child nurse, or even a young child of 4 or 5 will attempt to soothe the baby back to quiescence. When it becomes quiet, its distractor leaves it. Adult interaction with babies is generally aimed at producing a cessation of response rather than a stimulation of it. . . .

Thus the baby spends his first two years as a passive observer of the busy courtyard life. He is never alone, never the center of attention.   (Minturn and Hitchcock 1966:107,110,111,112)

Even as Minturn confirms in these passages points made by earlier observers, she transforms our understanding of these facts. For example, Kakar's point about the attention lavished by a mother on a male child is borne out, yet such attention appears less intense than Kakar would have it and more rare as well. Most important, the special relationship between the Hindu mother and her son appears here as a variation on a distinctive Hindu pattern rather than as a mere intensification of a style of intimacy found in the West. Further, feeding on demand is noted, yet cast in a new light. The response to crying is real enough but less swift and emotionally laden than many have assumed. The offer of the breast is meant to placate the child and thus to free up the mother's attention for work. Nursing is not, therefore, an occasion through which mother and child cement an emotional union. The child is frequently fed, yet the mother seldom lingers to mirror the baby's satisfaction. Thus, while the child no doubt develops a strong emotional attachment to the mother as a result of the physical gratification she provides, the mother does not respond by setting up a Western-style loving, emotional partnership. To what extent, then, does such mothering deserve Carstairs' designation of "too good?" Indeed, to what extent does such mothering appear, as Kakar would have it, "seductive?" Given Minturn's account, terms like "spoiling," "overindulgence," or "seduction" seem awkward misreadings of a pattern of physical closeness that cannot fairly be understood as a simple exaggeration of emotional tendencies familiar to us in the West.

The psychoanalysts might reply here that their theories refer to the inner meaning of external behavior. From this perspective, evidence should include not simply the ethnography of child rearing but also subjective material from dreams, myths, and clinical psychoanalyses. Indeed, analysts might caution against deducing too much from strictly observational evidence like that of Minturn. Perhaps, despite seeming emotional distance, mere physical closeness is sufficient to communicate a message of intimacy.

This is a valid caution, yet one that potentially enables any problematic set of subjective meanings to be read indefinitely into behavioral material. Moreover, current psychoanalytic views of Hindu child rearing do not so much reveal the inner meaning of overt emotional distancing behavior as they ignore such behavior altogether. It is significant, for example, that neither Carstairs, Kakar, nor Roland have ever directly come to grips with Minturn's work. Moreover, the revised psychoanalysis of Hindu culture I offer below is not based on observational data alone. The approach to Hindu child-rearing practices introduced in this chapter will soon be matched and deepened by a reading of more purely symbolic data from myths, fantasy, and clinical psychoanalyses as well as by an alternative reading of the data on Hindu child rearing. In order to support this alternative interpretation, I want to do more than simply contradict the traditional psychoanalytic view of Hindu upbringing. On the contrary, I intend to argue here that the parallels between Minturn's and Carstairs' accounts of Hindu child rearing go further than the obvious correspondences noted above. Beneath Carstairs' overt account—an account fundamental to all later psychoanalytic work on India—lies evidence that bears out Minturn's characterization of the emotional tone of Hindu child rearing—the very point on which the two authors seem most at odds. Thus, Carstairs himself provides us with important evidence for an alternative reading of the Hindu child-rearing situation.

A comparison of Carstairs and Minturn can begin with their seemingly divergent descriptions of weaning. Here is Minturn's account:

> Most mothers said they had no trouble weaning their children. A few reported that the children had troubled them for three or four days. One mother said that her child cried off and on for 20 days; this was the most extreme case of emotional upset due to weaning reported to us.
>
> Chilies or *nīm* leaves, which are bitter, may be put on the breast to aid in a difficult weaning, but since the mothers are reluctant to

use such punitive measures, they rarely resort to this practice. Two mothers told us that they were using $n\bar{\imath}m$ leaves to wean their children, but in both cases we saw the children nursing without protest. One mother held the leaves in her hand while nursing but did not use them. . . . The fact that the children are usually getting supplementary milk and some solid food before weaning is instituted seems to make it a relatively easy adjustment. The children we saw did not show signs of emotional upset, and, according to the mothers' reports, the children rarely tried to resume nursing after the birth of a second child.   (Minturn and Hitchcock 1966:115)

Compare this to Carstairs' account:

Suckling is moderately prolonged, weaning taking place usually at about two and a half years. By this time, the child is eating quite a generous diet, and the surrender of the breast might not seem too violent a wrench. Still, I was told, it usually provokes many days' crying and anger, because the child has not been accustomed to being thwarted. The mother may cover her nipples with a bitter paste until weaning is established; or rarely she may leave the child for two or three days.   (Carstairs 1967:63–64)

The facts seem almost identical. Interpretation creates the difference. Both accounts speak of supplementary diets before weaning, days of crying, and devices to discourage breast-feeding. The major factual difference is Minturn's point about the limited application of discouraging devices. In any case, despite considerable areas of factual agreement, Carstairs suggests weaning difficulties while Minturn speaks of easy weaning. Carstairs seems to view weaning in light of his belief that early maternal indulgence leads to poor tolerance of frustration. A close reading of Carstairs, however, shows that even his account of early maternal indulgence is undercut by an awareness of certain difficulties pressing in on even very young children.

Carstairs separates child care into an early period of excessive maternal indulgence and attention and a later period of loss of exclusive and consistent mothering. Nevertheless, this sharp distinction between early indulgence and later frustration is continually blurred. The child is weaned at about two-and-a-half years, and at times this seems to be Carstairs' dividing line (1967:63–64,158). On the other hand, he sometimes places the changeover at one-and-a-half or two years of age (1967:157). Further, Carstairs notes that even before the age of one-and-a-half the child is confronted with major, ongoing traumata—the regular witnessing of parental intercourse (which begins not more than six months after birth) and the periodic and inexplicably distant parental behavior when a grandparent enters the room (1967:157–158). (Recall that in Hindu India it is thought improper to fondle or pay attention to one's child in the presence of elders.)

Let us examine this last point more closely. According to Carstairs:

> [The mother] must look on impassively while the grandmother makes much of her child—unless the child begins to cry. Only then is she entitled to assert her first claim to "mother" her baby, by clasping it in her arms and giving it the breast.
>
> In this setting the pattern becomes established that a mother is an attentive but pre-occupied person, whose feelings only become apparent when the child cries to her in distress—and then she hurries to supply all his wants.   (Carstairs 1967:66)

This passage clearly recalls Minturn. The mother is attentive but "preoccupied." She shows her feelings only when the child cries. Carstairs, in fact, at times portrays this as the ongoing and typical mothering situation: "In this setting, the pattern becomes established. . . ."

On the other hand, Carstairs elsewhere treats this situation as a temporary and for the child unpredictable consequence of the grandmother's (i.e., mother-in-law's) presence. In his theoretical summation, Carstairs clearly speaks of distancing as a temporary effect:

> Already, before this, [i.e., before the age of one-and-a-half or two years] the child will have cause to notice that his mother, though devoted to his service, is unaccountably inconstant in the warmth of her contact with him. At times she caresses him affectionately while at other times, owing to the presence of her parents-in-law, she becomes aloof and seemingly indifferent to him.
>
> (Carstairs 1967:157)

The passage by Carstairs quoted directly before this implies a long-term and consistent attitude of mothering resembling that described by Minturn. I suggest Carstairs saw this pattern, yet ultimately took it as temporary because of his belief that the Hindu mother's intense physical ministrations indicate the same desire for symbiosis they would in the West. Underneath the grandmother's enforced restraint, the mother is assumed to hold feelings like those of the Western mother, "feelings [that] only become apparent when the child cries to her in distress." Yet, as I think Carstairs implies and as Minturn states, this pattern is not simply a periodic conse-quence of the elders' presence—although it is surely heightened by that presence—but the ongoing form of mother-child relations in India. It possesses its own consistency and its own psychological underpinning. Moreover, even if we regard the mother's habitual stance as a result of the mother-in-law's continuous supervision of mother and child, we must be prepared to identify an internal con-sistency and psychological underpinning for this very pattern of mul-tiple caretaking. Carstairs, however, thinking in individualist terms, focuses on the mother alone, thus overemphasizing the artificial nature of the grandmother's presence. Carstairs' consequent attempt to isolate a prior and pure indulgent intimacy between mother and child explains why he remains unclear on the extent of the mother's distracted attention, and it accounts for his periodic attempts to move up the time when excessively good mothering ends and harsh mothering begins.

It is even possible to detect in Carstairs' portrayal of the child as "king" an echo of Minturn's view of the infant as the passive, unmir-rored observer of courtyard life. For example, when Carstairs dis-cusses the long hours spent by the Hindu child in the cradle, he stresses the sensuous pleasure of the frequent rocking provided by adults (1967:64–65). Noting that Hindu kings and gods are honored by similar rocking, Carstairs sees the hours in the cradle as an exten-sion of the "royal indulgence" accorded the child. Minturn, on the other hand, stresses the covering of the child in the cradle, along with the absence of direct eye contact with the women of the family courtyard (1966:107, 112). No doubt, in her view, rocking would appear chiefly as a way to keep the child passive, placated, and relatively uninvolved with his caretakers, however much pleasure the child may experience from the motion itself. Again, while the two accounts are not in complete contradiction, interpretation is all. Certainly, as Carstairs would have it, the rocking of the cradle gratifies the child. Even so, Carstairs' emphasis can mislead a reader into viewing the Hindu parent-child relation as one of extreme personal intimacy. As Minturn shows, this is too simple.

Minturn's is by no means the only observational study to cast doubt on the consensus psychoanalytic account of Hindu child rearing. Although studies of child rearing have been and continue to be relegated to the periphery of contemporary anthropological concern, a modest ethnographic literature on Hindu child-rearing practices has nonetheless developed in the years following Minturn's pioneering study. Unfortunately, researchers of Hindu child rearing receive little attention—even from each other—and therefore the literature as a whole remains disorganized and unself-conscious. Careful consideration of the literature on Hindu child-rearing practices, however, does reveal consensus on a surprising number of issues. In particular, there is wide support for Minturn's assessment of the emotional character of the Hindu mother-child relationship.

Susan Seymour, for example, is one of the few researchers of Hindu child rearing to match Minturn in experience and expertise. In a number of publications she explicitly echoes Minturn's view:

> In general, the care of children in Bhubaneswar was strikingly casual and impersonal. Children were taken for granted and their basic needs attended to, but they received little other special attention or stimulation. The situation was similar to that described for Khalapur, India, by Minturn and Hitchcock.   (Seymour 1975:47)

> While children were greatly desired, once born, they tended to be treated as one more member of the household, not as a special individual deserving of special attention. In fact, there were taboos against praising or focusing attention on infants for fear of attracting the Evil Eye or other maloccurrences.   (Seymour 1983:269)

Even some more psychoanalytically oriented observers clearly confirm Minturn's account. For example, Renaldo Maduro, a Jungian-influenced anthropologist, has done important but neglected work among a group of Brahman artists. Compare his account of feeding and cradling to that of Minturn and Carstairs.

> In Nathdwara, it is a disgrace for Brahmin mothers not to attend immediately to a whimpering child. If the mother is not at once

available, then other women in the household (including older siblings) may fill in for her by rocking and singing the child to sleep.
. . .

The child's passivity during all the rocking and swinging is important for his personality formation. From infancy, he is expected to remain passive and unresponsive. And although they attend to his every need, his parents are in a real sense distant too. Ironically, the cradle-swing relationship is impersonal, for the child need not be held, cuddled, or treated sensually; in fact, any member of the household—even young children—can be assigned the monotonous task of mechanically pulling a string to keep an infant in motion and contented. Outside the feeding situation (a warm close experience at the breast), less physical contact and libidinal stimulation was observed between Brahmin mothers and their children than among lower castes. Painters are very often nostalgic for the days of being rocked to sleep. . . .

Painter children are breast-fed on demand for approximately two years (or longer) and may continue to find solace at a mother's or grandmother's breast for many years thereafter. At the slightest noise signifying discomfort, mothers habitually thrust the breast into the young child's mouth to pacify him. . . . However, rarely is a child actively stimulated during the attention paid to him; while breast-feeding, he is still largely a receiver, and inside and outside this sphere little or nothing is done to encourage vigorous activity or to permit frustration and aggression which would, in normal doses, further the work of ego structuring and separation.   (Maduro 1976:160–161)

Once again, while the sensual satisfaction of feeding and cradle-rocking are present, the emotional character of the mother-child relation is one of distance. Physical contact with and gratification of the child does not occasion a loving mirroring of emotions as it would in the West. The child, as a unique individual, seems almost not to exist.

Yet Maduro's psychoanalytic approach is able to assimilate data like Minturn's without this having marked consequences on its conclusions. Whereas for Carstairs overindulgence indicates a dangerous psychological closeness between mother and child, for Maduro physical closeness combined with emotional distance is equally dangerous. What Maduro seeks and finds lacking in Hindu child rearing is the gradual training in independence that both Freudian and Jungian theory claim is necessary. Whatever departs from this norm is taken as either too much or too little of a good thing. In similar fashion, Carstairs avoids the contradiction evident in his description of frustrations brought on by so-called too good Hindu mothering. While feeding on demand is condemned by Carstairs as a "too good" overindulgence that leads to oral fixation, the Hindu mother's distancing in the presence of the mother-in-law is productive of the same fixation, this time by virtue of its "inconstancy."

Like Maduro and Carstairs, Alan Roland encounters, if only briefly, reports that echo Minturn's stress on the disjunction between physical ministration and emotional attention in Hindu mothering. As with Maduro and Carstairs, however, such data do not alter basic conclusions. Roland never refers to Minturn's own research, but he does mention a personal communication from two students of Hindu child rearing. Here is the passage:

> There is a subtle inhibition of too great self-other differentiation and separation through the amount of gratification and closeness an Indian child experiences. This decidedly contrasts with the "optimal" frustrations of the Western child, which foster the inner separation process of the child from the mother. While there is a great deal of affection, emotional and physical gratification, and empathic awareness of the child's dependency needs, there is often very little empathy with the more autonomous and individualized strivings of the child (pers. com. Dr. Bhutta and Erna Hoch)—again central to both the separation and individuation processes in Western children.
>
> (Roland 1988:233)

Here, Roland assimilates the comments of Bhutta and Hoch by distinguishing an empathic awareness of "dependency needs" from empathic concerns for "individualized strivings." Thus, Roland is able to retain the notion that Hindu child rearing highlights the mirroring of emotions, even as he acknowledges that at least some important emotions are, in fact, not mirrored. It is questionable whether the child-rearing situation described by Roland ought even to be characterized as an "intense" experience of mirroring since mirroring is here said to be restricted to very particular sorts of emotions. I argue, however, that the alleged mirroring of a Hindu child's nonindividualized strivings is an illusion. Roland, like Carstairs and

Kakar before him, is here reading into the intense "gratification and closeness" of the Hindu mother-child situation the essentially Western emotional stance of empathy. In fact, the emotional contact and awareness Westerners associate with physical closeness is absent from the Hindu situation, whether it is a question of mirroring a child's autonomous strivings or otherwise.

The problematic use of "empathy" or "mirroring" as concepts emerges also in Roland's interpretation of adult behavior, where he sees in Hindu sensitivity to the honor and standing of the group a "subtly constant, but mainly nonverbal" form of "mirroring" (1988:246). Here again, by interpreting a Hindu phenomenon as both a heightened, yet subtle and nonverbal version of our highly verbal and interactive Western notion of empathic attention, Roland stretches our Western notions of empathy and mirroring to the breaking point. By retaining these concepts in cases of admittedly nonverbal interaction, I think, Roland makes it too easy to read Western patterns of subjectivity into behavior that has its own distinctive psychological roots. Below, in a reworked account of the Hindu child-rearing situation, I spell out an alternative reading of the nonverbal closeness characteristic of the Hindu mother-child relationship. (See also my reanalysis of Roland's most extensive clinical case study in chapter 7.)

To summarize, psychoanalysts generally take observational data on physical contact in Hindu infancy as evidence of sensual overindulgence and of extreme, even dangerous, emotional closeness. Evidence that suggests a distinction between physical and emotional closeness in the Hindu case is customarily downplayed, for such data imply that the underlying rationale of Hindu child rearing is fundamentally different from any we are familiar with. When forced to confront such information, however, psychoanalysts treat any absence of personal attention as a frustration every bit as productive of early fixation as excessive gratification.

As Roland notes, albeit without fully recognizing the problem's impact on his own work, this way of thinking involves a kind of trick. In the absence of the approved Western mode of child rearing, all diverse cultural practices come off as too much or too little of a good thing. Whatever is foreign to the classic Western notion of proper child rearing thus appears pathogenic. However much a given analyst might wish to escape this outcome, the logic is too deeply built into the theory to be circumvented without fundamental change.

A new approach to this problem is therefore necessary. The neglected though growing literature on Hindu child rearing might be used to construct an alternative model of Hindu psychological development—a model in which the distinctive Hindu mix of physical indulgence and personal distance makes sense.[6] In such a model, a combination of closeness and distance would work to reassure a child of the world's benevolence even as it gently moves that child to break away from a too direct link to the mother. From this point of view, the group character of Hindu life would be traceable to a culturally patterned developmental achievement, not to a problematic extension of the earliest phase of psychological life. This new understanding of the role of the group in Hindu psychological development will provide us with a key that unlocks the riddle of Santoshi Ma and of the larger Goddess of which she is a variant.

Chapter 4

Renunciation on the Way to the Group: A New Approach to Early Hindu Childhood

Is it possible to develop a model of Hindu child rearing practices without casting them as misshapen approximations of our own techniques? Can we devise a theory of Hindu maturation free of the individualism of traditional psychoanalysis yet productive of depth-psychological insight? I think we can. The richness of Hindu myth and ritual with its habitual recourse to family metaphor and body imagery allows us to suggest and substantiate a new developmental model of the Hindu psyche. Hindu religious imagery will be the subject of subsequent chapters, where we shall return to the problem of the Goddess in her many forms and concentrate on the relation between human and divine mothering. In those chapters the core of a new model of Hindu development will emerge. In this chapter, however, I hope to prepare the ground for this proposed theory by suggesting a new interpretation of the data on Hindu child rearing.

The available information on Hindu child rearing can fairly be described as abundant. In comparison to the minimal child rearing data treated by Carstairs, Kakar, and Roland, the existing material is rich and generally untouched. For example, as seen in the previous chapter, Leigh Minturn's extensive treatment of Hindu child rearing (1966) clearly calls into question the notion—held in common by Carstairs, Kakar, and Roland—that the Hindu mother's close physical ministrations indicate a powerful emotional intimacy between mother and child. Yet neither Kakar nor Roland, who wrote well after Minturn's work was published, take her ethnography into account. Minturn's comprehensive treatment of Hindu child rearing, clearly the best available account, remains virtually untouched by psychoanalytic theorists.[1]

On the other hand, there is a sense in which the available data on Hindu child rearing are frustratingly thin. Whether a given observer's orientation is psychoanalytic or not, Western patterns serve almost always as implicit standards against which Hindus are measured. Rarely is an effort made to positively characterize behavior according to a specifically Indian rationale. For example, while observers leave no doubt that Hindu children are *not* socialized for independence, they give us precious little information on how Hindus actively integrate children into the groups so important to Hindu life. The category of "dependence" into which so much Hindu socialization behavior is placed is in practice little more than the negative of our valued Western "independence." As a positive description of Hindu behavior, it has little content (Surya 1969:388–389). Western observations of Hindu child rearing rarely escape this trap. For the most part, they offer statistical comparisons between Hindus and others based on universal research categories derived chiefly from Western sources (for example, Whiting and Whiting 1975; Rohner and Chaki-Sircar 1988). In this methodology, the possibility of deriving categories of observation and understanding from specifically Hindu sources is foreclosed from the start.

This being said, however, the existing, relatively untouched storehouse of information on Hindu child rearing does contain some exceedingly useful material. Often, the unstructured, qualitative observations that accompany more statistical studies, like those of Susan Seymour (1971, 1975, 1976, 1983), contain insights and observations that challenge traditional psychoanalytic theories of Hindu socialization. These observations call for a systematic consideration from the point of view of depth psychology.

Then there are observers such as Alan Beals (1962). Precisely because Beals is not primarily interested in child rearing or psychology, his observations and conclusions are shaped by an attempt to grasp the particularity of the Hindu situation. Beals, perhaps more clearly than anyone else, highlights the pattern of threat, bargain, and persistent request central to so much Hindu mother-child interaction. While this pattern can be identified and studied, retroactively, so to speak, in the existing literature, such bargaining behavior has heretofore been downplayed because it finds no ready place in current developmental theory.

Finally, there are studies, like those of Mildred Luschinsky (1962) or Renaldo Maduro (1976), that, though relatively conventional in their theoretical approach, are extremely rich, detailed, insightful, and surprisingly unknown to most writers on Hindu psychology. By virtue of the sheer weight of high quality observation these studies contain, they lend themselves to rethinking and reworking from any number of different points of view.

Another advantage is the fact that our sources on Hindu child rearing practices show an impressive consistency across regional and other boundaries. Of course, family structure and socialization behavior does vary. Kolenda, for example, contrasts the joint families of North India with a Southern Nattati Nadar community of predominantly nuclear families (1984). Seymour, moreover, in a number of careful comparative studies, details quantitative variation in certain types of child-rearing behavior on the basis of factors such as caste, class, and modernization (Seymour 1971, 1975, 1976, 1983). Nonetheless, Seymour grants that the difference in the practices of various groups is more one of degree than of principle (1975:47,49,51).

After a comprehensive reading of our sources, it is this uniformity that stands out. For example, accounts from Northwest India (Carstairs 1967; Luschinsky 1962; Maduro 1976; Minturn and Hitchcock 1966; Wiser and Wiser 1963), East India (Bhattacharyya 1986; Rohner and Chaki-Sircar 1987; Seymour 1971, 1975, 1976, 1983), and South India (Beals 1962; Dube 1955; Mencher 1963) agree in their descriptions of nursing, weaning, and toilet training. To take some more specific examples, Mencher's account of beliefs regarding the use of praise in a Southern, matrilineal joint family setting (1963:62) agrees with accounts from many other, more northerly, patrilineal regions (Maduro 1976:166–167; Minturn and Hitchcock 1966:119–121; Poffenberger 1981:83). Similarly, Beals' description of a pattern of persistent requests by children in a South Indian village (1962:12–22) matches closely with reports from the North (Minturn and Hitchcock 1966:130,133) and East (Seymour 1971:144–148). Even such details as teasing games, in which gifts are given to a child and then in a test requested back again, are reported with remarkable similarity by observers in the East (Bhattacharyya 1986:146) and South (Nichter and Nichter 1987:75).

Moreover, accounts from all regions speak of joint families, multiple caretakers, and rules of restraint on parent-child interaction in front of elders. Even where joint families do not predominate, nuclear families are reported to locate near relatives in order to approximate joint family participation in child rearing (Beals 1962:13). In short, while there is a need to investigate and clarify subtle variations, the essential consistency in the diverse existing accounts of Hindu child rearing justifies our treating them as a unit for purposes of analyzing the psychological underpinnings of the fundamental patterns and principles unifying Hindu thought and character.

In this connection, I also wish to mention Margaret Trawick's profound book, *Notes on Love in a Tamil Family* (1990). Trawick's book was published well after completion of the basic text of this work, and I have thus not incorporated her ethnography of Hindu child rearing directly into the body of this or subsequent chapters. Clearly, however, Trawick's close, deep observations of childhood in a South Indian family are among the most important material on Hindu socialization ever recorded. They represent the first glimmer of a serious, renewed anthropological interest in the study of Hindu child rearing.

I have been particularly struck by the fundamental compatibility between the view of Hindu childhood put forth below, in my own work, and the material newly reported by Trawick. This is particularly significant given the fact that Trawick's account is from the South Indian state of Tamil Nadu—perhaps the area within India most distinctively marked off from the dominant Northern tradition.

Specifically, Trawick details the tension between the care offered by the child's "own" parents and the care offered by the broader family group in a way that clearly meshes with my own view. This is so despite the significant kinship differences between the Northern system and the Dravidian kinship system of Tamil Nadu. Trawick also discusses a Tamil system of child adoption that, however different in its particulars, matches the basic function of Hindu multiple mothering as described below. Also, Trawick's account of "training" strategies along with her description of bargaining by-play between caretaker and child can clearly be interpreted in light of the perspective on these matters I outline below. Finally, in addition to these fundamental areas of compatibility, Trawick's ethnography bears out the earlier socialization accounts examined in this chapter on a great number of detailed particulars. For example, Trawick provides an account of the same teasing game of giving and taking already reported by observers widely dispersed throughout India.[2]

In many ways, Trawick's theoretical approach, informed in part by the work of Lacan, shares with my own viewpoint the attempt to break with Western psychological individualism. On the other hand, Trawick's "postmodern" stance prompts her quite consciously to eschew the systematic construction of an alternative, culturally reshaped psychoanalytic theory. Nor, therefore, does Trawick systematically relate her own approach to that of extant psychoanalytic interpretations of Hindu culture. Indeed, if anything, Trawick gives signs of missing the fundamental challenge that observations such as hers pose to the work of analysts like Carstairs, Kakar, and Roland.[3] Thus, the reshaped psychoanalytic model I offer below can be seen as an attempt to draw Trawick's acute and fascinating treatment of child rearing together with the larger corpus of Hindu socialization research into a new, theoretical whole—a whole that is clearly depth psychological in character and that can thus be systematically compared and contrasted with traditional, Western psychoanalyses of childhood.

In sum, then, while not ideal for our purposes, the available data on Hindu child rearing are sufficient to permit a preliminary recasting into a reshaped psychoanalytic point of view. Moreover, whatever the limitations of the available data, it can be said with confidence that the approach presented here takes more information on Hindu child rearing into account than do current psychoanalyses of Hindu culture.

No doubt, further research on Hindu child-rearing practices will prompt extension, modification, regional diversification, or rejection of elements of the model presented here. In order to reach that point, however, the available child rearing material needs reconsideration and reworking. This reworking process cannot simply await further data, for the most serious barrier to the collection of such data is actually theoretical. India has long been a destination for anthropologists, and there has been ample opportunity to conduct culturally sensitive observations of Hindu childhood. Nonetheless, relatively little observation of Hindu child-rearing practices, in comparison to other sorts of anthropological study, has been carried out—Trawick's work is a recent and welcome exception. An important reason for this, I suggest, is that a psychological theory sufficiently free of Western bias is unavailable for anthropological use. Most ethnographers thus continue to eschew child observation, embarrassed by data that can at present only be subject to ethnocentric comparison with the West. At the same time, a mere handful of observers with an interest in child rearing go on working from more traditional psychological perspectives.

A renascent anthropological interest in Hindu child rearing, then, would be encouraged by a novel theoretical approach, one less burdened by an implicit Western vision of normality. Above all, therefore, I hope to show what a nonethnocentric, broadly psychoanalytic theory of Hindu development *could* look like. The specific approach to Hindu child rearing and psychology outlined below should serve as a starting point for future work, and revisions based on more extensive future observations of child rearing would be welcome. To encourage such work, I wish to establish that it is indeed possible to adapt a psychoanalytic model to the particularities of the Hindu case.

The family group, and not merely the individual mother and her child, lies at the core of this suggested model of Hindu child rearing. From this point of view, much of a Hindu mother's behavior toward her child is designed to gently push him away from the relationship with her and toward a sense of immersion in, or unity with, the family at large. Similarly, the behavior of family members other than the mother is meant to exert a kind of pull on the child to draw him away from an exclusive tie to the mother.

What, then, is the culturally distinctive form of this push away from the mother and the corresponding pull toward the group? In this chapter I hope to show that the Hindu mother as well as the larger group of caretakers in the Hindu joint family[4] so arrange their care as to prompt in the child a voluntary renunciation of infantile ties to the mother. In response to subtle prompting by adults, the Hindu child, seemingly without being forced to do so, abandons the intense early attachment to infantile forms of pleasure, i.e., unrestricted oral, anal, and phallic gratification. This contrasts with the Western case, in which the child is gradually, but forcibly, made to abandon exclusive attachments to love objects and immature pleasures in return for the mature, approving love of the parents.

Because psychoanalysts have sought to confirm in India merely the presence or absence of this Western developmental pattern, they have missed altogether the Hindu child's movement, by way of renunciation, away from infantile attachments to the mother and toward a more mature participation in the group. Not seeing the Hindu mother's subtle prompting of her child to renunciation but only her refusal to overtly deny pleasure, the analysts have mistakenly characterized Hindu mothering as dangerously indulgent. Unaware of the long, gradual process by which the Hindu child renounces infantile attachments, the analysts have interpreted the late call for discipline by the father as an unprecedented and thus traumatic crackdown. In this chapter, then, by arguing for the existence of the heretofore unrecognized developmental process of renunciation on the way to the group, I hope to create the basis of a new psychoanalysis of Hinduism.

To begin the explication of renunciation on the way to the group, let us turn to the much-discussed problem of Hindu nursing. Most accounts of Hindu breast-feeding stress that a child is fed whenever it cries (Beals 1962:15,19; Bhattacharyya 1986:133–134; Boss 1965:67; Carstairs 1967:63–64; Cormack 1953:12–13; Dube 1955:149,192; Luschinsky 1962:123; Maduro 1976:161–168; Minturn and Hitchcock 1966:107–108; Murphy and Murphy 1953:47; Narain 1964:135–137; Seymour 1971:145; Wiser and Wiser 1963:76–77). A Hindu baby, Carstairs notes, "is never allowed to cry for long" (1967:64). While feeding on demand is in fact standard practice, this way of describing Hindu nursing conveys the misleading impression of a maternal servant promptly and fully catering to her "royal" child's demands (Carstairs 1967:65). Of course, as Carstairs, Kakar, and Roland point out, Hindus describe or treat children as kings, queens, or even as "divine saviors" (Carstairs 1967:64–65; Kakar 1978:88–89; Roland 1988:249). It must be said, however, that the Hindu way of relating to a king, or even a god, is not precisely what a Westerner might expect. It is commonplace, for example, for Hindu petitioners to worry a divine patron with what a Westerner would consider rudely persistent requests. Gods who fail to deliver bounties for which proper service has been rendered may find themselves chastised, or at least pestered, by their most loyal devotees (Bharati 1975:282; Pocock 1973:46).

Likewise, Hindu mothers and children berate each other with streams of threats and requests that sometimes delay and always affect the character of services rendered. This combination of threat and bargain is explicit when a child has learned to speak. Yet, as I show below, it is implicitly present even before this in the wordless interaction of mother and infant. While this pattern of interplay, once identified, may strike a psychoanalytic observer as even more problematic than nursing on demand, I hope to show that in the Hindu context it has a salutary effect on the child's development. This is because the bargaining by-play of mother and child has the effect of pushing the child away from an exclusive and dependent attachment to the mother and toward a kind of participation or immersion in the activity of the broader family group. Implicitly and eventually explicitly, the Hindu mother says to her child, "Yes, I will feed you if you insist, because anyone in this group will eventually get what he needs, but you'll get more food and love from me and from everyone else if you grow up soon and abandon the breast." To this the child replies, so to speak, "I'll think it over, but first give me the breast."

As a child matures, the mother's response to his persistent requests slows while her emphasis on the bargain involved sharpens. The child is eventually asked not only to abandon immature pleasures but also to join the group by carrying out useful tasks. While the mother's growing reluctance to answer a child's call for the breast or, later, for solid food at first evokes yet more insistent demands, eventually the child grasps the point and without being forced to do so reduces demands for immature gratification and/or voluntarily shoulders more family tasks, thus reaping a reward in the form of full membership in and honor from the group. To increase the group's attraction, the mother is careful not to lavish too much attention on the child outside the feeding situation. The group, on the other hand, as we see below, offers the child a degree and quality of attention not available from the mother. Thus, although pleasure is never overtly withheld from the child, such pleasure is accompanied all along by a message that eventually makes its impression.

This call to maturity buried, as it were, in the food is what psychoanalytic observers have missed. All that has been visible to psychoanalytic observers of Hindu child rearing to date is an overt and prolonged gratification of infantile pleasure and a corresponding absence of training in frustration. Hindus, however, do have a distinctive method for loosening the child's attachment to pleasure. They do not withhold gratification but create conditions in which a child will abandon it without being forced to do so.

This characteristic Hindu pattern of persistent request and reluctant reply is relatively easy to see in the interactions of older children with adults. It is here, then, that our investigation begins. Consider, for example, these passages from Minturn:

> The extent to which the children were capable of insistent demanding was brought home to us almost daily . . . throughout our stay we were rarely out of earshot of the whining cry, "Give me my photo." Since we took photographs of the children daily, and sent the films to Delhi to be developed, it was impossible to give the children all the pictures that had been taken of them, although we passed out as many as we could. No amount of explanation could silence their demands, nor did the mothers reprimand their children for this persistent begging. Many mothers were, in fact, only slightly less demanding in this regard than their offspring. . . .
>
> The Rajput children do not strike an observer as being particularly well trained. One reason is because of the pattern that a strong or repeated request is required before a villager, adult or child, will comply, unless the request falls within the limits of some customary obligation, and such formal obligations do not affect the children. Thus

it is often necessary for a mother to ask a child several times to do something before the child complies. Since mothers are usually lenient with small children, they sometimes do not comply at all.

(Minturn and Hitchcock 1966:130,133)

While these comments describe behavior familiar to travelers in India, the degree to which this pattern of action affects childhood feeding needs emphasis. Below, Beals describes a bit of interaction that makes the feeding-bargaining equation explicit:

The mother scowls at her child, "You must have worked hard to be so hungry." The mother serves food and says, "Eat this. After you have eaten it, you must sit here and rock your little sister." The mother says, "You eat so much; where do you go; why won't you stay home?" The child replies, "I have a stomachache, I cannot rock my little sister." The child finishes its food and runs out of the house. Later, the child's aunt sees it and asks it to run to the store and buy some cooking oil. When it returns, the aunt says, "If you continue to obey me like this, I will give you something good to eat." When the mother catches the child again, she asks, "Where have you been?" Learning what occurred, she says, "If you brought cooking oil, that is fine; now come play with your sister." The child says, "First give me something to eat, and I will play with my sister." The mother scolds, "You will die of eating, sometimes you are willing to work, sometimes you are not willing to work; may you eat dirt." She gives it food and the child plays with its sister. (Beals 1962:19–20)

This is Beals' comment on such behavior:

Almost always the child receives its food, but very often the food is accompanied by a threat. The food comes from working. He who does not work may end up eating dirt. The food is a bribe, and the mother constantly claims the privilege of withholding food. Often food is slow to come. It must be paid for by running to the store to get cooking oil or betel leaves and areca nuts. Sometimes food is obtained through incessant demands. Services provided by adults for children are always conditional. (Beals 1962:20)

Perhaps Beals goes a bit far when he says that all services provided to children are conditional. This is not quite the case for, as Beals himself notes, the child almost always receives food.

In this connection, the reader may recall the dispute between anthropologists who see the services of Hindu gods as conditional on a devotee's gifts of food and those who emphasize the compassion of a divine giving that asks no direct tribute (Babb 1975:53–61; Hayley 1980; Mayer 1981:167; Wadley 1975:86). Perhaps there is truth on both sides of this theological dispute, for what seems to be happening on the human level is a kind of ideal or unforced bargain. Food is rarely withheld from the child, yet he is made to understand that a mature, valued family member would earn the honor of grateful feeding by performing services for the family—services such as caring for younger siblings or running errands for an aunt. From this perspective, the mother's threatening scold to her self-indulgent child, "May you eat dirt," is not merely an assertion that only work produces food, it is also a way of impugning the honor or "purity" contained in the food a group grudgingly offers to its less self-sacrificing members.[5]

Thus, while Hindu mothers do answer their children's requests for food, this often occurs grudgingly and with an ideal set of conditions attached. Nursing on demand, therefore, seems not to flow from the mother's inordinate desire for intimacy. On the contrary, Hindu mothers have clear and conscious objections to the persistent requests of their children. For example, when Minturn asked mothers:

> "Whom do you call a bad child?" or "What sorts of things do you punish your children for?" Stubborn demanding of attention was the most frequently cited negative characteristic. This concept was phrased by the women in a number of different ways, for example, "When he is stubborn," "When he troubles me," "When he cries for nothing," "When he will not listen," "When he will not stop crying," or "When he insists on having food which I cannot give him."
> (Minturn and Hitchcock 1966:132)

Seymour reports similar complaints:

> As mothers slept with their children at night, night-feedings were a simple matter. When a child awakened, a mother simply turned to him and offered her breast, there being no need to get up. However, several mothers complained to me that their children kept them awake during much of the night demanding the breast; nevertheless, they did not stop indulging these demands.   (Seymour 1971:144)

While it is true that mothers indulge their children's persistent requests, they clearly evidence a hesitance to give in without some resistance. This, I think, is a Hindu mother's way of showing her child the path to more mature behavior even as she leaves the precise timing of such maturation up to the child. As noted above, this is evident not only in verbal bargaining with older children but also in the unspoken language of early nursing. Consider the following extended excerpt from Seymour's doctoral dissertation. These all-too-neglected observations constitute perhaps the most detailed account of Hindu nursing in existence:

> Although demand-feeding was the general procedure with infants and young children, mothers did not necessarily respond quickly or immediately when a child cried or otherwise complained. A child might have to cry from one to eight minutes before someone responded, for mothers went when it was convenient for them. . . .
>
> A child thus learned at an early age that he must make prolonged demands in order to get a response and that eventually someone would come. In the joint family, where other female relatives were available, it might be someone other than his mother, or in a large family with many children it might be an older sibling. These persons were not suitable if the child wanted his mother's breast so, if he kept complaining, he was eventually turned over to his own mother. . . .
>
> Once a mother did respond to a child's demands to nurse, she not only responded in a casual manner but usually only for brief periods. She might offer her breast anywhere from one to five minutes and then abruptly stop and remove her breast while the child was still sucking. Of mothers abruptly breaking interaction with their children in this manner, 165 instances were observed and nearly 70 percent of the time the child resisted his mother's action by crying and trying to regain the breast. After some moments of such complaining by a child, a mother usually submitted and offered her breast again, again removing it a few minutes later. A nursing period might consist of a number of such sequences of events. . . .
>
> Thus, a child's demands to nurse were intermittently reinforced by the mother. With one exception, a child was rarely nursed steadily for a prolonged period until he was satisfied. The exception consisted of those occasions when a mother lay down with her child and nursed him until he fell asleep, a technique used for quieting an upset child or putting an active one to sleep.

As children developed motor skills, they could pursue their mothers about the house and demand the breast when they wanted. As a woman sat working on the floor, a child might approach her and simply take her breast in his mouth. She might resist and cover herself tightly with her sari but, if the child persisted, she usually gave in and let him suckle. By the age of one a child had usually learned to be actively demanding with his rather passive and casual mother. In this manner he could eventually get what he wanted.

(Seymour 1971:145–148)

This account of Hindu nursing gives a very different impression than those of Carstairs, Kakar, or Roland. In Seymour's account, Hindu nursing on demand seems less a pattern of perpetual gratification or empathic mirroring than an almost continual frustration. In fact, full gratification is provided only when a mother wants the child to cease interaction, i.e., to sleep. No doubt, these more detailed data might simply reinforce a traditional analyst's conviction that Hindu mothering leads to an oral-narcissistic fixation. Yet I think the pattern of nursing described has a consistent, if double-edged, message. While the mother lets her child know she is always available, she simultaneously suggests that complete self-indulgence is neither acceptable nor admirable behavior. In a sense, even as the mother forces her child to a pattern of persistent request, she also begins a long, gradual process of weaning. From a very early period, the mother lets her baby know in what direction adult behavior will take it while at the same time letting the child control the overall pace of its psychological growth.

While Seymour's account provides a key to the distinctive nature of Hindu development, her description of Hindu nursing may at first seem to reveal a hitherto neglected and fundamental parallel between infant feeding in East and West. After all, Seymour shows that nursing, which was heretofore conceived by psychoanalytic observers as evergratifying indulgence, is in fact a carefully controlled combination of indulgence and frustration. Therefore, should the reader heed our admonitions and scruple to define the Hindu pattern as a dangerous mixture of excessive indulgence and unpredictable frustration, he or she might conclude that Hindu nursing works precisely because it successfully and carefully balances indulgence with frustration. The typical pattern of Hindu nursing might therefore be described as a functional equivalent of Western feeding patterns. From this point of view, differences would be incidental. Whereas in the West moments of indulgence and frustration are separated more definitively into times when feeding is or is not considered proper, in Hindu India the gratification of nursing on demand is continually interlaced with tiny frustrations. These two patterns, however different on the surface, would each serve to gradually accustom a child to frustration and to prepare him for weaning.

This simple resolution of the comparative problem, although in some degree valid, is misleading. There are fundamental differences in Western and Hindu nursing, differences in both external practices and in the internal representation of these practices. While it is true that each approach works by way of a combination of gratification and frustration, the differences in deployment of gratification and frustration are not at all incidental.

The most important difference in practices between nursing in East and West centers around the issue of clear stopping points. This difference was still more sharply defined in the days when feeding on schedule dominated in the West. Even today, however, as Western feeding patterns grow more flexible, the Hindu pattern of continual stops and starts along with the Hindu mother's careful avoidance of definitive refusal to any emphatic request for the breast would strike a Westerner as dangerously inconsistent. This absence of definitive stopping points or refusals in the Hindu case contributes, I suggest, to a decisive difference in the inner representation of the feeding process.

It is true that in both West and East successful weaning depends both on a careful dosing of frustration by the mother and on the eventual reconciliation to frustration on the part of the child. In the West, however, precisely because the mother does often give a final, definitive refusal, successful weaning is experienced as an acceptance by the child of the mother's "No." In Hindu India, on the other hand, because the breast is never completely withheld, the child experiences weaning as the voluntary renunciation of pleasure. The meaning of this difference is clarified by a brief comparison of the classic Hindu and Western religious responses to the greatest imaginable frustration—that of death.

In the traditional Judeo-Christian view, the righteous obey commands and prohibitions set down by God in return for the promise of blissful triumph over death through a purified life in God's heaven (Partin 1986:186–187; Tober and Lusby 1986:237–239). This image is modeled on the child's internalization of parental commands and prohibitions in return for the promise of a more independent life as a mature and beloved child. It is true that the movement toward maturity here involves a voluntary abandonment of selfish, immature pleasures. Yet it is vital that this sacrifice is conceived of as submission to God's will. The good Jew or Christian accepts the divine "Thou shalt not," just as the Western baby learns to accept the parental "No."

By contrast, the highest level of Hindu response to the frustration represented by death, is a realization that all existence is pervaded by loss (Sundararajan 1974:100–101). Since happiness is inevitably transitory, there are little deaths everywhere, so to speak. Thus, the mature and intelligent response is to psychically withdraw from the pursuit of pleasure and even from the sense of individuality toward which pleasure is directed. This turning from the self permits the realization that the individual is indissolubly connected to the larger universe. I suggest that this religious image is modeled on the Hindu child's voluntary sacrifice of the pleasures his mother never definitely ceases to offer, a sacrifice made in order to move away from the mother and toward a more mature immersion in the unified family. While it is true that the Hindu child is prompted to this renunciation by the mother's careful interlacing of pleasure with frustration, it is vital that the mother conducts herself in such a way as to give the child a sense that abstention is finally and fundamentally his choice.

Whereas in the West weaning is the culmination of a long process through which a child learns to tolerate and accept imposed frustration, in Hindu India weaning is the result of a process whereby immature pleasures, so labeled by tiny accompanying frustrations, are gradually renounced by the child himself. Despite the fact that Western children must finally, in some sense, abandon pleasure on their own and despite the fact that Hindu mothers subtly engineer their children's "voluntary sacrifice," the external and internal differences between the two processes help account for a great deal of what is distinctive and important in Hindu cultural life.

Consideration of Seymour's account from a slightly different point of view bears out this conclusion. The succession of feedings punctuated by withdrawal, which Seymour describes, cannot simply be seen as brief, alternating experiences of gratification and frustration—experiences that differ from their Western counterparts only in length. This is because the length of a given Hindu feeding event is not keyed to a perception of the child's mood. In other words, as Minturn and others have said elsewhere, Hindu feeding is not accompanied by an attentive mirroring of the child's emotions (Maduro 1976:160–161; Minturn and Hitchcock 1966:107–112; Seymour 1975:47; see above, chapter 3).

The internal consequences of this external difference are revealed by a reconsideration of our religious comparison. In Western psychological theory, a child is able to accept frustration imposed by the parents when it is convinced of their love and is determined to keep that love. The empathic character of Western feeding establishes this love and gives the child the reassurance necessary to go without the breast when this is asked of him. In just this way, the Jew or Christian sets aside selfish and sinful yearnings for the higher pleasure of a caring and personal God's eternal love (Partin 1986:186–187; Tober and Lusby 1986:237–239).

In the highest Hindu view, however, the individual does not distance from pleasure for the sake of a demanding but loving personal god. Rather, self-restraint is imposed to reach a state beyond mere personal relationship, a state in which higher unity with the universe itself is perceived (Sundararajan 1974:99–100). Even when Hindus conceive of this higher unity in terms of personal divinities, the stress is not on obeying commandments for the sake of a single great God's love but on a self-motivated sacrifice productive of an immersion in a complex yet unified set of divinities that is coterminous with the universe itself (Kinsley 1977; Long 1977). The transcendence of an uncertain world, a world that is neither essentially loving nor hating but ultimately without deep or permanent meaning, recalls the Hindu child's eventual turning away from the mixed pleasures of a serviceable but emotionally shallow feeding process. Moreover, the accompanying striving for unity with a higher reality that is coterminous with the unified gods, calls to mind the Hindu child's endeavor to join the adult world beyond the mother by imitating it.

Toilet training, for example, as we see below, is accomplished less by overt parental demands than by a gradual process in which the child spontaneously imitates others. Similarly, observers stress the predominance of imitative over fantasy play among Hindu children (Beals 1962:19; Cormack 1953:59; Luschinsky 1962:173; Minturn and Hitchcock 1966:128; Seymour 1975:52). In other words, the Hindu child abandons the transitory, impersonal pleasures of nursing for the sake of more satisfying participation in the life of the larger family group. By renunciatory choice, the child opts for the higher satisfaction of becoming like, and thus joining, the group of adults. Thus, a Hindu child comes to prefer adult food to the increasingly less fulfilling pleasure of the mother's reluctantly presented breast.

The essential difference between the approach outlined here and that of previous psychoanalytic authors is that the Hindu movement toward unification with the whole is considered not a developmental retreat to early symbiosis prompted by poor mothering but a culturally patterned developmental advance made possible by just this pattern of mothering. The advantage of this approach, moreover, is not simply its removal of negative evaluations from Hindu psychology but its ability to make more and better sense of the significant data on Hindu child-rearing practices we do have. The value of our discussion of Hindu nursing, for example, emerges when it is related to anthropological descriptions of the weaning process in India. Here, again, there is much evidence that prompts us to modify Carstairs' classic psychoanalytic account of weaning.

Observers agree that while Hindu weaning generally takes place between two and three years of age, in the absence of younger siblings it can be delayed until the fifth or sixth year (Beals 1962:15; Bhattacharyya 1986:134; Boss 1965:67; Carstairs 1967:63–64; Cormack 1953:13; Dube 1955:193; Luschinsky 1962:177–178; Maduro 1976:157, 161; Minturn and Hitchcock 1966:114–115; Murphy and Murphy 1953:49; Narain 1964:135–137; Seymour 1971:149–152). This far, Carstairs' psychoanalytic account is in agreement with the anthropological consensus. On other points, however, Carstairs and anthropological observers part company. According to Carstairs, weaning is a difficult emotional wrench even though the way has been prepared by an ever-expanding diet of solid food (1967:63–64). Minturn, however, characterizes the emotional adjustment required by weaning as relatively minor (Minturn and Hitchcock 1966:115). Moreover, discouraging devices mentioned by Carstairs, such as the application of bitter paste to the breast, are, according to Minturn and others, rarely and sparingly used (Cormack 1953:13; Minturn and Hitchcock 1966:115; Seymour 1971:150–151). In fact, Minturn tells us that some mothers report children who stop nursing of their own accord (Minturn and Hitchcock 1966:114).

Minturn's position on weaning is almost uniformly echoed by other observers of the Hindu child-rearing process. Cormack, for example, quotes an informant who says that babies "usually wean themselves" (1953:13; see also Murphy and Murphy:195). Moreover, in another lengthy and generally neglected account of Hindu child rearing, Luschinsky takes explicit exception to Carstairs' discussion of weaning in particular and of early childhood in general. She notes Carstairs' contention that the Hindu boy child's early blissful situation is rudely overturned by the dual blows of weaning and the loss of exclusive possession of the mother to the father (Luschinsky 1962:179–180). Loss of the mother is said to be based on the expiration of the postpartum sex taboo. Luschinsky shows that sexual relations between the mother and father are generally resumed sometime before weaning and that weaning itself is a gentler, more gradual process than Carstairs indicates. Luschinsky concludes:

> [The village] data does not, therefore, support the contention that a child experiences concurring deprivations which are sudden and occur at a relatively late period. The deprivations appear to be gradually effected over a period of several years.
>
> (Luschinsky 1962:179–180)

The gradual and untraumatic nature of Hindu weaning is confirmed by Seymour:

> By the end of the second year . . . nursing periods simply supplemented regular meals. . . . Weaning was a prolonged process in the cases I observed, lasting from six months to a year. A woman did not abruptly stop nursing her child but rather gave in less quickly and regularly to his demands for her breast. In this manner she reduced feedings for a given day. The effect on the child was to make him more aggressively persistent as long as he was convinced that his

mother would give in in the end, and mothers usually did submit at irregular intervals . . . [one] mother told me that she had even used red pepper on her breast to discourage her child, but I had not witnessed this and the child was still clearly interested. In fact, the only way I could know that a child was being weaned was to be told as it was not obvious from either the mother's or the child's behavior.

Two of the women who said they were weaning their children were New Capital middle-class women who felt it was time. The third was an Old Town middle-class woman who was pregnant. These three children did not give up nursing during a six-month period of observation, despite the fact that the last mother was nearly ready to give birth again. All three mothers complained to me that their children refused to take other foods and insisted on nursing. Of course, the children's desires were intermittently reinforced by their mothers irregularly giving in to their demands. How a child became completely weaned I am not sure. In cases where women are pregnant and give birth again, the arrival of the new child probably brings an abrupt end to the suckling of the previous child if he has not already been completely weaned. In other cases I suspect that over time the combination of offering children other foods and responding less and less regularly to their demands to nurse must eventually dissuade them.   (Seymour 1971:149–151)

Seymour's account of weaning is consistent with the notion that Hindu children abandon the breast as a reaction to the mother's heightened interlacing of the feedings with frustration. While Seymour rarely finds Hindu mothers delivering an absolute "No" to persistent requests, their increasingly slow, grudging responses to pleas for the breast gently "dissuade" the child. This pattern accounts for other observers' reports that Hindu weaning is "child-conditioned" or even that babies "usually wean themselves" (Cormack 1953:13,16; Minturn and Hitchcock 1966:114; Murphy and Murphy 1953:49). It is not that Hindu mothers have no role in the weaning process. Clearly they preside over it through a gradually escalating pattern of feeding specifically designed to discourage the child. The vital point for our purposes is that the process is designed to succeed without emphasizing the mother's role in it, indeed, without making the child feel as if serious requests will ever be refused. Thus, while both mother and child participate, the process is experienced as (and to some degree is) one in which the decisive sacrifice is voluntarily made by the child.

As noted, Seymour's description of Hindu weaning shows, once again, the process whereby the mother's intermittent withholding of the breast sets up a pattern of bargaining by-play or persistent request between mother and child. Beals gives an account that helps us understand more deeply the role of this by-play in the mechanism of weaning itself:

> As the child begins to walk, the mother's treatment begins to change. When the child cries in the early morning, the mother scolds and grumbles. After breast feeding, she orders it out of the house, "Go outside and play with your sister." The child clings to its mother's sari and refuses to go. The mother picks it up and puts it outside. After an hour, the child toddles back into the house and begins to cry, the mother says, "I am cooking dinner, stay outside when I am cooking dinner. If you don't stay outside, I won't cook any dinner." When the child cries again, the mother picks it up, breast feeds it and takes it outside again. When it cries again, she says, "Will your life come to an end if I don't pick you up?" When the mother goes to get water, the child again begins to cry. The mother leaves the child alone in the house and reappears in a half hour carrying water. She serves food. The child sees everyone sitting to eat and comes over laughing. The mother picks it up to nurse. She takes a small piece of bread, mashes it in her fingers and gives it to the child, who at first refuses the bread, then takes it and throws it on the ground. The mother scolds, "You have become too proud: what have you done?" (Beals 1962:15)

Here is a graphic depiction of the struggle between the Hindu child's active demandingness and the mother's attempts to push him gradually away from dependence on her and toward more mature activity as a member of the group. The breast is offered on demand, but nursing is immediately followed by a figurative and sometimes literal forcing of the child out of the house and into play with other family members. There are bargains and threats here as well. Food will not be prepared if the child fails to remain outside. Of course, as observers agree, including adult Hindu informants themselves, such threats to withhold food, while frequently made, are rarely, if ever, carried out (Beals 1962:20; Maduro 1976:167–169; Minturn and Hitchcock 1966:123). Yet the message is clear. A child must learn that "his life will not come to an end" without the constant presence of his mother. At the conclusion of this passage, the child joyfully joins the assembled family group, yet balks at accepting solid food. The mother then upbraids him for "pride." At one level, the mother's accusation of pride alludes to the Hindu notion that people of higher position refuse to accept food from those below them on the scale of purity. In a deeper sense, this meaning of "pride" lets the mother reproach her child for improperly holding himself separate from the group to which he properly belongs.

Here, then, the gradual weaning of the Hindu child is in motion. The mother will not overtly deny the breast, yet she does block access long enough to let the child know that the selfish pleasures of infancy must eventually be sacrificed for the more mature pleasures of playtime companionship with siblings and mealtime partaking of solid food as a full-fledged member of the family group. From this perspective, family members are not surrogate mothers who merely reinforce the natural mother's "overindulgence." Rather, their companionship is for the child one long, fundamental psychological step beyond that of the mother. To participate maturely in group activities, for example, to eat the food of the group means a sacrifice of immature and selfish pleasure at the breast. Full participation in the group, then, is not a narcissistic union with the mother writ large. Rather, it is a developmental achievement that signals the abandonment of early pleasures.

While the reader may now grant that the traditional psychoanalytic picture of excessive early indulgence followed by a late, abrupt withdrawal of pleasure is too simple, there may remain a troubled curiosity about the Hindu mother's habit of giving in to her child even as she tries to accustom the child to her absence. Seymour, after all, appears a bit disturbed when, in the passage above, she notes the chronic failure of Hindu mothers to withhold the breast even during the persistent begging about which these mothers explicitly complain. From a Western perspective, such behavior invariably comes off as "inconsistency." As Luschinsky puts it:

> In most cases, succorant behavior in children is not punished when it persists to the point of annoyance or when it is accompanied by aggressiveness. And many elders are not consistent in refusing or

granting children's demands. Children appear to enjoy their "right" to persist in their requests, and many take delight in trying to override their mothers' vetoes by one means or another.

(Luschinsky 1962:182; see also Beals 1962:21; Dube 1955:194; Maduro 1976:158)

Yet part of the consistent message conveyed by the Hindu pattern of breast-feeding is that no member of the group is allowed to directly refuse a clear and repeated request from another member. It is only by finally acquiescing to the child's request that a Hindu mother can eventually teach him to offer the same sacrificing compliance to the members of the group he must someday join.

In this connection, few psychoanalytic observers of Hindu child rearing mention another arena of interaction between the Hindu mother and her child—the daily oil massage or bath. When the bath is discussed, chiefly by the ethnographers, it is treated as a dangerous frustration in which the child is impersonally handled, almost as if he were a slab of meat, his caretakers ignoring his cries as they work him over (Luschinsky 1962:150; Maduro 1976:161; Minturn and Hitchcock 1966:110; Seymour 1971:152–154). Yet this imposing quality of the bath is the counterpart of the child's entitlement to food on request. This theme of requests made without warning or without reference to the immediate needs or mood of the giver is reminiscent of the way adult Hindus stress one caste-fellow's obligation to entertain or house another, regardless of when the guest may call or for how long he may wish to stay (Maduro 1976:155; Roland 1988:197).[6] A group member has a right to impose upon the group, and so does the group have a right to impose upon a given member (Murphy and Murphy 1953:56). This is the message conveyed both by feeding on demand and by the group's right to demand for the sake of cleanliness, health, and purity that a child submit to a massage or bath. The system works not because of forcible withholding or punishment (Bhattacharyya 1986:134) but because members of the group are motivated to voluntarily sacrifice for the sake of others in return for both the honor and concrete rewards of group membership. This is why, as we have seen, Hindu mothers prompt their children to a sacrifice of the breast through attacks on their selfishness and individual pride. For this reason too, observers report that mothers frequently "train" children by an appeal to their pride in group membership or with threats of isolation from the group (Cormack 1953:44–45; Luschinsky 1962:182–184; Maduro 1976:157; Mencher 1963:62; Minturn and Hitchcock 1966:121–122). These techniques of training will be reviewed in greater detail below. Right now my concern is to clarify the basic and consistent, if often unspoken, message conveyed by a nursing Hindu mother to her child.

Through both her gratification of his request and her measured interference with that same gratification, the mother seeks her child's acquiescence in a kind of understanding. The child is asked to join a group—a group that will unfailingly grant requests he is forced to make. In return, he must learn to abandon childhood selfishness (i.e., in the first instance, the breast itself) so that he may offer this same sort of help to others in the group. For this sacrifice he receives not only a guarantee of aid but also the emotional satisfaction of taking his place as a member of an esteemed group. Thus, in a culturally distinctive yet controlled and consistent way, a Hindu mother gradually pushes her child away from dependence on the pleasure of her presence and toward the more mature pleasures of membership in the group. While the outcome may not be a Western sense of individuation, neither is it simply a continuation of, or regression to, a dangerously intimate union of mother and child. Nor is the outcome of Hindu child rearing the empathy embodied in early Western mothering taken to its highest power. In fact, the Hindu process of maturation works precisely because the Hindu mother withholds from her child just this sort of empathic attention or emotional mirroring. (For the contrary view, see Roland 1988.)

If the child is pushed by the Hindu mother toward the group, there is also a corresponding pull exerted by the group. In contrast to the limited attention invested by the mother in the child during their physical interaction, the group offers a positive, spontaneous emotional stimulation that is somewhat less directly tied to bodily care. Thus the emotional sustenance of the group acts to draw the Hindu child away from the physical pleasures of his infantile attachment to the mother, prompting him to sacrifice those pleasures in return for a more mature stance within the family at large.

Evidence of the pull of the group is provided by Seymour's comparison between expressions of affect in nuclear and joint Hindu families (Seymour 1983; see also Rohner and Chaki-Sircar 1987:423). Seymour's problem is set by Minturn, whose early work stressed the lack of affect in Hindu mother-child interaction. In a later comparative study, Minturn and Lambert rank Hindu mothers below those in five other cultures on a scale of maternal warmth (1964:230–239). In explanation of this finding, Minturn and Lambert suggest that avoidance of conflict in the large joint families characteristic of India requires a certain emotional coldness and control (1964:238). Seymour, however, tested this hypothesis through careful observation and found to her surprise that expressions of affect actually increase in proportion to increases in the structural complexity of Hindu households (1983:270). Expressions of affect, that is, were greatest in large joint Hindu families. This increase in affect, however, comes not from the mothers in joint families. Maternal care in these households retains the same relatively impersonal character it possesses in most Hindu contexts. Rather, the increase in affect in large joint families is measured at the level of the group, spontaneous stimulation of the child coming chiefly from nonmaternal caretakers (Seymour 1983:272–273).[7]

This contrast between the quality of emotional interaction supplied by maternal and nonmaternal caretakers may help explain some of the differences between anthropological and psychoanalytic accounts of Hindu child rearing. Kakar, for example, relies on only a few sources for his characterization of the Hindu mother-child relationship. Besides Carstairs, one of these sources is Dube's village study (1955). Dube emphasizes how frequently the Hindu child is fondled and played with. Yet Dube always characterizes those who treat the child in this way as "the elders" or as "people" in general (1955:149,193). Kakar, however, tends to treat supplementary caretakers as simple extensions of the mother and therefore assimilates Dube's discussion of group behavior to Dube's treatment of the mother; thus, he sees Dube's account as relatively uncomplicated evidence of an extremely close, even exclusive, emotional bond between Hindu mother and child (Kakar 1978:80,196). In fact, however, Dube's evidence can easily be read to support the view that the Hindu mother's tie to the child is counterbalanced by the special attention of the larger group.[8]

The character of group stimulation of children is clarified by an article in which two Western anthropologists, Mimi and Mark Nichter, describe the response of Indian villagers to their own young child during their fieldwork:

> Villagers had few notions of the child as an individual with a will of his or her own. Instead, they viewed a child as a source of entertainment. Thus, often when Simeon was busy at play, someone would come over to him and pick him up. At first when he protested, people would think it funny. Eventually he developed an effective technique for ending this behavior: he learned that a sharp pinch to the nipple would invariably lead a woman to put him down promptly.
>
> Adults subjected Simeon to constant teasing, offering him something to play with and then, moments later, asking for it back, citing a kinship term: "I'm your mother's brother *mava*, can't I have that now?" Simeon's responses to the teasing game were subject to different interpretations, depending on who the teaser was. At first we expected that if Simeon gave the object back immediately, he would be praised for his willingness to share with close relatives. Although this was true some of the time, on other occasions, when he did not relinquish the object, he was praised for being clever. We came to understand that teasing a child and then evaluating the response was a way villagers could evaluate the child's character and personality. Despite the fact that neither we nor Simeon liked this practice, teasing was a major form of social interaction, and we could do nothing to prevent it.
>
> (Nichter and Nichter 1987:74–75; for another account of this sort of teasing, see Bhattacharyya 1986:146)

Despite the distress of Simeon and his parents at teasing and at the general forwardness of strangers, the Nichters, including Simeon, found themselves somewhat miffed when on their return to America such attentions were no longer forthcoming:

> Even before arriving in the States, we began to notice differences in attitudes towards children. In the early hours of our flight, when the plane was filled with South Asians, people lavished attention on Simeon. Stops in Europe brought on new passengers, and we began to hear "Shh" and to observe looks of annoyance at the "inconvenience" of being near a child.   (Nichter and Nichter 1987:79)

These passages bear out and give flesh to accounts like those of

Seymour and Dube, which show evidence of more frequent emotional interaction between the child and the group than between the child and its mother. More than this, however, these passages show us that even when "attention" is "lavished" on a Hindu child, the specific character of that attention differs from that we are familiar with in the West. Even at the group level, the child's emotions are not mirrored in such a way as to establish a loving intimacy between individuals. Something else entirely seems to be going on, but what exactly is it?

The interaction of Simeon with the adults around him makes sense in light of the understanding between the child and the group I referred to earlier. That understanding entails an entitlement of each side to make demands on the other. Adults may pick up a child at will without fear of interrupting his play and thereby crushing his individuality. By the same token, however, a child can be praised not only for generous giving but also for a refusal to return a gift— that is, for a sense of his own entitlement to the bounty of the group. This may help explain the fact that, as Maduro tells us, a child's greatest weapon against his parents is a refusal to take (Maduro 1976:163), for such a refusal indicates an exit from the basic understanding of mutual entitlement that holds the group together. Both this sense of entitlement to take from the group and the willingness to sacrifice on behalf of other group members, then, are necessary components of the understanding toward which the bulk of Hindu adult-child interaction is directed.

Unfortunately, rather than moving toward a positive description of what Hindu adult-child interaction *is*, Western observers in the past have contented themselves with pointing out that Hindu child rearing does *not* follow rules we in the West consider proper. Invariably, therefore, the emphasis is on the way the adult-child interaction discourages independence and individuation (Luschinsky 1962:197–198; Maduro 1976:152–172; Mencher 1963:56–57; Minturn and Hitchcock 1966:130–131; Seymour 1971, 1975; Surya 1969:388–389). This point of view in turn has led to the mistaken impression that a child's relations with the group are the simple continuation or displacement of an unbroken symbiosis with the mother (Kakar 1978:130; Roland 1988:233,248–249). In fact, however, the teasing interplay of child and group helps to break maternal bonds in a culturally distinctive way.

Consider, for example, a well-known form of Indian teasing (Cormack 1953:15; Seymour 1971:156–157) described here by Renaldo Maduro:

> Young mothers joke very often about giving their children away. Outside the home in public places, or when visitors are present in the home, it is extremely common for a mother to exclaim: "Here, I will give you away right now to so and so! Here, take him away! I don't want him any more! I cannot feed him! You can have him! I will give him away if you promise to feed him!" During this ritual monologue highlighting maternal ambivalence, the terrified child usually wails and clings desperately to his mother as the adults around him laugh. This particular scenario involving rejection and food occurs so frequently in Nathdwara that it cannot fail to make a significant impression on young children.   (Maduro 1976:168)

Maduro goes on to treat this pattern of teasing as a traumatic influence that leaves the Hindu adult fixated on pre-oedipal fears centering on food and maternal deprivation. To my way of thinking, however, this sort of joking serves as a culturally particular mode of freeing the child from maternal fixation by pushing him toward the group. The satisfaction involved in this teasing is double-edged. On the one hand, the adults relish the child's fear of leaving his mother's pleasurable bounty. On the other hand, I think they sense the value of the underlying message communicated to the child, i.e., "Your mother will not always be able to feed you. You will have to grow up and accept parenting from the wider group of adults around you." In effect, the pattern echoes that found in the teasing encountered by Simeon Nichter above. There, a child could be praised either for returning a gift or for refusing to do so. Thus, there is an adult pleasure in the child's selfishness, a selfishness that in its mature transformation ultimately ratifies acceptance of the group, and on the other hand, there is a pleasure in a direct movement outward, away from childish selfishness and toward a more mature and giving immersion in the group.[9]

The push and pull to the group is also illustrated in yet another element of the teasing game encountered by the Nichters: the emphasis on kin terms. In the passage quoted above, the teasing game of gift exchange begins only after Simeon's adult interlocutor claims relation by citing a kinship term. Elsewhere, the Nichters emphasize that while they taught Simeon words for "things outside" such as stars or plants, village adults concentrated on teaching Simeon the words for "things inside," most especially kinship terms (Nichter and Nichter 1987:73). This tallies with the accounts of several other anthropologists, all of whom stress that while Hindu children receive almost no overt training in either frustration or independence, they are actively taught about the meaning of family relations through an emphasis on kinship terms (Beals 1962:21; Dube 1955:193; Luschinsky 1962:167; Seymour 1971:157). Indeed, Minturn reports a rare case of overt praise for a child (direct praise for children is frowned upon) after its correct use of a kinship term (Minturn and Hitchcock 1966:132). A passage from Luschinsky will give some indication of how the teaching of kinship terms to the child acts both by virtue of its content and its process to draw the child's emotional interest toward the group:

> Even before children start making sounds, some adults try to acquaint them with certain words. Very often these are kinship terms. ... This is intensified after a child begins to make sounds. Adults listen carefully to the sounds to try to catch any resemblance to common words and especially to kinship terms. If they find such resemblance, they repeat the words or terms often to the child, pointing to the objects or persons. It is not surprising that a child's first vocabulary words are often kinship terms because chance achievements in this area are well rewarded. Every family member is interested in his or her relationship to the child. It is quite natural for an adult who has been "called" by a child to respond enthusiastically. Attention and affection are the rewards showered on a little boy or girl by the paternal grandmother who has been called "Aji," the paternal aunt who has been called "Phua," or by any others, except the father, who are honored by the child's early vocal efforts.
>
> (Luschinsky 1962:167)

Note that the child's father is restrained by custom, as an "own" parent, from strong, overt displays of emotion toward the child in a family setting. The rules of respect thus act to channel the child's emotional interest toward the larger group. In this, then, we have another example of the characteristic Hindu push outward and pull toward the group.

We see here that the relatively informal patterns of behavior and emotion we have been discussing help to make sense of the more formal aspects of Hindu child rearing. All observers report the existence of conscious and generally effective taboos on certain types of behavior toward children. Among these are the taboo on a parent's fondling, attending to, or even punishing her or his child in the presence of that parent's own parent or parent-in-law (Carstairs 1967:66–67; Dube 1955:152,158; Jacobson 1982:98; Luschinsky 1962:184; Maduro 1976:158; Mandelbaum 1988:14; Minturn and Hitchcock 1966:117–119; Rohner and Chaki-Sircar 1987:71). Traditionally, moreover, in extended families a parent should remain distanced from her or his child even in front of elder sisters- or brothers-in-law. Carstairs, of course, points out the likelihood that such caretaking leads to dangerously inconsistent parenting. According to Carstairs, the Hindu child is confused by the on-again, off-again ministrations of parents who pass in and out of their elders' orbits. As we saw above, Maduro, a Jungian analyst, echoes Carstairs' point of view.

The difficulty with this psychoanalytic perspective is that it assumes the singular importance of the mother-child relationship and evaluates all other caretakers on the basis of whether they strengthen or diminish that primary connection (see also Boss 1965:72). From another point of view, however, the taboo on parental attention to children before elders can be seen as an example of the psychological push away from the parents and toward the group. In this connection, it is interesting to note that observers uniformly testify to the mild character of a mother-in-law's attitude toward her grandchild. This resembles, of course, the customary indulgence of grandparents in our own society. In Hindu joint families, however, the mother-in-law is not just an occasional, welcome visitor to the courtyard, she is the everpresent head and embodiment of the family's mothers. This mother-in-law, who has the first right to punish a grandchild, even when that child's mother is in the mother-in-law's immediate presence, is in fact more often to be found disciplining the child's mother for being harsh on the grandchild (Cormack 1953:21; Luschinsky 1962:184; Minturn and Hitchcock 1966:118; Rohner and Chaki-Sircar 1987:71; Wiser and Wiser 1963:82). Thus, rather than communicating contradictory messages about a mother's love, the taboo on fondling one's child before a grandparent is part of a consistent pattern of attitudes and practices that gradually draws a child out of the orbit of the mother and toward the loving protection of a larger group, which is represented here by the mild discipline (toward the grandchild) of the mother's mother-in-law.

Another universally reported, conscious, and effective taboo of Hindu child rearing is the prohibition on praising a child "to his face." Hindus seem to agree that praising a child to his face, and particularly one's own child, will spoil him, making him full of himself and reluctant to submit to discipline. Most of the anthropological and psychological observers who report the taboo on praise speak of it as evidence that Hindu parents eschew what Luschinsky calls "love-oriented" techniques of training (Luschinsky 1962:183; Maduro 1976:166–167; Mencher 1963:62; Minturn and Hitchcock 1966:119–121; Narain 1964:139; Poffenberger 1981:83–84; Rohner and Chaki-Sircar 1988:77). That is, Hindu parents refrain from capitalizing on the child's love by offering praise for good behavior.

This observation, while valid, ought rightly to raise yet another question. If love-oriented techniques of training are not favored by Hindus, what techniques take their place? The question takes on importance when we realize how deeply our Western notion of love is built into current psychoanalytic theory. In the classic account of toilet training, for example, the child gives up the uninhibited exercise of pleasure in excretion not only out of fear of parental punishment but also in order to retain the love of a parent who offers praise in return for compliance (Shengold 1988:34–35). Yet all observers seem to agree that Hindus neither praise children for exercising proper toilet habits nor do they blame or punish them for mistakes. If this is the case, how are we to understand the inner process by which Hindu toilet training takes place? What motivates a child to give up unrestricted anal pleasure if not the blame and praise of beloved parents? The same question can be asked regarding Hindu weaning, which, as we have seen, is generally untraumatic and sometimes even voluntary on the part of the child even though the way to it is not anticipated by a gradual love-oriented training in the denial of the breast. At this point, then, an examination of Hindu toilet training practices should clarify both the underlying psychology of weaning and the general psychological process whereby the Hindu child abandons all forms of infantile pleasure in the absence of love-oriented techniques of training.

It is perhaps misleading to use the term "toilet training" in the Hindu context. There are efforts made to move the child in the direction of anal control. On the other hand, the principles behind these efforts are unlike those generally associated with our idea of training. As noted, there is little emphasis on praise when a child signals a willingness to urinate or defecate so that he may be taken outside. Nor is soiling within the house punished by scolding or interpreted as a kind of willful disobedience. While an American child, according to Sears, Macomby, and Levin, generally begins toilet training around the eleventh month and completes it by the eighteenth month (1976:109), Hindu children may be "trained" or, more often, "train themselves" anytime between the first and the fourth or fifth years (for accounts of Hindu toilet training see: Bhattacharyya 1986:134; Boss 1965:68; Carstairs 1967:66–67; Cormack 1953:13,16; Dube 1955:192–194; Luschinsky 1962:152–153, 167–168; Mencher 1963:57; Minturn and Hitchcock 1966:109,116–117; Murphy and Murphy 1953:49; Narain 1964:137–139; Seymour 1971:155–156).

Hindu mothers do sometimes make attempts to have a child signal the need to urinate or defecate, but such efforts are unsystematic, unconnected with rewards or sanctions and often omitted altogether. Generally, a child trains himself through the observation and imitation of others, often as he accompanies adults, siblings, or older children to the fields during their morning ablutions. While such self-training is generally accomplished in the second, third, or fourth year, a child continues to rely on others to be cleansed with water afterwards until the age of four or five. While a child may not be directly scolded for making a mistake, he may be made to feel that he has been inconsiderate of others. As he grows older and has more contact with children his own age, group teasing begins to play a role in anal training. Mencher, for example, reports an incident in which a four-year-old boy remained hidden under a chair for nearly two hours after being laughed at by a group of children for expelling gas (1963:61).

While training by adults is often omitted altogether, the perfunctory early efforts at training provide an important clue to the principles underlying Hindu psychological development. Consider the following description of these attempts at training:

> It is considered desirable that training in defecation begin as soon as a baby is old enough to sit up, but such training is provided only by those women who do not feel greatly pressed by household and other work. The mother who wants to provide such training does so in the following way. In the morning or evening or at both times, she sits on a low stool with her knees apart and the outside part of the sole of each foot on the ground. In this way, the inside part of the sole of each foot is in the air. The baby is placed on these two surfaces of the feet and held. Often the mother makes some kind of noise to suggest what she wants of the baby. Women say that once a baby develops the habit of defecating regularly, not much of the mother's time is required. One Thakur woman said that her daughter was fully trained at seven months. She defecated only in the mornings, when put on her mother's feet and not later in the day, except during some illnesses. But the majority of women are too busy to devote much time to this training. Some make no effort at all, letting their babies defecate where they will. Others put their babies on their feet in the mornings, but only for a short time. If the babies do not quickly respond the mothers return to their work. . . .
>
> Mothers are not very concerned if their attempts to toilet train their babies are not successful. They simply postpone the toilet training for a later period.   (Luschinsky 1962:152)

Other accounts mention similar efforts at training, but most authors stress them less than Luschinsky, emphasizing instead that little or nothing is done by adults other than to wait for a child to imitate his elders and peers. Yet Luschinsky's detailed account calls to mind Seymour's and Beals' descriptions of Hindu weaning. By withholding the breast briefly and letting the child know that he will not "die without it," a Hindu mother gives the child a model of mature behavior. This is also what happens when a mother briefly places a child on her feet and makes sounds to indicate urination or defecation. In contrast to the West, such efforts are not followed through by an enforced denial of the breast or an insistence on anal compliance. Rather, the child, having been alerted to the content of adult behavior, is left to move toward it on its own.

A crucial factor in the child's self-timed progress toward maturity appears to be a desire for membership in the group. In Beals' snapshot of the weaning process, for example, the child's joy in participating in the group meal will only be fully realized when it abandons the breast for solid food. In the case of anal training, it is the mature companionship of elder relatives and peers on their way to the fields for their own toilet that motivates a child to begin self-discipline. The group also exercises negative sanctions in the form of teasing on the occasion of anal immaturity. In short, the dynamic seems to entail a voluntary sacrifice of infantile pleasures according to a pre-established model of mature behavior for the sake of participation in the group. The model of mature behavior established by the mother pushes the child away, and the lure of honored participation in the group as well as the sanction of group teasing pull the child toward maturity. Yet the mother does not so much deny the child the free experience of oral or anal pleasure as she waits for the forces buffeting the child to prompt self-sacrifice on its part. Thus, both weaning and toilet training are "child-conditioned." This process seems to substitute in the Hindu case for the Western dynamic of imposed frustration, motivated by a mixture of love and punishment and administered by a single primary caretaker.

The basic Hindu pattern of movement toward maturity identified above is also played out in the realm of infantile phallic pleasure. Before the age of five, a boy child is not directly punished or openly discouraged from playing with his genitals (Luschinsky 1962:174; Poffenberger 1981:87–88). As Dube describes it:

> When boys are seen manipulating their organs the elders smile and playfully remove their hands from them. Boys invariably start doing so again, and are not admonished. This amuses rather than irritates the older members of the family.   (Dube 1955:193)

The practice described here resembles that adopted in weaning and toilet training. A child is given a model of proper behavior—the hand is removed. Yet pleasure is not denied for long. In fact, adults seem to enjoy watching a child manifest a sense of entitlement to pleasure. Yet, after the adult frees the boy's hand, returns the breast, allows the child to make a mess, or—in the case of the teasing game played with the Nichters' child—after the adult presents a gift, the child's sense of entitlement refers to a pleasure being permitted or presented by the group, not to a pleasure gained alone. That is, once it has been made clear to the child, even if nonverbally, that pleasure comes not from one's own power but as a gift from the group, the meaning of indulgence is transformed into something else and is thus permitted and even relished. In fact, with very young children, adults actively provide genital pleasure to an infant, massaging the genitals in order to calm a child down (Dube 1955:192). Such a genital massage is not an extreme and dangerous form of personal entanglement, any more than the Hindu mother's offer of the breast represents a delicate and empathic emotional partnership. Like Hindu breast-feeding, genital massage is the group's way of obtaining a child's compliance while also introducing it to the entitlements and obligations of group membership.

The free offer of pleasure by the group makes sense given the expectation of adults that the child will eventually prove ready to give up pleasure in order to provide it to others as a fully functioning member of the group. Generally, this occurs as the child renounces infantile gratification of its own will, both to participate more fully and more honorably in group life and because the child now knows that its vital needs will always be met by the group. By the age of five or six, however, when particularly the boys' discipline is taken over by men, mature self-sacrifice and group participation is directly demanded. Here is how the process is described by Dube:

> Later childhood begins at about five and continues until the advent of adolescence. At this stage the children form their own play-groups; spending several hours of the day in their respective age-groups. Now they are free to play in the streets and the open ground outside the village. Maternal attention is now considerably reduced; the elders keep an eye on them, but apart from this they have considerable freedom. As they grow older solicitation of affectionate responses through handling, play and fondling gradually diminishes. Toilet training becomes strict, and the child is expected to have full control over defecation and urination. Cleanliness is insisted upon, and any failure on his part in this respect arouses anger in the elders. The erring child is ridiculed, chastised and punished. Now they must wear clothes and begin to hide their genitals. If the elders find their organs exposed they point to them and ask, "Arre, what is that? Why are you exhibiting that little thing?" Children often develop a sense of shame at this stage, blush at such remarks, hide their organs and

run away from the elders. Discipline becomes more rigorous and physical punishment is more frequent. (Dube 1955:194)

This passage by Dube is a classic description of the so-called crackdown phase that follows the early "indulgence" of Hindu infants. Dube's account, along with that of Carstairs, stands behind Kakar's emphasis on the traumatic effects of what he calls the Hindu boy's second birth. Kakar sees further evidence for the negative impact of the crackdown phase in the many painful memories of this period of childhood unearthed through analyses with his Hindu patients. Yet I wonder whether the key to the psychic pain some may feel in this period does not lie deeper still. While a Hindu psychoanalytic patient may have experienced the shift toward harsher discipline at age five as a trauma, this may be evidence of pathological rather than normal development prior to the period of the second birth. In other words, such a patient may not have been properly ushered through the precrackdown period and therefore may have experienced the mature, group-oriented stance demanded of him at age five as unprecedented and overwhelming. In *normal* Hindu development, on the other hand, the so-called crackdown at age five may not so much contrast with early indulgence as consolidate an internal movement toward sacrifice of infantile pleasure that has been going on for years previously.[10] Only in this way can we account for reports of untraumatic weaning—even self-weaning—and accounts of voluntary toilet training through imitation. Indeed, the Wisers speak of the second birth itself as a time when young boys are actually anxious to leave the women's quarters and avail themselves of the collective company of the family's men (Wiser and Wiser 1963:78).

It is because psychoanalytic observers have missed the characteristic Hindu push away from the mother and the pull toward the group along with the voluntary sacrifice of childhood pleasure that this pattern prompts that the Hindu refusal to overtly deny a child pleasure in its early years has been falsely interpreted as overindulgence. Thus, the forceful and final consolidation of this heretofore gradual and distinctive cultural learning process at age five has been misinterpreted as a dangerously traumatic imposition on a pampered and unprepared child.

Chapter 5

The Ek-Hi Phase

Up to now, I have focused chiefly, although by no means exclusively, on the outer circumstances of Hindu childhood. Now I attend more directly to the subjective correlates of the child's external situation. In this chapter, therefore, I consider the implications of my inquiry into Hindu child rearing for our understanding of the Hindu child's fantasy life. On the basis of this investigation I wish to build a reworked psychoanalytic theory of Hinduism.

The focus of this reworking will be the childhood roots of Hindu Goddess imagery. That is, we shall ask how our new understanding of Hindu child-rearing practices might reshape the approach to the Hindu Goddess taken by psychoanalytic authors such as Carstairs and Kakar. To put it somewhat differently, we take the clues our earlier, nonindividualist approach to Hindu Goddess imagery gives us about childhood subjectivity and, combining these clues with our group-oriented understanding of Hindu child-rearing practices, emerge with a new, or rather, a reworked theory of early psychological development among Hindus. The underlying theme of this reworking process in its treatment of both child-rearing practices reworking process in its treatment of both child-rearing practices and Goddess imagery is a heightened sense of the importance of groups as opposed to individuals on the Hindu scene.

Psychoanalysts understand much of Hinduism's Goddess imagery to be rooted in what is called the pre-oedipal phase—the time (from birth to about three years of age) prior to the onset of phallic sexuality and the Oedipus complex (Carstairs 1967:155–159; Kakar 1978:79–139). The central issues of the pre-oedipal phase, although variously conceived by different analysts, center around the consolidation of a sense of bounded unity, continuity, and fundamental goodness in the self and others. A child should emerge from the pre-oedipal phase with a clear sense of his own individuality, identity, and worth. So, too, the child should have a clear sense of trust in the distinctly separate yet fundamentally benevolent adults and peers he meets in the world.

Conflicts and achievements centered around these pre-oedipal issues are in the classical theory preeminently played out in the child's interaction with his earliest primary caretaker, the mother. A child consolidates a sense of individuality when he comes to realize that he cannot compel the mother to offer food or comfort by merely wishing it. At the same time, the basic consistency over time of the mother's response to her child's requests prompts that child to trust in the fundamental goodness of both himself and the world around him.

In this chapter I argue that the psychoanalytic notion of the pre-oedipal period must be substantially revised when it is applied to the Hindu case. This is so because among Hindus the early rearing of the child is fundamentally shaped by the group. I therefore propose the name *ek-hi phase* for the Hindu counterpart to the Western pre-oedipal phase. (*ek-hi* rhymes with "deck-three.") This name derives from the Hindi phrase, "*Devī sab ek hī haī*"or "*Mā sab ek hī haī*," meaning, "All the mothers, or mother goddesses, are simply one and the same." *Ek-hi* thus means "just one" or "one and the same." As in the Western pre-oedipal phase, questions of trust, identity, and goodness are at stake in the Hindu ek-hi phase. In the Hindu case, however, the movement is not away from the mother and toward individuation and trust. Rather, the movement is away from the natural mother and toward a more mature immersion in a larger and fundamentally benevolent group of mothers, a group in which all the mothers are, ultimately, "just one."

I construct the notion of an ek-hi phase through a reworking of classic psychoanalytic treatments of the Hindu Goddess. In particular, I am interested in Carstairs' link between Hindu Goddess imagery and an alleged Hindu tendency toward "splitting" (Carstairs 1967:155–159; but see also, Kakar 1978:79–112). We recall that Carstairs sees early Hindu mothering as intensely, even excessively, gratifying. Based on this observation, Carstairs goes on to argue that as a result of this early indulgence, the Hindu child is unable to unify all-good and all-bad images of the mother. The Indian child, says Carstairs, cannot easily accept that the mother who occasionally frustrates is actually the same as the mother who regularly gratifies. Thus the image of the mother is split into two distinct beings— one radically benign and one radically malignant.

Carstairs' point derives from Melanie Klein's insight into the child's need to "discover" the very notion of personal unity that adults take for granted (Carstairs 1967:155–159; Klein 1975a, 1975b, 1975c). What the child needs in order to make this discovery is a gradual movement toward independence in the fulfillment of his sensual needs. Excessive indulgence or frustration leaves him unwilling and unable to relinquish the happy fantasy that he can always be satisfied by a perfect mother or the terrible associated fear that every pause in gratification is a permanent end of happiness— the triumph of a totally different and thoroughly bad mother. Thus, for example, a child who received inadequate training in frustration during infancy might imagine that his unresponsive mother is not his real mother but an evil impostor who has killed and substituted herself for the benign, authentic mother who in fact wishes to fulfill all his needs (Bettelheim 1977:66–70).

Observations of prolonged physical closeness between Hindu mothers and children as well as the Hindu pattern of feeding on demand are interpreted by Carstairs as barriers to the mature integration of split mother images. Following the classic model, Carstairs sees excessive indulgence as leaving the Hindu child unable to tolerate, or imagine, the reality of a less than perfectly responsive mother. Indeed, Carstairs' best evidence for this is the imagery of the Hindu Goddess. The contrast between the popular portrait of the Goddess as an overflowing, benevolent, divine mother and the equally ubiquitous images of her as a horrible, fierce goddess, beheading demon victims and drinking their blood, seems to any psychoanalytically oriented anthropologist the clearest proof of an oral fixation at a point prior to the unification of the mother. For Carstairs, then, the split images of benign and fierce goddesses reveal an unresolved split, persisting from childhood into adult life, in Hindus' unconscious attitudes toward their mothers.

In addition to Carstairs' interest in splitting summarized here, there is an additional, and related, psychoanalytic theme stressed by others investigating early Hindu mothering, particularly by Kakar (1978:128–139; but see also, Carstairs 1967:161). While those who follow Klein tend to focus on the need to unify partial mother images in the pre-oedipal period, others think of this same phase as a time when the child's own ego must become increasingly differentiated from that of the mother. This perspective stresses the achievement of the idea of personal unity from a point of view somewhat different from that of Klein. From this perspective, the infant does not initially see itself as a being separate from its mother, and the same gradual process of weaning (in every sense) from contact with the mother stressed by Klein in terms of the need to unify split mother images is here seen as the key to the child's consolidation of its own sense of a separate self out of an early desire to maintain an unbounded narcissistic union with the mother.

As noted in chapters 3 and 4, this psychoanalytic perspective on pre-oedipal issues sees Hindu philosophy's insistence on the ultimate unity of existence as the product of an early failure to differentiate the ego of the child from that of the mother. From this point of view, the traditional Hindu stress on the importance of the group is also a kind of displacement, this time onto the social world, of the child's early, undifferentiated ego. Put another way, the inability of the child to separate from the mother leaves a longing for union with a greater being. In later years, this desire is displaced onto the father in the joint family, onto a guru, and onto authority figures generally.

As noted, this perspective is stressed, although not to the exclusion of the Kleinian analysis of split mother images, in the recent work of Sudhir Kakar (1978:126–139). For Kakar, then, the need to reexperience the narcissistic merger with a mother whom the child has never internally abandoned is at the root of the Hindu orientation to the social whole stressed by Dumont. Kakar, in fact, explicitly claims to have explained the psychological roots of Dumont's conception of hierarchy since Dumont sees hierarchy as a form of holism.

One can hardly blame the psychoanalysts for their refusal to heed the complaints of those who preach against the imposition of Western explanatory systems on alien cultures. Connections such as that between indulgent child-rearing practices and cultural images of split mother goddesses are too clear to ignore. The Hindu data seem not merely explicable in psychoanalytic terms; because of the explicit nature of the imagery involved, they seem to support the theory even more convincingly than the Western data upon which it was originally based. There is hardly a controversial Freudian or Kleinian image, however skeptically received in the West, that cannot be found in frighteningly explicit form in the mythological language of Hinduism.

I think any new psychological approach to Hindu religious symbolism must offer an explanation of the profound plausibility of traditional psychoanalytic interpretations. From my point of view, the truth is that the analysts are partly right. Their explanations always seem to work because they are playing with psychological material that is closely related to the material they are familiar with. This "cousinship" is close enough to persistently reconfirm, so to speak, the basic theory without forcing any serious reconsideration.

On the other hand, despite the genuine plausibility of psychoanalytic explanations, the uncommitted continue to rebel (Kondos 1986; Pocock 1961). One reason for this antipsychoanalytic rebellion is the implication contained in the analytic view of Hindu material of a pervasive cultural pathology. The skeptics are right to demur, for there really is a trick in the traditional analytic approach to other cultures. Although it remains hidden in a Western context, implicit in psychoanalysis is a prescriptive model of child rearing as well as an accompanying set of moral values. The traditional psychoanalytic view requires that a child be raised by a primary caretaker and that he or she be eased gently into autonomy. Deviations from this pattern are deemed pathogenic. Since very few non-Western cultures raise children in this manner, their every aspect is interpreted from a psychoanalytic perspective as an unfortunate detour along some developmental path traveled more directly in the West.

Of course, this may actually be the state of affairs. On the other hand, that matters should appear so is grounds for suspicion. The results are too pat and convenient from the point of view of a Western sensibility. They stem, moreover, not from a comparison of cultures but from the secondary application of a theory taken to be universal prior to a disciplined investigation of cross-cultural material.

Again, I raise these objections not to justify dismissal of the psychoanalytic approach but to open that approach to deeper modification. If psychoanalytic explanations of Hindu culture have seized upon material closely related to yet still significantly different from that encountered by psychoanalysts in the West, then we must focus on these specific differences with new eyes. There must be a careful enumeration of similarities and differences along with an attempt to make sense of these according to new models.

Following this admonition, I point here to some important differences between the Hindu Goddess imagery explained by Carstairs and Kakar and the seeming prototypes of these images in Western psychological theory. While many of these differences can be explained (or explained away) according to the traditional psychoanalytic model, I intend to use them as a basis for the construction of a specifically Hindu path of psychological development. This path of development parallels the one outlined by psychoanalysis for Westerners yet retains a distinctive Hindu character. This Hindu course of development will enable us to make sense of both the concrete content and the underlying principles of our system of classification of Hindu goddesses.

There are at least three qualities of Hindu Goddess imagery that prompt us to question conventional psychoanalytic interpretations: first, the imagery's explicitness; second, its multiplicity; and third, its underlying unity. I begin my treatment of these issues with a discussion of explicitness in the imagery of the Goddess.

Although it is true, as noted, that the clarity, even gruesomeness, of Goddess imagery is sometimes taken as a confirmation of the universality of psychoanalytic theory, the neatness of fit should give pause. According to psychoanalysis, images such as that of the split mother are generally unconscious. The very reason that psychoanalytic interpretations of Western literature or religion provoke skepticism is that the underlying symbolism is disguised by psychological resistance. What does it mean, then, when a culture explicitly celebrates the image of a murderous, blood-drinking "mother," draped with a necklace of severed male heads? The ordinary psychoanalytic response to this would have to be that the pathogenic child-rearing practices of Indian culture leave the populace in a kind of controlled, quasi-psychotic state in which such images easily float to the surface. As noted above, Carstairs holds a position quite close to this. The apparently smooth psychological functioning of most Indians in everyday life, on the other hand, prompts other analysts to explain away the clear implications of the traditional analysis.

Kakar, for example, as pointed out in chapter 3, speaks of cultural support for the imagery of the Goddess. Others, like Gananath Obeyesekere, speak of religious symbolism as a "cultural idiom" through which underlying psychological forces may be expressed (1981:21,34–86). These ideas of cultural support or idioms of expression act as safety valves for a theory under pressure. As long as the problem of the imagery's explicitness can be attributed to cultural forces, there appears to be no need for a reformulation of the underlying psychological theory. Western diagnostic categories, such as hysteria or narcissism, can thus be freely applied to other cultures while variation is viewed as the particular cultural idiom through which underlying, universal psychological processes are expressed (Kakar 1982a:74–81; Obeyesekere 1981:86). Thus, explicit imagery need not imply pathology, and even where pathology may be present, the support of a common cultural idiom is said to keep it in check (Spiro 1987).

While this approach appears to give both psychology and sociology their due, in fact it satisfies neither. Once the psychoanalysts have recourse to an independent realm of cultural symbolism, they forfeit the chief claim of their analysis, the grounding of cultural symbols in psychological forces. If there is a cultural idiom of Goddess mythology in India, where does it come from? Must it not be from the same oral fixation and consequent unresolved mother split it supports or expresses? We are back to square one. Where do the explicit images come from, and why does their presence not entail more profound disturbances of day-to-day functioning among the populace?

Although the appeal to a level of cultural support appears to be a prudential bow in the direction of sociology, in fact, it prevents the reconstitution of psychological theory along cultural lines. Once a universal psychology is sealed off from variation by the cultural support theory, interest is deflected from the cultural differences that ought to prompt a rethinking of the universal system. I have already pointed out the explicit character of Goddess symbolism as one of these differences. There are others.

It is important to stress that the imagery of the Hindu Goddess is not merely dual, it is multiple. That is, there is not simply a good and a bad Hindu goddess; there is, on the contrary, an everchanging array of goddesses. These goddesses replicate, expand, merge, and contract in number and type depending on context. It is thus most problematic to analyze the Goddess according to a simple duality.

This difficulty has at least two dimensions. First, as posited by the proposed new classification of goddesses (see figure one, chapter 2), there are actually two fundamental types of goddesses, each blending into the other. Each of these types manifests its own characteristic form of duality. So-called individual goddesses may appear at different points along this spectrum of classification. That is, a goddess, for example, Santoshi Ma, may stress the characteristics of the benevolent side of the sister-daughter mother goddess while still subtly exhibiting the type of malevolence characteristic of this pole. On the other hand, an individual goddess, like Santoshi Ma, may in particular contexts shift still more radically between the malevolent and benevolent poles of her characteristic side of the classification scheme. In the course of these movements "individual" goddesses, such as Santoshi Ma, may reveal themselves to be multiforms of "other" goddesses who are also in the process of moving along the continuum of classification. For a discussion of such shifts in Santoshi Ma's character, see the conclusion of this chapter.

Thus we are faced not with a simple duality but with a double-poled malevolence and benevolence along which move a multiplicity of beings whose identities constantly split and merge. Beyond the complexities of this scheme, another aspect of multiplicity must be stressed. There is a clear preoccupation with sheer number in the worship of Hindu goddesses.

In worship, vernacular text, and ordinary conversation, Hindus stress the multiple nature of the Goddess. She is celebrated as composed of "seven sisters," or "nine goddesses," or "one hundred and eight names" (Erndl 1984:11–14, 1987:72,282,312). It is important, for example, that in the film about Santoshi Ma, she is opposed not merely to one malevolent wife goddess, but to three such goddesses.

No doubt, although traditional psychoanalysts do not generally note the phenomenon of goddess multiplicity, they could explain it as reducible to a fundamental duality. As long as Babb's scheme of classification of goddesses held sway, this was a plausible approach. If, on the other hand, goddesses are more profitably seen as varied along a mediated double-poled model with distinct modes of benevolence and malevolence at *each* end, then the psychoanalytic notion of a simple good/bad dichotomy becomes problematic. Furthermore, while informants' stress on the Goddess's multiple forms can be reduced to a relatively simple basic typology, it would be a great advantage if a psychological approach could explain the phenomenon of multiplicity per se.

In addition to the explicitness of their imagery and their complex multiplicity, there is a third characteristic of Hindu goddesses that calls the traditional psychoanalytic explanation into question. The Hindu Goddess, as I have already emphasized, is quite clearly a *unified* deity. So far from representing split mother images, the Goddess seems repeatedly to affirm the unity of all aspects of the maternal. Nor is this unity a mere formal, theological idea. On the contrary, the fact that "all the goddesses are one" is persistently stressed by informants. It is almost impossible to question Hindus at any length about the particular forms of the Goddess without being reminded of this notion. If anyone was having trouble unifying split mother images in the field, it was not my informants but me.

Once again, however, the traditional psychoanalytic approach does have a way of dealing with this situation. The stress on the Goddess's unity along with the related assertion that she is "everywhere" can be grounded in the craving for narcissistic merger with the mother—part of an effort to recover the early period when the self of the mother and that of the child were not clearly distinguished.

Again, while one can sympathize with those who complain of the analytic tendency to fit alien material into a familiar package, it is also hard not to see the analysts' point of view. For the most part, the explanation can be made to fit. Moreover, the way out of the stand-off between analytic "imperialism" and the skepticism of those who must remain silent on unconscious processes altogether requires a difficult rethinking of traditional theories—a rethinking neither side is disposed to undertake. Yet this *is* the way out. All the parts are there, but they need to be put together in a new way. The key to this process is to focus on the culturally distinct qualities of Hindu Goddess imagery in such a way as to allow them to guide a reconstitution of the traditional theory in Hindu terms.

By the same token, it is vital that attention be given to crucial differences between the Indian child-rearing situation and its alleged parallels in the West. For example, as noted, psychoanalytic discussions of Hindu child-rearing techniques focus on a pattern of physical indulgence, involving frequent breast-feeding, late weaning, and prolonged physical proximity between mother and child. In fact, however, as established in the previous two chapters, these modes of physical interaction between mother and child do not entail the kind of emotional relationship they would in the West. In other words, the mother who constantly touches and feeds the child does not treat that child as a beloved, narcissistic extension of her own self. During the period of physical contact, there is not the same sort of attention or mirroring as would be expected in the West to accompany intense physical contact or breast-feeding.

There are two possible responses to this finding. On the one hand, one could argue, as some have, that this combination of physical closeness and so-called inadequate mirroring locks a child still more powerfully into his infantile needs (Maduro 1976:161). On the other hand, one could point out, as Robert LeVine, for example, has done, that the varied emotional tone accompanying physical closeness in other cultures makes the application of the Western indulgence/frustration dichotomy to strictly physical data on breast-feeding problematic (LeVine 1977). From this perspective, mere physical contact and gratification need not lead to oral fixation or weak ego differentiation.

The adoption of this latter point of view, however, raises important questions. What are the actual effects of the Hindu mode of child rearing? If they differ enough from their seeming Western counterparts in that they do not yield pathology, how is this process to be positively understood? It is necessary, in other words, to move away from a stance that simply accepts or rejects the application of Western models of child rearing to other cultures and toward a positive formulation of culturally distinctive patterns of development.

I want to offer an experimental model of Hindu development through the stages of oral, anal, and phallic sexuality. This model will reinterpret the familiar data on what has seemed to be early maternal indulgence in India and derive from them distinctive and non-Western principles according to which the pleasures of infantile sexuality are renounced in the Hindu context. Starting from the study of Hindu child rearing in the previous two chapters, my central point will be that the Hindu child advances through the stages of infantile sexuality not by way of processes of weaning, training, or in response to oedipally induced threats of castration, but through a voluntary renunciation of pleasure in return for membership in the group. I call this process the construction of an *ego of the whole*.

I do think that Freud's three stages of infantile sexuality are in an important sense universal (Fenichel 1945:54–101; Freud 1962). More precisely, I adopt a modified notion of three universal stages of infantile sexuality as a working assumption. From this point of view, children everywhere go through succeeding phases where pleasure is situated chiefly in oral, anal, and genital erogenous zones. Each phase must be successfully transcended through a difficult process of turning away from pleasure. Moreover, through the abandonment of pleasure each of these stages, when traversed successfully, leaves the child with a stronger, more mature ego. The universality of this process and the unconscious imagery it institutes continue to apparently confirm the applicability of existing psychoanalytic theory to diverse cultures.

The very presence of the universal imagery of the oral, anal, and phallic-genital phases, however, obscures the confusion in current psychoanalytic theory between the phases themselves and culturally varied modes of renunciation that propel the child through them. Take, for example, the classic psychoanalytic treatment of the methods for the effective transcendence of each of the phases.

In psychoanalytic theory, the three phases of infantile sexuality—oral, anal, and phallic—are transcended in their immature forms chiefly through weaning, toilet training, and oedipally induced castration anxiety, respectively. Each of these three processes partakes of a pattern that, I contend, is specifically Western in form. By intermingling an account of these culturally distinct processes with a delineation of universal stages, psychoanalysis sets up a situation where data from any culture can seem to confirm a developmental theory while at the same time these data will appear to give evidence of an unsuccessful developmental journey.

The psychoanalytic accounts of the transcendence of each of the three phases of infantile sexuality share a common form. In every case, pleasure is abandoned through some sort of force or pressure, whether it be weaning, toilet training, or oedipally induced threats of castration. Counterbalancing these negative forces is a positive motivation centering on a personal emotional relationship with a parental figure. Pleasure is abandoned not merely because it is forcibly made difficult or impossible to fulfill but also because the child is motivated toward abandonment by the desire to please a loving and beloved parent (Fenichel 1945:105; Shengold 1988:34–35; Winnicott 1964:44). That parent first sees to it that early pleasures are accompanied by and associated with a very personalized sort of emotional relationship. Then the parent promises the child that same love in return for an abandonment of the now immature pleasure. In acceding to the parent's wishes and successfully transcending pleasure, the child's ego is strengthened through an internal identification with the parent. This pattern underlying all three phases of infantile sexuality is not commonly focused on per se. If analysts were to focus on it, the extent to which this pattern is a peculiar characteristic of development in the West might be clarified.

Among Hindus, however, as demonstrated in the chapters above, the mode by which the pleasures of infantile sexuality are transcended is different. In the Hindu context, the parental figures make pleasure at each stage fully available while simultaneously hinting that a more mature relation to pleasure is both possible and desirable. Yet, neither the pleasure offered nor the wish of the parents that it be abandoned are accompanied by a powerful, personalized love relationship. In the Hindu context, the locus of personal satisfaction lies less in personalized, exclusive emotional ties than in activity within and on behalf of the group. Thus the child discovers that if he is to partake of this activity, he must voluntarily renounce infantile pleasure. Having made this renunciation, the child's ego is consolidated through a sense of having incorporated and having been incorporated by the group. The external appearance of this internal process is characterized by voluntary renunciation. Negatively, as shown in chapter 4, renunciation is motivated not by attempts at direct coercion but by teasing and other forms of threatened exclusion from the group. Positively, renunciation is motivated not by direct instruction but by unforced imitation.

To describe the construction of an ego of the whole, I prefer the notion of an incorporation of and by the group to that of identification with it. This helps avoid the cultural characteristics inherent in the idea (appropriate for the West) of identification (Kurtz 1990:37–102). The notion of identification contains an unremarked assumption of individualism in its picture of fundamentally separate yet now associated entities. From the perspective of the ego of the whole, on the other hand, the child and the group are not merely associated by resemblance. The child's ego is actually constituted through nesting within the group. Similarly, the child has the sense that his "own" action is taken on behalf of or even "by" the group contained, so to speak, within him. This idea of a dual incorporation has obvious affinities with Dumont's idea of the encompassing and the encompassed (1980).

The reports of physical indulgence in childhood accompanied by a lack of maternal attention may now appear in a new light. While the mother's frequent ministrations no doubt prompt in the child a powerful emotional attachment to her, it is precisely her failure to mirror these feelings that prevents the development of an emotional partnership that would isolate the mother-child pair from the group. I suggest, in other words, that the Hindu mother's relatively distant stance toward the child, rather than trapping him in an oral fixation in which the mother's image remains split and his own ego undifferentiated, pushes him instead toward an abandonment of infantile orality and consequent consolidation of an ego of the whole. From this perspective, the group is not a secondary entity upon which an essentially unbroken narcissistic merger with the mother is displaced or extended. Rather, the group is a primary player in the consolidation of the child's ego, a player whose intervention is able to break the child's selfish, immature connection to the mother.[1] As for the fate of the split mother images, this can best be illuminated through a discussion of another key difference between the situation of Hindu child rearing and its seeming counterpart in the West: the presence of multiple mothers.

Hindu mothering is multiple mothering, and this fact is not adequately taken into account by psychoanalytic discussions of the Indian scene. It is true that the child's natural mother ordinarily has a special relationship to her child. For the most part she is the one who nurses it, holds it, and attends to it. On the other hand, especially in the setting of the joint family, these duties are shared by siblings, cousins, and by the mother's sisters-in-law (the wives of her husband's brothers) (Cormack 1953:1,8; Dube 1955:192; Luschinsky 1962:121–125; Minturn and Hitchcock 1966:107–108; Rohner and Chaki-Sircar 1988:69–70; Roland 1988:249; Seymour 1983). Finally, the young mother's mother-in-law, ruler of the women's portion of the joint family, has a special claim on the child (Minturn and Hitchcock 1966:118; Wiser and Wiser 1963:82).

As noted in the previous chapter, in the joint family setting care is taken to ensure that the direct association between individual mothers and their children is not too exclusive. In fact, among the women of such a family, gathered typically with their children in the inner courtyard of the home, special efforts are made to avoid signs of favoritism or special attention from a mother toward her own children, but a mother would not hesitate to play with the children of her sisters-in-law (Jacobson 1982:98; Vatuk 1982:74).[2] Moreover, as we saw above, in the immediate presence of her mother-in-law, a young mother should suspend direct physical contact with her child, perhaps even handing the child over to the mother-in-law. The underlying message of this pattern of respect is that the child belongs more to the family as a whole than to any one individual (Minturn and Hitchcock 1966:118–119; Wiser 1963:82). Even after motherhood, then, the wife still poses a danger to the joint family. Her "selfish" and "jealous" interest in "her" husband and child can, if not properly controlled, lead to a weakening of the family through partition.

The psychoanalytic approach, while it does not focus on the phenomenon of Hindu joint mothering, might have a way of incorporating it into its analysis. On the one hand, joint mothering can be viewed as another barrier to the integration of split mother images. Without a single, consistent primary caretaker, it could be argued, the child cannot easily play out its loves and hates on the same mother figure long enough to see her fundamental unity (Boss 1965:72; Erikson 1969:42). Instead, some mothers are seen as all-bad, and others are idealized as all-good. In other words, multiple mothering can prevent the healing of the split within the image of the natural mother by spreading out the opposition between good and bad among multiple mothers. This is the position taken by Hippler, Boyer, and Boyer on multiple mothering among the Alaska Athabascans (1975:210, see also, Kardiner 1945:147). We might summarize this position as allowing for splits both within a single mother and between multiple mothers.

From a slightly different point of view, the situation is equally bleak. For example, let us review Carstairs' discussion of the Hindu mother's practice of maintaining a respectful aloofness from her own child when in the presence of elder in-laws. For Carstairs, the mother's aloofness from her child in the presence of the mother-in-law undermines the child's confidence in reliable care:

> The child will have cause to notice that his mother, though devoted to his service, is unaccountably inconstant in the warmth of her contact with him. At times she caresses him affectionately while at other times owing to the presence of her parents-in-law she becomes aloof and seemingly indifferent to him.
>
> (Carstairs 1967:157)

For Carstairs, then, the practice of respectful aloofness from the child compounds the dangers of excessive physical indulgence by adding to it unpredictable frustration, thus preventing any healing of the split in the image of the mother.

I think a reworking of this rather grim point of view is both possible and desirable. Such a reworking could proceed from the basic notion that the infant does at first split off good and bad experiences by creating thoroughly benign and malignant images of its caretakers. Our reworking could also assume with Carstairs and dency to split and correspondingly increases the sense of a caretaker's complex, imperfect, yet fundamental goodness. What should distinguish this new approach to the inner world of Hindu infancy is a refusal to treat the relation to a single natural mother as the sole focus of the early struggle to overcome splitting.

We can begin to develop this approach to splitting by experimentally imagining from the child's point of view how splitting might play into the Hindu situation of multiple mothering. Following this, I shall present evidence from Hindu myths that should begin to clarify and substantiate the results of our thought experiment.

Consider again the position of the child whose mother distances herself because of the presence of her mother-in-law and who even hands over the child to care of the mother-in-law. As the child gains an awareness that another mother's presence affects the behavior of his "own" mother, the situation moves beyond that of a simple split between a single good and bad mother. If we focus on the natural mother alone, it is true that the chronic experience of an abrupt halt in her accustomed physical ministrations should provoke in the child the feeling that an angry sort of "demon mother" has somehow replaced his accustomed, all-good mother. Yet, as the child begins to grasp that the emergence of this demon mother is related to the presence of the mother-in-law, there may also develop the sense in the child that he or she is being given over to the control of one demon mother by another. This moment could be experienced by the child under two aspects. On the one hand, the child would have a sense that there are two demon mothers, his own mother, now ignoring him, and the mother-in-law in whose presence they are. On the other hand, the child might experience this demonic duo as essentially one in purpose and origin. That is, the child would get a sense of a generally demonic mother who could manifest herself either singly or in multiples.

As the child matures and makes at least some headway in unifying the split in the image of his natural mother, there is likely to emerge a more complex imagination of the meaning of the mother's pause before the mother-in-law. From this more mature point of view, the generally benign mother is felt to grow angry with the child on the appearance of the mother-in-law, for the child interprets the mother's distancing in light of the anger it makes *him* feel. Despite her perceived anger, however, the mother is not experienced by the relatively mature child as *totally* bad. Yet, in what appears to be her fury, she hands the child over or submits him to the control of a more purely demoniacal mother (the mother-in-law). Overwhelmed by his own anger at the lapse in care, the child may then come to feel that he has himself become a vengeful demon, one who has been turned over by his angry but not all-bad mother to a pure demon-mother for destruction. Already, then, we are dealing with multiple mother images—some are more ambiguous in character than others, yet each seems related to aspects of all. The bad mother-in-law may appear as a multiform of the bad natural mother. Yet at times, especially as the child matures, the all-bad mother-in-law may seem more one-sided than a complex, generally benevolent, but occasionally angry, natural mother. Thus, splits emerge both within and between multiple and occasionally merging mothers.

Eventually, however, and this is where we must break most profoundly with the traditional psychoanalytic perspective, a deeper change occurs. Why should we not assume that the underlying message of the respect behavior among various mothers is eventually grasped by the child? In other words, we must assume that at a certain point the child realizes that the mother-in-law is not his enemy. Whenever the direct care of the mother is suspended, *someone* else, be it the mother-in-law or one of the other daughters-in-law of the household, takes over. Each of these various mothers, moreover, works from a common purpose. The child grasps, for example, that just as his own mother's favoritism is constrained, so too is that of his aunts toward his cousins. Both boy child and girl child come to realize that, in the end, consistent care resides not in a relationship to any single individual but in the relationship to all the mothers taken as a group. Although one of these mothers may at any given moment abandon the child, another is sure to emerge to replace her. Gaining an insight that rewards a long struggle for enlightenment, the child sees that "all the mothers are one."

A passage from Dumont helps explain the conceptual error of the traditional psychoanalytic interpretation:

> The normative subject [in India] as opposed to the empirical agent is constituted not by a single human person, but by a constellation of persons making up the whole. The simplest form is a pair. At one

stroke, this perception solves a few false problems ("ownership of land") and puts us on the path of understanding (solidarity of father and son in the joint family). While the anthropologist usually speaks of dyadic relationships, we are faced with a dyadic subject, because the relationship is conceived as internal to reality, as its core.

(Dumont 1970b:141)

Carstairs' interpretation of the effect on the child of the mother-in-law's presence is thus set in the framework of a false problem. The question is not the relationship between the mother and child as individuals. Seen in this light, the appearance of third parties can only be viewed as disruptive. Yet this problematic individualist perspective is built into traditional psychoanalytic theory. By shifting our perspective, however, and taking the group as our subject it can be seen that the child does unify split mother images *at the level of the group*. Reliable care, in other words, proceeds from all the mothers taken as a whole.

Our reconstruction from the child's perspective shows that in a multiple mothering situation, as already intuited by the psychoanalysts, there does exist a context that encourages splitting both within *and between* diverse mother figures. Yet the realization that as a consistently caring group all of the mothers are one does permit the child to sense the kind and benevolent mother underneath the guise of the demon mother. Moreover, it is precisely because split mother images are unified at the level of the group that there is no need to combine explicit good and bad images into a single moderated individual. Relatively extreme images of splits within a single mother or of contrasts *between* mothers continue to exist. Despite the rules of respect, in other words, not all of a child's mothers need be equal givers of care. Some will remain more "demonic" than others. And because of those same rules of respect, even the kindest of caretakers will at times seem demonlike. Nonetheless, the child knows that it can always depend on care from someone, not so much because of its relationship to any single mother as because of its status as a member of the group. It is this knowledge that enables the child to tolerate those "demonic moments" in its encounter with its several mothers as individuals.

My discussion of the complex splits occurring at the prototypical moment of withdrawal from the child by the mother in the presence of the mother-in-law may already have been recognized by those familiar with the Hindu Goddess as an account of the springing forth of the terrible goddess Kali from the angry brow of the fierce but fundamentally benign Durga in order that the great buffalo demon be slain (Dimmitt and van Buitenen 1978:225; Kinsley 1986:97). I do think that the birth of Kali out of the terrible and murderous anger of Durga is rooted in this moment and others like it. That is, the withdrawal of the mother from the child and the turning over of the child to the care of the mother's mother-in-law or sisters-in-law is experienced by the child as an abandonment of his now uncontrollable demon-self into the clutches of a horrible being sprung from his own angry but fundamentally good natural mother.

I hasten to add, however—and this is fundamental—that even this split *is* healed at the level of the group. Thus, even though the image of a horrible, bloodthirsty, death-dealing, black-faced, killer-goddess Kali remains explicit, the child comes to understand that this image is ultimately a part of a fundamentally good collection of mothers who provide consistent care when taken as a group.

Consider, for example, this excerpt from David Kinsley's discussion of the theology of Kali:

> The devotee . . . appropriates the truths Kali reveals by adopting the attitude of a child whose essential nature toward its mother is that of acceptance no matter how awful, how indifferent, how fearsome, she is. The devotee, then, by making the apparently unlikely assertion that Kali is his mother, enables himself to approach and appropriate the forbidding truths that Kali reveals; in appropriating these truths the devotee, like the Tantric adept, is liberated from the fear these truths impose on people who deny or ignore them.
>
> Through devotion to Kali the devotee becomes reconciled to death and achieves acceptance of the way things are, an equilibrium that remains unperturbed in Kali's presence.
>
> (Kinsley 1986:126–127)

It would be difficult to find a finer description of Klein's notion of the unification of split mother images. By acknowledging the truth of the mother's disappointing withdrawal or periodic anger, the child is reconciled to and thus liberated from the pain of being cared for by a less than perfect mother.

In Kali, then, we have a psychoanalytic paradox. The very image that seems to give proof of an unresolved split in the image of the mother is used to get across a message of unity. The key to the paradox is the realization that in the Hindu context the split is resolved not at the level of the individual mother, or the individual goddess, but through the knowledge that all the mothers—whether divine or human—are part of a single unified group. From this point of view, although explicit images of all-good and all-bad mothers may more freely prevail, these very images are always viewed as glimpses of a more complex unity in which good and bad coexist.

Kali is an interesting goddess because—although she is born in the context of Durga's struggle with the demon and is often represented, like Durga, as an unmarried goddess—she is also very frequently represented as a married goddess. In fact, as noted, this was a central difficulty in Babb's scheme of classification. For while Babb portrayed Kali as the prototypical single, malevolent goddess, he actually encountered an equally typical representation of Kali standing on the prone body of her husband Shiva.

A myth I was told in explanation of this iconographic pose tells of a Kali so maddened from her slaying of demons, so drunk with their blood, that she proceeded to rage out of control. The gods worried that the entire universe would be destroyed by her. It was only when Shiva lay down in her path and Kali realized that she was about to slay her own husband that she stopped her murderous rampage (for related myths, see Kinsley 1975:104–105).[3]

This story is interesting because it does, in fact, conform to Babb's notion of the mechanism underlying the character of married goddesses. Although Kali always appears in a "terrible" form, here, at least, she is being calmed and controlled by a husband, prone at her feet though he may be. Kali, then, although born from the brow of the unmarried, sister-daughter mother goddess Durga, holds a place, more so than any other goddess, on *both* poles of the proposed goddess classification scheme.

The reason for Kali's status as a married goddess, I believe, is that the child eventually comes to understand the link between his somewhat less enthusiastic "mothers" and their in-law status with respect to his real mother. In other words, the grown child sees that his relation to his more demonic mothers is not direct. It is mediated by marriage. Thus the symbolism of Kali comes to be associated with marriage. To put it another way, the most difficult split for the child to unify is not so much the split between the two sides of his own mother as it is the split between his own mother and the in-law mothers (his mother's mother-in-law and her husband's brothers' wives—i.e., her sisters-in-law). It is this opposition that is activated at the classic moment when the mother withdraws her ministrations from the child in the presence of the mother-in-law. The unification of this split is the real achievement of the ek-hi phase. It is this achievement that is consolidated by the insight that all the mothers are one. If even the demonic Kali, symbol of the distant in-law mothers, can be seen as good, as part and parcel of an ultimately benign *group* of mothers, then the split is healed.[4]

My suggestion, therefore, is that the two poles of our proposed goddess classification scheme, the sister-daughter mothers on the one hand and the wife—daughter-in-law mothers on the other, symbolize something deeper than the split between women in two diverse sets of kinship statuses. Unconsciously, these two opposed kin groupings represent the split between the real mother and the in-law mothers. Durga and Kali, then, represent the ambiguous but fundamentally good natural mother and the demonlike in-law mothers, respectively, just as they embody a parallel opposition between unmarried sister-daughter goddesses and wife goddesses.

To understand this split, it will be necessary to see its reflection in Santoshi Ma's textual myth as well as in the film version of that myth. Consider the following summary of the early printed story of Santoshi Ma, followed by the cinematic transformation of that same story:

The Printed Story

There was once a mother who had seven sons. Six earned money but the seventh was idle. The mother fed the six working sons good food, but she fed their partially eaten and thus polluted leftovers to the seventh. (Partially eaten portions of food are thought of as polluted by saliva and are called *jūṭhā*.) The seventh son was too naive to see this, however, and believed that his mother treated him well. One day, the seventh son's wife discovered that his mother was feeding him his brothers' *jūṭhā*. She told her husband, and when he confirmed it, he left his wife and his home in order to make money and reclaim his honor. His cruel mother was not sorry to see him go.

The seventh son found work with a prosperous merchant and soon grew wealthy. His wife, however, having been left at home, was tormented by her in-laws, forced to do all the family's hard work and fed in an insulting manner.

One day, while working in the forest, the seventh son's wife learned from a group of women how to worship Santoshi Ma. She learned that by performing the fast of Santoshi Ma on successive Fridays wishes could be granted. During the fasts, all sour food should be avoided and Santoshi Ma's favorite food, gur-canā, an inexpensive mixture of brown sugar and roasted chickpeas, should be offered. The seventh son's wife undertook the fast and asked Santoshi Ma to bring her husband home.

In response to this worship, Santoshi Ma went to the seventh son in a dream and prompted him to return home. In order to facilitate this, the goddess performed a miracle. She made it possible for the son to complete all of his business dealings in a single day.

When the son reached home, he saw his wife's miserable condition and understood the suffering worked on her by his mother. As a result, he asked for a partition of his holdings and set up a new hearth with his wife in a separate section of the family house.

In gratitude, the wife performed the closing ceremony of Santoshi Ma's fast. This ceremony requires that a special meal be served to eight boys, and she invited the children of her in-laws to take the meal. These children, however, had been coached by the in-laws to ruin the ceremony. They prevailed upon the seventh son's wife to offer them a little money and then purchased and ate sour food with that money.

The rules of Santoshi Ma's fast forbid gifts of money as well as the eating of sour food. Santoshi Ma, therefore, punished the seventh son's wife by causing her husband to be imprisoned. Her devotee then begged Santoshi Ma for forgiveness, which was granted. The seventh son was released from prison and a new closing ceremony was carried out, this time with Brahman boys instead of the children of the in-laws.

Santoshi Ma was pleased with this worship and decided to pay her devotee a visit. She took on the terrible form of a fierce demoness and came toward the heroine's house. On seeing this, the mother-in-law took fright, thinking the demon would eat the children. At her urging, the children of the household ran away. The seventh son's wife, however, immediately recognized the "demon" as Santoshi Ma. She took the child nursing at her breast and respectfully laid him aside. Her mother-in-law berated her for this neglect and endangerment of the child. Just then, however, Santoshi Ma, through her miraculous power, attracted children from all around, until all one could see in the courtyard was a sea of children. All then realized that the ogress was actually Santoshi Ma. All, including the mother-in-law, begged for Santoshi Ma's forgiveness, and all worshiped at the foot of the goddess.

The Film

It is the brother-sister holiday of *Rakshā Bandhan* and in the heaven of the elephant-headed god Ganesh, the deity's sister is tying the holiday bracelet on his arm. Ganesh's sons ask for a sister to tie the bracelet on their arm, and for this purpose Ganesh creates Santoshi Ma out of flames drawn from the breasts of his two wives, Riddhi and Siddhi.

Santoshi Ma grows into a mature goddess who grants her devotees satisfaction. (Santoshi Ma means "Mother of Satisfaction.") On earth, her greatest devotee is the beautiful young girl Satyavati. Satyavati asks Santoshi Ma for a husband, and the goddess listens. With Santoshi Ma's help, Satyavati meets and falls in love with Birju.

Birju sings devotional songs for Santoshi Ma but does not work in the fields like his six brothers. His artistic talents are nurtured by his kind, oldest brother, and he is well cared for by his widowed mother. Birju's brothers and sisters-in-law, however, resent his refusal to work in the fields. His elder sister-in-law goes so far as to insult Birju by secretly feeding him his brothers' polluted leftovers (*jūṭhā*).

Birju saves Satyavati from an attempted rape, and following this, a marriage is arranged. Birju's mother is delighted that he will now settle down, and she is particularly pleased by the beauty of Satyavati. Birju's sisters-in-law, however, resent him and are jealous of his beautiful wife. They sabotage the mother's welcome of the bride and tease and torment Satyavati.

In gratitude for their meeting and marriage, Satyavati and Birju go on a pilgrimage to Santoshi Ma's temples. The heavenly message carrier and trouble making gossip, Narad, carries news of this pilgrimage to the three goddesses Lakshmi, Parvati, and Brahmani. The goddesses are enraged when they hear from Narad of Santoshi Ma's popularity on earth. Narad leads them to believe (incorrectly) that Satyavati, Santoshi Ma's great devotee, will not worship them but only Santoshi Ma. The goddesses decide to discourage the worship of their rival Santoshi Ma by destroying the happiness of Santoshi Ma's devotee Satyavati.

At just this time, however, three holy men reach Satyavati's door begging for alms. They are turned away by her evil sisters-in-law, but Satyavati calls them back and offers them gur-canā, the humble food previously offered to Santoshi Ma in worship. (Such divine leftovers are called prasād.) These holy men then go to heaven and offer the food of Santoshi Ma to the three goddesses. The goddesses indignantly reject the food and attempt to physically eject the holy men from heaven. All of a sudden, the saints reveal themselves to be the goddesses' husbands in disguise, the gods Vishnu, Shiva, and Brahma. The gods plead with their wives to accept, as they had, the food of Santoshi Ma, but the goddesses refuse. (By eating the leftovers of Santoshi Ma, the goddesses would be temporarily lowering themselves before Santoshi Ma in an act of worship.)

The goddesses undermine Satyavati's happiness by causing Birju to discover that his sister-in-law prepares polluted food for him. Birju feels utterly betrayed, saying that he had previously considered his sister-in-law to be as worthy of respect as his own mother. Enraged, Birju leaves home and all that is dear, including Satyavati herself, to make his fortune. As he attempts to cross a river, however, the goddesses stir up a tempest. Birju is tossed overboard and nearly drowns, but Satyavati senses the danger and prays to Santoshi Ma. In response, Santoshi Ma comes down from heaven and personally rescues Birju from certain death.

The three goddesses, however, visit Birju's home in disguise and tell the family that Birju has been drowned. Satyavati refuses to believe this. She knows that Santoshi Ma would not let this happen. When her father comes to fetch the "widow" home, therefore, Satyavati refuses to go. Moreover, because they wish to use Satyavati as a workhorse, the sisters-in-law tell Satyavati's father that they will take good care of her. So Satyavati's father leaves her with her in-laws, who then force her into hard labor, beat, and insult her.

Meanwhile Birju gets work with a prosperous merchant and grows rich. The merchant's beautiful daughter loves him, and he stays with her, for the three goddesses have taken away his memory of Satyavati.

Satyavati is driven by the torture of her in-laws, unchecked in her husband's absence, to attempt suicide. The sage Narad intervenes, however, and teaches Satyavati Santoshi Ma's fast. She performs the fast on successive Fridays in hopes of bringing her husband home. Many tribulations follow. The three goddesses and her evil in-laws try to thwart Satyavati, but with Santoshi Ma's help, the fast is completed, and Birju returns home a wealthy man.

Birju sees what has happened to his wife in his absence. He completes his revenge on his family by setting up his own magnificent new home with a temple to Santoshi Ma inside. Satyavati, however, wishing a family reconciliation, invites her in-laws to the closing ceremony of Santoshi Ma's fast. Her jealous sisters-in-law ruin the ceremony by squeezing lemons, a tabooed sour food, into the offerings. For this Santoshi Ma causes their sons, who eat the ceremonial food, to die. She also disrupts the heavens where the three goddesses live, for they had inspired the evil sisters-in-law to spoil the ritual.

Satyavati's in-laws accuse her of poisoning the children. She turns to Santoshi Ma for vindication, and the goddess brings all back to life after descending from heaven and announcing her pleasure with Satyavati's devotion. The evil in-laws worship Santoshi Ma and beg her forgiveness. The three goddesses then confront Santoshi Ma in heaven. We learn, however, that the antipathy between the goddesses was not real. It was all simply a test of Satyavati's devotion. Santoshi Ma, after all, is the daughter of Parvati's son Ganesh. Thus the movie ends with all characters reconciled.

We have already noted the fundamental opposition in the film between Santoshi Ma as a sister-daughter goddess, and Lakshmi, Parvati, and Brahmani as wife goddesses. Underneath this opposition, however, is yet another—the split between the natural mother and the in-law mothers of childhood. The heroine of the film has no living mother, yet Santoshi Ma and Birju's own benign mother play this role. The malignant goddesses, on the other hand, act through the heroine's jealous older sisters-in-law. At various points in the film, these sisters-in-law make themselves out to be the heroine's caretakers (i.e., mothers). In fact, however, they are her tormenters. The same split is enacted from the point of view of the hero. His mother is good, but his sisters-in-law torment him. He expresses his shock at their betrayal by saying that he had always treated them as if they were his very own mother. Again, at the divine level, Santoshi Ma takes the role of the hero's heavenly mother while the three goddesses work by way of the machinations of his perverse sister-in-law "mothers."

In the film, then, there are two parallel oppositions between mothers. The hero and heroine are helped on the heavenly level by a motherly Santoshi Ma while the three divine mothers Lakshmi, Parvati, and Brahmani torment them. This split among deities, in turn, is paralleled and often played out by way of an earthly split. The hero's mother is kind while his sisters-in-law offer a perverse and malignant sort of mothering.

The written story also splits the image of the mother, and here, too, the split has its origin in the opposition between the natural mother and the in-law mothers. In the written story, the heroine's human mother-in-law portrays the demonic in-law mothers of infancy. Santoshi Ma, on the other hand, represents the complex, but fundamentally good, natural mother. Thus, while the usually supportive Santoshi Ma punishes the heroine of the story for an inadvertent ritual error, she also forgives her. At the climax of the story, moreover, when Santoshi Ma tests her devotee with her terrible form, we learn that the split between our two types of mothers is reconcilable if we can recognize the illusory nature of the difference between the kindly and demonic sides of all mothers.

While the film follows the same pattern of splits and reconciliation, there is an important difference—in the cinematic version of the myth the oppositions are more explicit and more exciting. In the printed story the two types of mothers work from different bases, heaven and earth. They do not really confront one another until their final reconciliation at the end of the story. The superiority in status of the symbolic natural mother (Santoshi Ma), moreover, is never in doubt. Finally, although Santoshi Ma and the heroine's mother-in-law are opposed insofar as one is helpful and the other hurtful, there is little direct undoing of the actions of one by the other. All of this changes, however, in the film. Here the opponents are more nearly equal and more explicitly in conflict. The heroine is helped by her mother-in-law and tormented by her sisters-in-law. This battle, moreover, parallels and enacts the dangerous dispute between the rival goddesses. This divine dispute, although mediated to some degree by the messenger Narad, is depicted in a fairly straightforward manner. The three goddesses try to harm the hero and heroine, and Santoshi Ma's intervention overturns the effect of their actions. At the climax of the story, the goddesses inspire a direct ritual insult of Santoshi Ma, and Santoshi Ma retaliates by attacking the very homes of the three goddesses.

In the film, as in the written story, Santoshi Ma, the representative of the ambiguous but fundamentally good natural mother of childhood, punishes and then forgives a ritual error. At the end of the film, moreover, the opposition between Santoshi Ma and the other goddesses is shown to be illusory. The film leaves this reconciliation, however, until the very last minute. For the greater part of the movie's length, the conflict between the two types of mothers is played out as a direct battle within parallel human and divine groups. The deepest reason for the film's popularity, then, is that it enacts in an unusually explicit form the final and most tenuously unified split of the ek-hi phase, the split between the "real mother" and the in-law mothers in the joint family.

Moreover, we can see the image of Kali lurking beneath the explicit goddess identities of the film. As the three married goddesses struggle to destroy the happiness of Santoshi Ma's devotees, their husbands seem to take the side of Santoshi Ma. These three gods, Brahma, Vishnu, and Shiva, return to heaven from their earthly visit to Santoshi Ma's devotees, having taken the guise of religious mendicants. Hearing these mendicants speak of Santoshi Ma, the three goddesses physically begin to push them out of heaven. Only when the three gods resume their divine form and reveal themselves to be the three goddesses' husbands are their wives calmed. This recalls the image of Kali ending her rampage only when realizing that she is trampling on her own husband. It shows that in their opposition to Santoshi Ma the married goddesses convey a hint of the opposition, examined above, between Durga (of whom Santoshi Ma is said to be a form) as the natural mother and Kali as the in-law mother.

In the printed story, as noted, the same split between the natural mother and the in-law mothers is conveyed, although in a less controversial form. The origin of this split in the early child-rearing situation is illuminated by the reconciliation between mothers portrayed at the end of the printed story. To reiterate, at the climax of this story, Santoshi Ma decides to visit the home of her human devotee (the heroine). In order to test her devotee, however, she adopts a "terrible form." As the seeming demoness moves toward the home, the heroine's evil mother-in-law cries out, children run in all directions, and doors and windows are bolted. All fear that the demoness will eat one of the children. The heroine, however, immediately recognizes the seemingly threatening visitor as Santoshi Ma. At the sight of the deity, she puts down the child who had been suckling at her breast. This removal of the baby from the breast infuriates the mother-in-law, who viciously berates the heroine for her lapse in the care of the child. In a moment, however, through the power of Santoshi Ma, the courtyard appears to be filled with a sea of children. The heroine then explains that the visitor is actually Santoshi Ma, and, recognizing the goddess at last, all, including the once cruel mother-in-law, worship at the feet of the deity.

This climax of the printed story, like the climax of the film, depicts the unification of the natural mother and the in-law mothers. The appearance of what seems to be a child-eating demoness prompts a seemingly irresponsible mother to reject a child nursing at the breast. This apparently obvious yet in fact unenlightened point of view, initially shared by most of the family members, is not so different from Carstairs' own interpretation of the Hindu mother's respect behavior before the mother-in-law. For Carstairs, the mother's removal from the child in the presence of the mother-in-law is a regrettable lapse. What the heroine of the story realizes, however, is that the demoness is really a goddess and that a respectful end to nursing actually leads to a miraculous profusion of children throughout the household. In other words, she sees that the key to good mothering of all the household's children, taken as a group, lies in recognizing the ultimate benignity of the demon-Santoshi Ma (here the symbolic mother-in-law) and in respectfully ending attentions to her "own" child. This is the meaning of the profusion of children that follows on the "rejection" of the heroine's nursing baby. Once the heroine's insight is adopted, the household's evil mother-in-law and frightened children are joyfully united in the worship of the mother goddess now seen to be good. Appropriately, the insight into the true, benign nature of the symbolic mother-in-law (the "demonic" Santoshi Ma) is followed by the transformation of the story's human mother-in-law into a kind and reverent woman.

In the printed story, the reader knows all along that the demoness is Santoshi Ma, who has come to test her devotee. This helps moderate the tensions within the divine image. The real conflict in the printed story, moreover, is created by human in-laws. It is not set in motion by the ambiguous activity of the goddess herself. In the film, on the other hand, the long war of the goddesses is ended only at the very last minute, and even this reconciliation comes as a surprise to the viewer. Most importantly, the film's conflicts are developed by way of an unorthodox dispute between ordinarily asso-

FIGURE 2
Printed Story

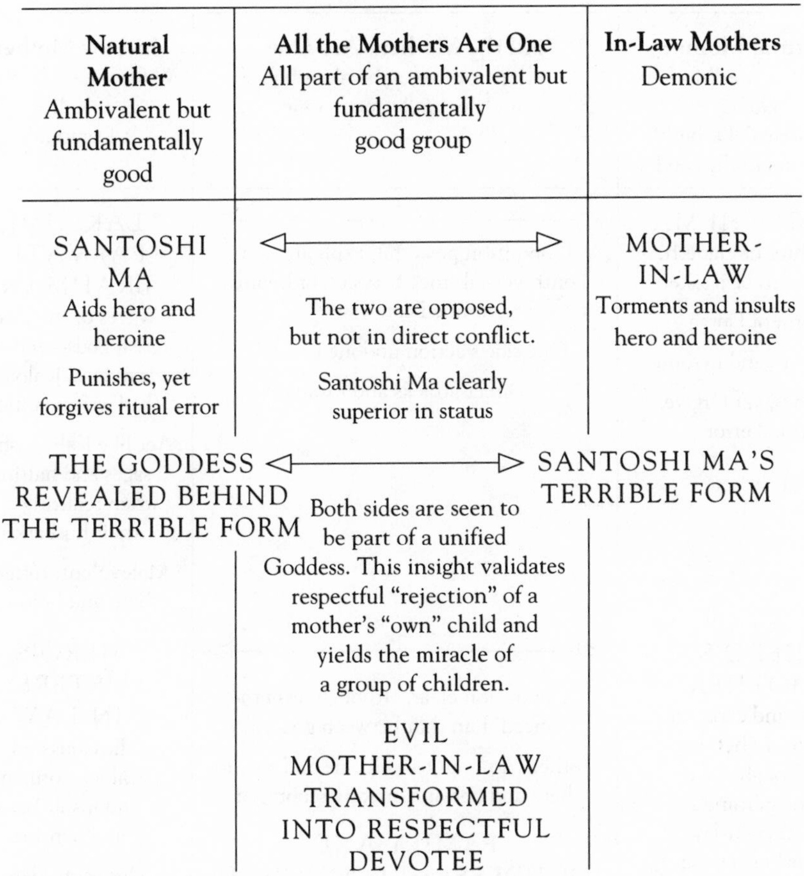

Natural Mother Ambivalent but fundamentally good	**All the Mothers Are One** All part of an ambivalent but fundamentally good group	**In-Law Mothers** Demonic
SANTOSHI MA Aids hero and heroine	◁————————▷ The two are opposed, but not in direct conflict.	MOTHER-IN-LAW Torments and insults hero and heroine
Punishes, yet forgives ritual error	Santoshi Ma clearly superior in status	

THE GODDESS ◁————————▷ SANTOSHI MA'S
REVEALED BEHIND   Both sides are seen to   TERRIBLE FORM
THE TERRIBLE FORM   be part of a unified
Goddess. This insight validates
respectful "rejection" of a
mother's "own" child and
yields the miracle of
a group of children.

EVIL
MOTHER-IN-LAW
TRANSFORMED
INTO RESPECTFUL
DEVOTEE

ciated *goddesses*. While the film's continual highlighting of tensions within the usually unified notion of the greater Goddess accounts for its success, the splitting and unification in both it and the printed story are basically the same. The overall approach to our two versions of the Santoshi Ma myths can now be summarized in diagrammatic form (see figures 2 and 3).

It will be seen that the approach enacted in the concept of an ek-hi phase offers an explanation for each of the three aspects of Hindu Goddess imagery the psychoanalytic notion of an unresolved split between the good and bad mother fails to take into account.

FIGURE 3

Film

Natural Mother Sister-Daughter Mothers: Durga Ambivalent, but fundamentally good	All the Mothers Are One All part of an ambivalent but fundamentally good group	In-Law Mothers Wife-in-Law Mothers: Kali Demonic
SANTOSHI MA Daughter of Ganesh, created to be a sister Form of Durga Aids hero and heroine Punishes, yet forgives ritual error	◁————————————▷ Opposition powerful, explicit, and controversial since between ordinarily unified goddesses One side's action undone by other Direct attacks and insults	LAKSHMI, PARVATI, BRAHMANI Wives of the three great gods—selfish, envious, jealous (bad wife qualities) Act like Kali, pushing sages and halting when realizing it is their husbands Malevolent; torment hero and heroine
HERO'S MOTHER Aids and cares for hero and heroine; although she is the heroine's mother-in-law, acts like a good mother to her; heroine's "real" mother dead. Wary of hero's artistic longings, yet ultimately forgiving, kind, and protective	◁————————————▷ Opposition clear, although less pro- nounced than that between goddesses Mother's attempt to welcome and care for hero and heroine directly sabotaged FAMILY AND GODDESSES RECONCILED Parvati as mother of Santoshi Ma's father Revelation of unity kept until last moment	HERO'S SISTERS- IN-LAW Envious and jealous; torment and insult hero and heroine Hero considered them like his own mother, but they failed him

First, the explicit nature of the imagery is explained as permissible in light of the fact that the various sides of motherliness are unified at the level of the group. Second, the images are multiple, sliding in and out of one another in complex fashion, because they go back to a situation of multiple mothering. Moreover, beyond a simple split between good and bad within a single mother, we can now perceive the symbolic remnants of an additional split involving multiple mothers, that between the natural mother and the in-law mothers. This split may be enacted in a relatively hidden manner as the benign and demonic sides of a single goddess or in a more obvious, yet more controversial manner, as a war between a number of goddesses. The healing of this particular split is the final step in the consolidation of an ego of the whole. This, in turn, explains the third and final deficiency within the current psychoanalytic discussion of Goddess imagery, the denial of a Hindu resolution of the split mother problem. The split *is* healed; the mother is unified, but at the level of the group. This is why Hindus responded to my inquiries about the goddesses' dispute in Santoshi Ma's film with the denial that such a quarrel could take place. Their insistence in response to my queries that all the goddesses are one, enacted the healing of the split between the natural mother and the in-law mothers, the very split the film so successfully reactivates.

Even when a split and its subsequent unification take place within a single deity, as at the climax of the written story of Santoshi Ma, the opposition between the natural mother and the in-law mothers may actually be at stake. By depicting the healing of this split as the unification of a single being, the unity of all the mothers in the group is dramatically highlighted. On the other hand, precisely because the process portrayed ultimately refers to separate beings within the family, the explicit depiction of the splitting process is not surprising. It reflects not a tenuous hold on the notion of a single being's integrity, but an effort to consolidate separate human mothers into a single divine whole.

Ultimately, however, the unity of purpose and identity behind the multiple mothers of the Hindu joint family is best grasped as something subtly underlying the overt diversity both of real Hindu mothers and of the multiple, shifting, and complex representations of those mothers in the child's mind. From this follows the conscious stress in worship on the Goddess's many forms as well as the characteristic of the pantheon itself to constantly generate "new" variations on the same basic divine theme. In the ongoing, kaleidoscopic process wherein new goddesses are generated and recombined, the Hindu adult recapitulates, and thereby reinforces, a developmental movement in which maternal representations split, multiply, apparently move at cross-purposes, yet are ultimately revealed to be at one in an overall and consistent collective stance toward the child and his peers in the joint family.

A caution must now be added with regard to a criticism of the psychoanalytic scheme. While it is true that psychoanalysis encapsulates a prescriptive model of child rearing, involving a single primary caretaker moving the child toward autonomy through love, my position here in no way calls into question the validity of this scheme *for our culture*. I am not trying to show that Western children may properly be raised by multiple caretakers. Although this point may be argued, what I say does not decide it. We are comparing apples and oranges.

The Indian situation I have described does not merely numerically raise Western child-rearing practices to a higher power. On the contrary, in the Hindu case development proceeds according to *different principles*. The child, for example, renounces pleasure by means of his immersion in the group, not in response to the individualized love of a particular parent. Hindu group mothering works precisely because the child is *not* given Western-style mirroring. This is what pushes him or her away from immature pleasures and into the group. It is entirely possible, then, that the diffusion of Western modes of love and mirroring onto more than one caretaker could have deleterious results. A further discussion of American versus Hindu Indian mothering can be found at the conclusion of chapter 9.

We can now examine several revised diagrams of the goddess classification scheme that incorporate the results of the discussion to date (see figures 4 through 10). The diagrams depict the basic two-poled system, with a characteristic form of benevolence and malevolence at each pole. The two are mediated by a complex motherly benevolence that all the goddesses ultimately share and that permits merging and interchange of identity, generally remaining within the two separate poles but sometimes moving over the entire field.

At the top of each pole there is a divinity who represents a kind of "master image" of her goddess type. These two goddesses, Durga and Parvati, are usually in myth, ritual, and conversation referred to as the baseline forms of unmarried and married goddesses respectively. Consistent with the notion that all the goddesses are one, they are also considered multiforms of each other.

FIGURE 4

Goddess Classification Scheme

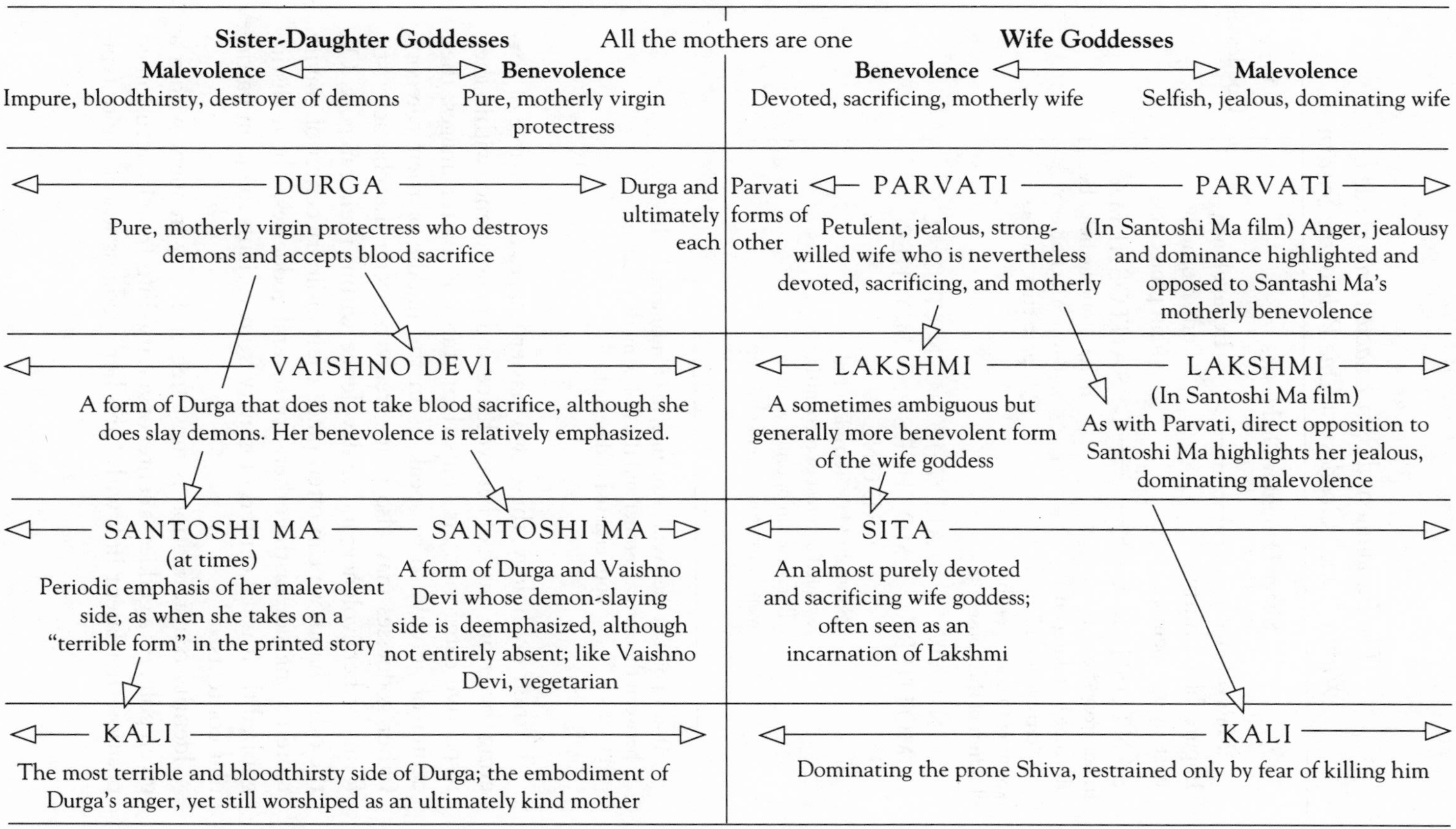

Sister-Daughter Goddesses		All the mothers are one	Wife Goddesses	
Malevolence	**Benevolence**		**Benevolence**	**Malevolence**
Impure, bloodthirsty, destroyer of demons	Pure, motherly virgin protectress		Devoted, sacrificing, motherly wife	Selfish, jealous, dominating wife

— DURGA — →

Pure, motherly virgin protectress who destroys demons and accepts blood sacrifice

— VAISHNO DEVI — →

A form of Durga that does not take blood sacrifice, although she does slay demons. Her benevolence is relatively emphasized.

— SANTOSHI MA — SANTOSHI MA → (at times)

Periodic emphasis of her malevolent side, as when she takes on a "terrible form" in the printed story

A form of Durga and Vaishno Devi whose demon-slaying side is deemphasized, although not entirely absent; like Vaishno Devi, vegetarian

— KALI — →

The most terrible and bloodthirsty side of Durga; the embodiment of Durga's anger, yet still worshiped as an ultimately kind mother

Durga and Parvati ultimately forms of each other

— PARVATI → Petulent, jealous, strong-willed wife who is nevertheless devoted, sacrificing, and motherly

— PARVATI → (In Santoshi Ma film) Anger, jealousy and dominance highlighted and opposed to Santashi Ma's motherly benevolence

— LAKSHMI → A sometimes ambiguous but generally more benevolent form of the wife goddess

— LAKSHMI → (In Santoshi Ma film) As with Parvati, direct opposition to Santoshi Ma highlights her jealous, dominating malevolence

— SITA → An almost purely devoted and sacrificing wife goddess; often seen as an incarnation of Lakshmi

— KALI → Dominating the prone Shiva, restrained only by fear of killing him

Arrows show directions in which character or identity can shift, split, or transform. See figures 5-10.

FIGURE 5
The Fundamental Split Enacted and Healed
Within "One" Goddess at One Pole of the System

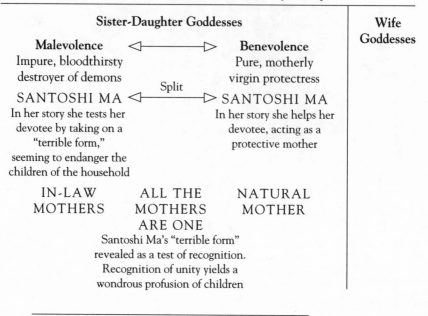

At any point in the overall structure, the fundamental split
between the natural mother and the in-law mothers can be
both enacted and healed.

In their mythology, these two master images are capable of covering the entire range of benevolence and malevolence within their respective categories. As befits their status as master images, their center of gravity, so to speak, is in the middle of their category. Other goddesses may also range freely between the characteristic forms of benevolence and malevolence within their category. On the other hand, we can often place their ordinary center of gravity more to one side or the other. For several goddesses, I have distinguished their usual centers of gravity from variants found in particular contexts.

Identity transformation is most free and very frequent within a given pole. As a goddess's center of gravity shifts from its accustomed position, her latent link with "another" goddess who is more typi-

FIGURE 6

The Fundamental Split Enacted and Healed
Between "Two" Goddess at One Pole of the System

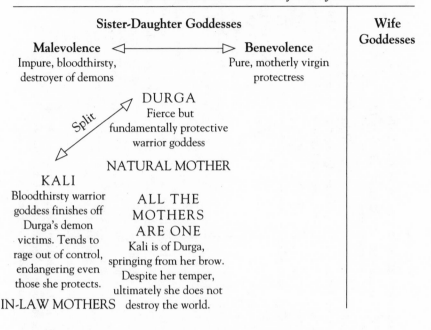

At any point in the overall structure, the fundamental split
between the natural mother and the in-law mothers can be
both enacted and healed.

cally found at that position emerges. Thus the unaccustomed shift of Lakshmi toward the edges of wifely malevolence, as in Santoshi Ma's film, brings out her link with Kali when Lakshmi tries to push her husband out of heaven. These transformations of identity are not so much identifications of one goddess with another as they are revelations of the unified structure that underlies and gives meaning to any particular divine manifestation.

For example, explicitly "demonic" transformations of Santoshi Ma, such as her "terrible form," show that she is not an entirely benevolent sister-daughter goddess, separate from more warlike sister-daughters such as Durga. Even in her "normal" mode, however, the sword visible in Santoshi Ma's typical portrait or icon reveals

FIGURE 7

The Fundamental Split Enacted and Healed Between "Several" Goddesses at Opposite Poles of the System

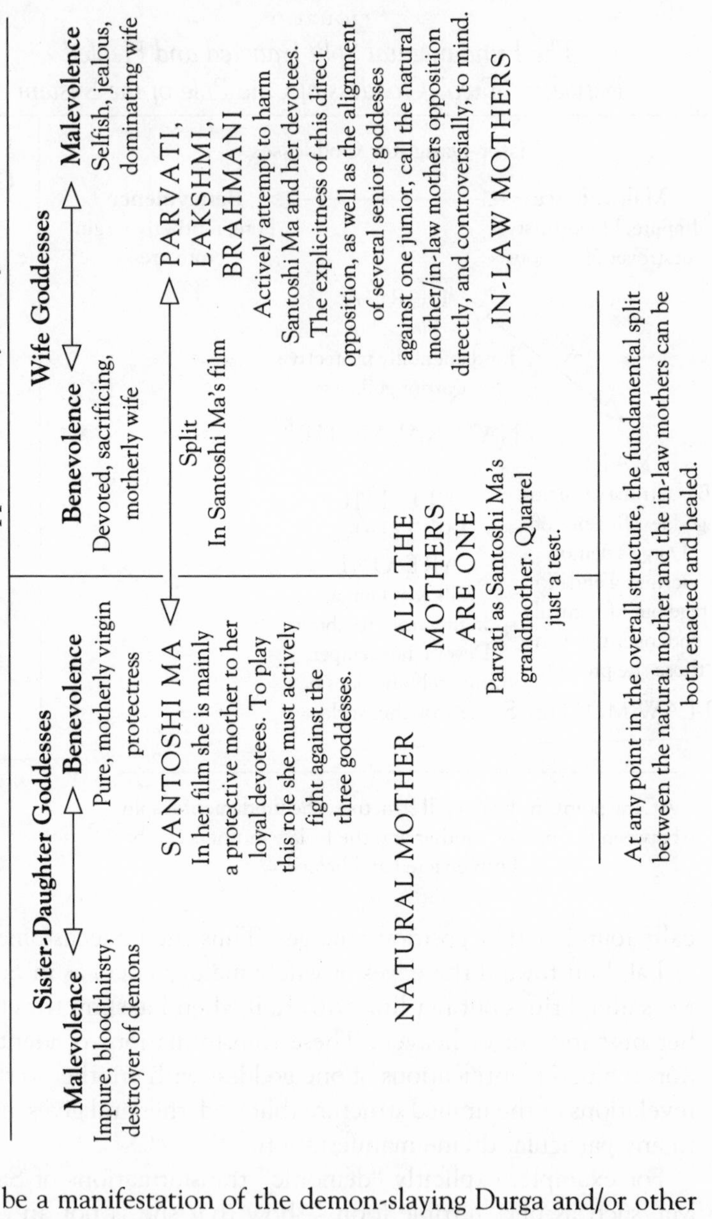

Sister-Daughter Goddesses

Malevolence
Impure, bloodthirsty, destroyer of demons

▷ **Benevolence**
Pure, motherly virgin protectress

Wife Goddesses

Benevolence
Devoted, sacrificing, motherly wife

▷ **Malevolence**
Selfish, jealous, dominating wife

SANTOSHI MA
In her film she is mainly a protective mother to her loyal devotees. To play this role she must actively fight against the three goddesses.

Split
In Santoshi Ma's film

▷ PARVATI, LAKSHMI, BRAHMANI
Actively attempt to harm Santoshi Ma and her devotees. The explicitness of this direct opposition, as well as the alignment of several senior goddesses against one junior, call the natural mother/in-law mothers opposition directly, and controversially, to mind.

NATURAL MOTHER

ALL THE MOTHERS ARE ONE
Parvati as Santoshi Ma's grandmother. Quarrel just a test.

IN-LAW MOTHERS

At any point in the overall structure, the fundamental split between the natural mother and the in-law mothers can be both enacted and healed.

her to be a manifestation of the demon-slaying Durga and/or other demon-slaying goddesses. Moreover, while usually treated as pacific and vegetarian, Santoshi Ma can grow angry (as in the printed story and film) when her ritual is misconducted. A chain letter, which helped popularize Santoshi Ma's worship, even threatens those who

FIGURE 8

A Goddess at an Unusual Position Takes on the Typical Character of "Another" Goddess

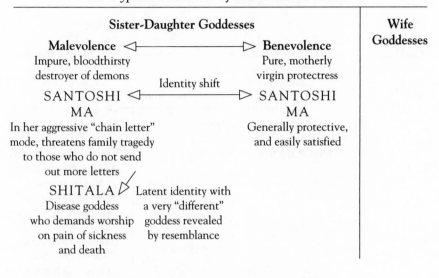

As goddesses move to unaccustomed points within the structure, their latent identity with seemingly different goddesses is revealed through resemblance or outright transformation.

fail to send out more letters with a death or disaster in the family (Erndl 1987:324–325; Kurtz 1990:74–77). I have met devotees who were given quite a scare by this letter. In the chain letter context, Santoshi Ma is reminiscent of no one so much as Shitala—a particularly fierce goddess who demands worship on pain of death by disease (Dimock 1982).

Thus, Santoshi Ma, like other goddesses, maintains a particular center of gravity on the continuum of benevolence and malevolence. In her case, benevolence is emphasized, but malevolence is never far from the surface and is sometimes clearly made manifest. At these moments, Santoshi Ma's latent links with "different" goddesses are made explicit. One devotee, frequently possessed by Santoshi Ma (among other deities), put it to me this way: Santoshi Ma is what Durga became at the moment after she slew the Buffalo Demon and calmed down. Santoshi Ma is the Goddess in the cool aftermath of battle. Thus, it is no paradox that Santoshi Ma should

FIGURE 9

A Goddess at an Unusual Position Takes
on the Typical Character of "Another" Goddess

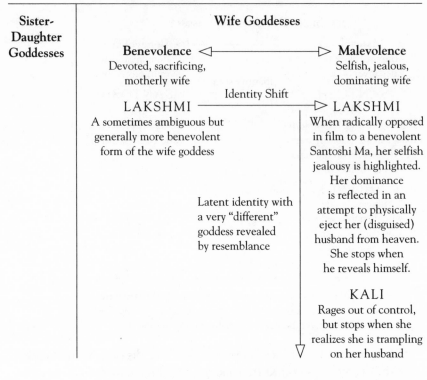

Sister-Daughter Goddesses | **Wife Goddesses**

Benevolence ◁——————▷ **Malevolence**
Devoted, sacrificing, / Selfish, jealous,
motherly wife / dominating wife

Identity Shift

LAKSHMI ——————▷ LAKSHMI

A sometimes ambiguous but generally more benevolent form of the wife goddess

Latent identity with a very "different" goddess revealed by resemblance

When radically opposed in film to a benevolent Santoshi Ma, her selfish jealousy is highlighted. Her dominance is reflected in an attempt to physically eject her (disguised) husband from heaven. She stops when he reveals himself.

KALI
Rages out of control, but stops when she realizes she is trampling on her husband

As goddesses move to unaccustomed points within the structure, their latent identity with seemingly different goddesses is revealed through resemblance or outright transformation.

be a benevolent goddess and yet also be unmarried (Das 1980:54). For Santoshi Ma is not, nor was she ever, *entirely* benevolent. She is simply an emphasized aspect of the larger, complex, unmarried, Durga image of the Goddess. She is a Durga whose sword is at rest, so to speak, but it is still in her hand and ready, on occasion, to strike. (See Santoshi Ma's bloody sword in Kurtz 1990:21.) These links between Santoshi Ma and Durga, then, are not secondary devices to absorb a "new" goddess into the pantheon (Kurtz 1990:37–102). Rather, they are revelations of the principle of unified diversity according to which the pantheon works. Santoshi Ma's

FIGURE 10

A Goddess at an Unusual Position Takes on the Identity of "Another" Goddess Through Transformation

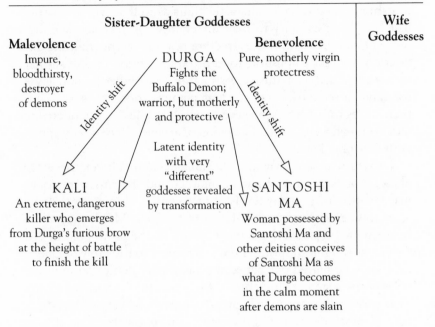

As goddesses move to unaccustomed points within the structure, their latent identity with seemingly different goddesses is revealed through resemblance or outright transformation.

image has always included the sword, and, in one sense or another, it always will. Santoshi Ma did not "become" Durga. Rather, Santoshi Ma could never have been imagined at all without already being Durga, without expressing some particular, yet shifting, aspect of the broad, subtle, pattern of deity that is "the Goddess." Santoshi Ma's image and its transformations make no sense in isolation from this larger pattern.

Here the insights of Western structuralism nicely incorporate the Hindu point of view (Dumont 1980). When Hindus say that all the goddesses are one, they refer, among other things, to the fact that a seemingly individual goddess may either move across the various positions within the overall structure of the Goddess while keeping "her" identity intact or that shifts in the position of a single goddess may eventuate in her transformation into "another." That is, Hindus are acquainted with the tendency for overtly different goddesses to exhibit "each other's" character traits as well as with a "particular" goddess's capacity to radically change her own form. Either mode of mobility within the structure is a way of undermining distinction in order to push us toward the perception of unity—that is, toward a sense of the very structure that underlies and gives meaning to seemingly independent manifestations of deity. Thus there arises the everpresent need to teach this lesson of underlying unity through a continuous, kaleidoscopic generation of only apparently separate deities.

To return to our diagram, the fundamental split of the ek-hi phase, that between the natural mother and the in-law mothers, may be encoded at many levels. It may come within a single deity, as in the benign and terrible forms of Santoshi Ma. It may come between two separate yet unified deities at the same pole of the system, as when Kali springs from and returns to the brow of Durga. Or it may be played out between a number of deities on opposite poles of the system, as in Santoshi Ma's film. In this latter form, the roots of the split in separate human "mothers" of divergent kin status become more apparent and thus more controversial.

Returning once more to the story of Santoshi Ma, we can detect in both the written story and the film a theme that confirms our earlier analysis of the child-rearing pattern underlying the conflicts of the ek-hi phase. Recall that the Hindu mother threatens that a child's failure to work will leave him to "eat dirt." That is, the mother threatens to withhold from a selfish child both food and the honor that sharing food with the family implies. This threat, on the one hand, is never meant to be literally carried out by the mother. That is, she would never actually deprive her child of food or consistently isolate him from the family although occasional brief exclusions from family activities are acceptable as punishments. On the other hand, her generally unrealized threats do bring it home to the child that failure to act on behalf of the group brings dishonor and isolation, thus effectively pushing the child toward a mature sacrifice of pleasure (see above, chapter 4). All this is depicted in Santoshi Ma's myth.

The hero of the story refuses to work in the fields with his brothers. For this refusal to sacrifice on behalf of the group, his family makes him "eat dirt" in the form of polluted food ($jūṭhā$). Such a tactic is neither practiced nor approved by actual Hindus. The myth, in fact, conveys its disapproval of the in-laws who serve "dirty food" as a punishment. In the film, for example, the sister-in-law who pollutes the hero's food is clearly a cruel, unsympathetic character. Indeed, the sister-in-law does not dare carry out her punishment of the hero openly but only in the secrecy of the kitchen. By the end of the story, in fact, the in-laws repent of their earlier cruelty.

Yet because it so clearly portrays both the enactment and eventual discrediting of food-pollution as a punishment, the myth teaches us something about the underlying psychology of similar punishments real Hindu mothers merely threaten their children with. That is, the myth shows how parental punishment both prompts maturity in the child yet also covers its tracks, so to speak, leaving the emphasis on the child's "willing sacrifice" of infantile pleasures. Thus, it is when the hero realizes that his family has dishonored him that he leaves everything and devotes himself to business until he can return home as a rich man. By painting those who pollute the hero as cruel and unjustified, the myth casts his sacrifice and hard work as a kind of noble revenge. Nonetheless, on reflection, it is apparent that the insult was the necessary catalyst of the hero's reformation and maturation. In the story, then, the hero's highly emphasized act of sacrifice is prompted by a family punishment that is literally enacted, yet also secret and eventually disavowed. In a parallel way, the Hindu child is prompted into a stance of voluntary sacrifice by suggestive pressure (rather than by overt force), by appeals to the prestige and advantages of full group membership, and by threats to withhold this prestige and advantage, threats that are never literally carried out. While the written and cinematic versions of Santoshi Ma's story exaggerate both punishment and the circumstances of its eventual withdrawal for purposes of dramatic effect, the underlying principles of socialization are the same. Pressure is placed on the child, but it is never consistently, openly, or forcibly carried through. Thus the emphasis is allowed to remain on the noble act of sacrifice rather than on its carefully orchestrated antecedents.

Chapter 6

The Durga Complex

Having completed a description of the ek-hi phase of development, we can now move on to a discussion of the Hindu counterpart of our Western Oedipus complex, to what I call the *Durga complex*. As noted, the ek-hi phase corresponds roughly to the Western pre-oedipal phase, and the Durga complex corresponds to the early oedipal phase in the West. It must be stressed that any given part of the structure of goddess interrelations diagrammed above is susceptible to interpretation in terms of ek-hi issues, Durga issues, or both. We have seen, for example, that Durga in her opposition to Kali represents the natural mother in opposition to the in-law mother(s). Thus Durga, after whom the Durga complex is named, may carry the symbolism of the earlier ek-hi phase. I choose the name *Durga complex* for the later phase, however, because its conflicts are given their fullest and clearest expression in the total mythology of Durga. While vital components of the Durga myths are structured by the conflicts of the ek-hi phase, ek-hi issues alone cannot adequately account for all the central themes of Durga mythology. Let us turn, then, to a closer examination of the myth and ritual of Durga and goddesses like her.

Hindus realize that Durga and Parvati are ultimately the same being. Thus, Durga may be considered Shiva's wife (Babb 1975:222; Kinsley 1989:22–23; Nicholas 1982:196). Nonetheless, in her aspect as Durga, the Goddess is most often considered a virgin (Babb 1975:222). From this perspective, Durga's motherliness derives not from her having borne children but from the motherly protection she holds out to her devotees (Khare 1982:151,156–161). Her status as a virgin, or *kumārī*, implicitly identifies Durga as a daughter. This, in turn, is consistent with the myth of Durga's birth from the anger of the great male gods (Dimmitt and van Buitenen 1978:234). She is their daughter, so to speak. Moreover, even where Durga's status as a wife is acknowledged, this may serve only to stress her role as a sister-daughter. Thus, in her most famous ritual, the Durga *pūjā* of Bengal, Durga is treated as a married daughter who returns with her children to her natal family for a visit (Kinsley 1986:113; Nicholas 1982:197). Durga, then, is a sister-daughter mother. Whether she is treated as a married daughter who returns to her natal home with children, or whether she is treated as a virgin who mothers her devotees, the element of wifely sexuality is underplayed. Precisely because of its overt distance from sexuality, Durga mythology is able to embody the characteristically Hindu form of conflicts over unconscious incestuous strivings.

In the classic myth of Durga's creation, the male gods are in danger of defeat in their battle with the demon Mahisha and his hosts (Dimmitt and van Buitenen 1978:219–242; Kinsley 1986:95–115; O'Flaherty 1975:238–269). Out of their embodied anger and frustration, the gods create Durga, equipping her with their personal weapons. Fighting alone, Durga defeats a series of demons, culminating in Mahisha himself. These demons would rather sexually possess and/or marry this beautiful woman than fight with her. Yet, to their amazement, she overcomes and destroys them. Sometimes Durga kills these demons directly, riding on her lion and decapitating them with the weapons she has received from the gods. At other times, the demons are killed by a particularly fierce and bloodthirsty goddess or group of goddesses who embody Durga's anger. These purely destructive goddesses, including Kali, the most famous of their number, issue from Durga's brow or mouth at the height of her anger in battle. Durga, then, protects the gods by defeating in battle the demons that had threatened to overcome them. Myths of other sister-daughter goddesses often follow this pattern. A demon with aggressive and/or sexual designs on the goddess is destroyed by her in battle. Often the demon is decapitated by the goddess.

The worship of such goddesses frequently involves either an actual animal sacrifice, generally the decapitation of a goat, or a symbolic sacrifice, for example, the offering of a coconut or pumpkin as a symbolic head (Babb 1975:132–140; Erndl 1987:87–91; Pocock 1973:43–49,66). Moreover, worship of Durga and related goddesses often entails some form of self-mutilation by devotees, particularly male devotees. For example, a sharp rod may be used to puncture the cheeks, or a portion of the tongue may be cut off (Babb 1975:137–138; Erndl 1987:265,302). Thus, an identification is often set up between the demon decapitated by the goddess and the devotee himself. Indeed, as will be seen below, stories abound of heroic devotees whose faith prompts them to mutilate, decapitate, or kill themselves in worship of the goddess (Erndl 1987:265,302). Finally, those who mutilate themselves in worship of the goddess often do so in an ecstatic state of possession by the goddess herself (Babb 1975:132–141).

Psychoanalytic explanations of this mythological and ritual complex may be divided into two related types. First, there are explanations that stress the dyad of mother and son. Second, there are explanations that invoke the classic oedipal triangle.

An explanation of the first type is offered by Sudhir Kakar in his extended discussion of the Hindu image of the "bad mother" (1978:87–103). According to Kakar, the early indulgence of the male child by the Hindu mother does more than merely deprive the child of his ability to tolerate frustration. While the image of the fierce goddess does have its roots in the child's unreconstructed imagining of an all-bad, ungiving mother (the inevitable companion image of the child's wished-for perfect mother), this is not the end of the story. The other facet of the aggressively frustrating and destroying mother is the sexually demanding mother.

For Kakar, in other words, the intense physical contact between the mother and her male child excites him sexually at a time when his fragile ego is not equipped to cope. In order to escape the threatening sexual demands of a woman far more mature than himself, the young boy repudiates his maleness. He undergoes, in other words, an inner self-castration and substitutes an identification with the mother for the more dangerous affirmation of his maleness. In this way Kakar explains the persistent motif of self-castration found in Hindu goddess worship.

Morris Carstairs explains the motif of self-castration before the image of the goddess in a related although slightly different way (1967:156–160). Carstairs notes that the early years of maternal indulgence experienced by the Hindu child are reversed quite radically, particularly for the boy, when he leaves the women's quarters and joins the men. Now, without a period of transition, the early spoiling is replaced by extensive demands for mature and masculine behavior. This "catastrophic reversal" of the infant's all too happy early situation leaves the growing boy unconsciously even more attached to pleasure and intolerant of frustration than he had already been. Thus, in order to recapture the longed for happiness, a man comes to feel he must infantilize himself by way of a psychological self-castration. In family life, this is reflected in a man's extreme susceptibility to the influence of his mother in the joint family, even well after his marriage. In fantasy life, the pattern is represented by symbolic self-castration in the worship of mother goddesses. Although Carstairs lays less stress than Kakar upon the sexual threat represented by the mother's early attentions to her child, both Carstairs and Kakar explain the motif of self-castration before mother goddesses as an escape from the dangers and frustrations of maturity by way of a regressive return to an early period of excessive maternal indulgence and protection.

Both Carstairs and Kakar also make reference to the classic oedipal triangle in explaining the content of the mythology of Durga and related goddesses. Their explanations are quite similar, but there is some difference of emphasis. Essentially, both Carstairs and Kakar as well as several other psychoanalytically oriented investigators of Hindu culture claim that the Hindu male Oedipus complex is characteristically "negative" (Boss 1965:67–83; Carstairs 1967:160–169; Kakar 1978:134–135; Ramanujan 1983; Spratt 1977:67,105–130). That is, instead of a resolution whereby the son renounces his rivalry with the father and wish for the mother (through an identification with the father and an attempt to find a substitute for the mother outside the family), the Hindu finds himself identifying with the mother and submitting homosexually to the father. Although this "negative" oedipal stance is a "resolution" in that it permits the boy to avoid the dangerous rivalry with the father provoked by the desire for the mother, this outcome can hardly be viewed as a *successful* resolution of the Oedipus complex.

Carstairs sees the feasting on the sacrificial goat in Goddess worship as an identification of the devotee with the mother in an alliance with her against the father (1967:165–166). While the symbolic eating of the father's castrated penis (the sacrificial goat meat) is, on the one hand, an attempt to incorporate the virility of the father, the eating of the penis and the identificatory alliance with the mother disclose a homosexual trend. Thus, the sacrificial eating of the father embodies both oedipal rivalry and a defense against this rivalry as reflected in a passive or homosexual trend.

Carstairs sees the generally submissive stance of adult men to their fathers within the joint family as further evidence of a reaction-formation against oedipal hostility, resulting in a submissive and essentially feminine attitude toward the father (1967:159–163). According to Carstairs, any chance that the oedipal rivalry might be resolved through identification with the father, as in the West, is foreclosed by the tendency toward emotional distance between father and son fostered within the joint family (1967:159).

Kakar's discussion of oedipal issues is similar to that of Carstairs (Kakar 1978:126–139). Kakar, however, tends to emphasize the earlier role of indulgent mothering in preventing full ego differentiation as well as the importance of early feminine identifications defensively instituted against seduction by the mother in shaping the oedipal stance. From this point of view, Kakar sees the renunciation of rivalry and consequent feminine submission to the father less as a defensive regression from severe oedipal hostility than as the logical outcome of pre-oedipal psychological tendencies. Like Carstairs, Kakar comments on the father's lack of availability to the son as well as on the general absence of overt hostility between father and son. For Kakar, however, this indicates not so much a reaction-formation against oedipal hostility as a genuine lack of hostility toward a distant father who is instead approached in a mode developed through early feminine identifications and a tendency toward narcissistic merger.

Both Carstairs and Kakar emphasize the feminine, passive, or homosexual stance of the son toward the father in the "negative Oedipus complex." For both of them, this stance is behind the persistent imagery of self-castration in Hindu mythology. The tendency toward self-castration, already noted in the discussion of the mother-son dyad, is now reinforced and transferred to the three-person oedipal context. The son's self-castration becomes a way of renouncing the desire for the mother and the rivalry with the father this implies. Thus, in mythology symbolic castrations before both goddesses and gods are common.

As before, it is now necessary to review and critique these explanations, focusing particularly on elements of Hindu imagery and

FIGURE 11
Kannappa Story

child-rearing patterns that are overlooked or distorted by the traditional psychoanalytic approach. First, however, I want to address some more fundamental doubts the reader might hold. Many must object to the very idea of interpreting ritual mutilation or mythological decapitations as symbolic castrations. Those fundamentally opposed to this sort of interpretation cannot be swayed solely by examples, however clear. On the other hand, those who are suspicious but curious may wish to see evidence that constitutes a clear and specific example of the type of imagery I have been referring to.

I therefore summarize here a Hindu myth as depicted in a popular Hindu comic book, such as may easily be found in the bazaars of Indian cities and towns. Such comic books appear in a number of Indian languages, including English. This particular comic book presents the popular South Indian myth of Kannappa (Pai, D'Rosario, and Vitankar 1979).

Kannappa is the leader of a tribe of hunters. He is manly and well skilled in the forest. One day, however, he is ineluctably drawn to worship by the sight of a temple of Shiva. His sense of devotion soon grows so strong that he gives up his chieftainship to become permanently resident near Shiva's temple. In comparison with the Brahman priest who normally tends to the temple, he is uncouth and ignorant in matters of worship. Yet his devotion is strong. Shiva arranges to test the relative steadfastness of his two devotees, the priest and the rustic hunter. In the midst of the priest's worship, one of the eyes on the temple's phallic image of Shiva begins to bleed. The horrified priest, fearing this as an omen of disaster, runs away. Soon, however, Kannappa enters the temple. On seeing Shiva's bleeding eye, Kannappa is moved by the suffering of his deity. When curative pastes fail to stop the bleeding, Kannappa decides to gouge out one of his own eyes and give it to Shiva (see figure 11). This works for a short time, but soon the second eye on Shiva's ritual phallus begins to bleed. Quickly, Kannappa prepares to offer his last good eye to Shiva. Kannappa worries, however, that when he is blind, he will not be able to see the image of Shiva and thus will not be able to properly replace the bleeding eye of the Shiva phallus with his own good eye.

Hitting upon a solution, Kannappa places his foot on the bleeding eye of Shiva in order to mark the proper spot. (Normally, placing a foot on a divine image would be an insult to the deity and thus a serious ritual error.) Just as Kannappa places his foot on Shiva's bleeding eye and prepares to remove his remaining good eye, however, Shiva himself emerges from the stone phallus to praise Kannappa for his unparalleled devotion. Shiva then fully restores his devotee's sight and takes Kannappa to his heaven to live forever by his side.

The story, of course, is making a point about the importance of devotional attitude over ritual correctness. In this it recalls the story of the naive farmer and the rock. The symbolism through which the point is made, however, is striking. I have always found this to be a particularly thought-provoking example of the imagery of self-castration in Indian mythology. Here, in a comic book meant chiefly for urban Indian children, we have a graphic portrayal of a man gouging his eyes out in order to repair a bleeding pair of eyes on a ritual phallus. (The Shiva *liṅga*, which Kannappa is worshipping here, is quite consciously taken by Hindus to represent the phallus of Shiva.) The mode of presentation makes it particularly clear to a Westerner that Hindus deem acceptable, even salutary, themes we would find off-putting anywhere, particularly in an educational comic book for children.

Psychoanalysts may be forgiven if they grow impatient with those who refuse to credit interpretations of such motifs as symbolic self-castration. The attack on the eyes, a common phallic symbol going back to the Oedipus myth itself, could hardly be more explicitly linked with the phallus than it is here. On the other hand, we must grant the skeptic that something "feels" wrong. If the psychoanalytic interpretation is right, and we have here a mythological exhortation to psychological self-castration by the child, then there must be a serious disturbance indeed in the Hindu psyche. It is hard not to feel sympathy for those who refuse to condemn an entire culture to pathology simply because it does not share our sensibilities. There is, I think, a middle way. We need not abandon all interpretation in terms of unconscious sexual symbolism. On the other hand, the symbolism must be placed in its Hindu context. In these myths, we are faced not with a misfiring of the Western path of psychic development but with evidence of a culturally distinct maturation process. To trace this process, it is necessary to clearly mark out the aspects of Hindu symbolism and child-rearing practices that psychoanalytic interpretations have failed to recognize or account for. In the area of phallic symbolism, for example, the traditional psycho-analytic explanations fail to adequately account for the explicitness, multiplicity, and the restorative character of the imagery.

The story of Kannappa prompts us to consider the first difference between the Hindu imagery of the Durga complex and the oedipal imagery of the West: the seemingly explicit, gruesome (even pathological) tone of the Indian myths. In the matter of pre-oedipal imagery, we found that psychoanalysts did not always use the explicitness of the split mother images as evidence for severe psychosis in the Hindu personality. The full pathological implications of the analysis were often softened by the notion of myth as a cultural idiom for the expression of psychological tendencies. This explanatory device is unsatisfactory because it begs the question of the mythological imagery's origin. Moreover, this approach softens, but does not really eliminate, the finding of pathology based on the Hindu failure to show evidence of what we take to be universal developmental solutions.

In the matter of the motif of self-castration, however, psychoanalytic interpreters of Hindu culture have the courage of their convictions. That is to say, the prevalence of symbolic self-castration is set firmly within the context of a negative resolution of oedipal anxieties. The resulting male identification with the mother and feminine submission to the father and authority figures generally is frankly said to lead to widespread homosexual tendencies as well as to impotence, or to fears of impotence, among Hindu males.

Both Carstairs and Kakar take this position (Carstairs 1967:73–74,83–86,163,167–168; Kakar 1978:93–95,101–103,110–112,154–160; See also, Boss 1965:67–83; Spratt 1966:181–204). In the matter of homosexuality, each of them points to the worship of deities, of Krishna in particular, in which both men and women are said to take the female role. In Krishna's case, the worshiper is often said to adopt the attitude of one of the milkmaids, or *gopīs*, who seek Krishna as their lover. Kakar and others also point to the possession of the male by Durga in Goddess worship as evidence of a homosexual trend. In the matter of impotence, both Carstairs and Kakar point to the widespread notion of semen loss. Hindus see a physical or even psychological preoccupation with women as a drain on a man's precious reserves of semen. Ascetic practices, on the other hand, preserve, store, and concentrate a man's semen, thus giving him power. The prevalence of folk practitioners and medicines claiming to prevent semen loss and/or cure impotence are further cited as proof of the Hindu male's difficulties with sexuality. Finally, both Carstairs and Kakar note that affairs, particularly with young women and prostitutes, are relatively common and not strongly disapproved of. In general, such affairs are said to be less sexually threatening than the demands of a mature spouse.

It should be noted that neither Carstairs nor Kakar present much evidence that actual impotence or homosexuality is more frequent in India than in the West. Their evidence consists for the most part of sexual attitudes or anxieties reflected in cultural imagery. In defense of the psychoanalysts it can be said that actual impotence and homosexuality are not required in order to confirm their diagnosis of the Hindu psyche. The presence of a neurotic preoccupation with impotence, or thinly disguised homosexual fantasies, in and of themselves constitute important evidence of a negative Oedipus complex.

On the other hand, it is necessary to distinguish between the shape of a culture's anxieties and their severity. For example, the nature of the Hindu concern with anality revolves not around a need for independent control and thus privacy but around the identity of the cleaner.[1] From this point of view, it would be a mistake to see the Hindus' relative lack of concern for privacy in defecation as evidence of a lack of anal concerns. The point is that the shape and focus of the Hindu concern with anality are different from ours.

By the same token, the fact that the Hindu conceives of sex in terms of a loss of semen and that these notions are rather freely and publicly linked with fears of impotence does not show that the fear of impotence is greater among Hindu men than among Western men. Western men treat sexual difficulties in the same manner as they treat defecation—as something necessitating privacy. This concern for privacy is linked to our pervasive individualism and consequent concern for independence and control over our own affairs. Thus, the absence of common and public images through which explicit sexual fears are expressed does not establish a difference in the degree of these concerns between cultures. Relatively freely expressed Hindu concerns about semen loss and impotence as well as relatively free expression of body waste production contrast with the pervasive Western concern for privacy that follows from our taken-for-granted individualism. The real difference between East and West lies in the nature or quality not in the quantity of sexual anxiety. Individualism is built into our psychic structure but not into that of the Hindu. We therefore require psychological constructs that will enable us to explain the unique form of Hindu sexual fears in a way that avoids the distortions imposed by an individualist psychology. This is why I offer the notion of a Durga complex. From this point of view, it will be seen that the seemingly explicit, gruesome, and pathological content of Durga complex imagery must actually be read as an indication of qualitative differences in the basic construction of Hindu and Western psyches.

The second important difference between oedipal interpretations of Indian imagery and the actual content of Hindu mythology is the focus on multiplicity in the mythology. We are familiar with this problem from our discussion of the ek-hi phase. There we found that imagery of multiple goddesses had its psychological source in an opposition between the natural mother of the child and what I have called the in-law mothers. These are the mother's sisters-in-law and mother-in-law. In spite of the special relation between a mother and her own children in regard to feeding and physical contact, the rules of propriety in the joint family lay considerable stress on the need to moderate this connection and associate the child with the entire group of mothers. The crucial work of the ek-hi phase lies in the gradual realization by the child that his true mother is a collectivity. This realization consolidates an ego of the whole, the child's sense that he is whole and good in so far as he contains and is contained by the group.

The conflict and resolution of the Durga complex is also bound up with the opposition between the natural mother and the in-law mothers. Although this opposition is to a degree resolved in the ek-hi phase, the shift from oral sensuality, dominant during the early part of the ek-hi phase, to a later phallic sexuality reopens the conflict for the young boy. Once again, he desires a special link with his "real" mother. Now, however, the desire is experienced in the phallic mode. To overcome this new version of an old problem and resolve his Durga complex, the young boy will draw on the lessons learned in the course of earlier ek-hi phase resolutions.

The conflict between the natural mother and the in-law mothers, then, is fundamental throughout the phases of infantile sexuality. This opposition, in fact, lies at the root of themes of groupness and multiplicity throughout Hindu mythology although this fact has been insufficiently recognized by psychoanalytic or other scholars. For example, the action in the two great Hindu epics, the Ramayana and Mahabharata, is set in motion when parents favor their "own" children over the children whom the morality of the group grants title to rule. In the Ramayana, Kaikeyi, one of the wives of Rama's father, King Dasharatha, manipulates the king so that he might grant succession to her own son rather than to Rama, the proper heir to the throne. This initiates Rama's exile and the main action of the story. The dramatic conflicts of the Mahabharata are even more clearly structured around an opposition between natural parents and in-law parents. In this epic, a weak king makes the mistake of favoring his own children over his brother's children, the rightful heirs to the kingdom. This weakness sets up a series of tragic conflicts in all the characters between loyalty to their immediate relatives and loyalty to the larger royal family.

My point is that this tension must not be relegated to the category of kinship alone and thereby segregated from psychological concerns. The tensions that structure the Hindu family also structure the psyche of the child who grows up in that family. Only by integrating group issues with questions of psychology can we make sense of the imagery of infantile sexuality to which the myths hark back. Such an approach will show that Kakar is wrong to treat the Hindu emphasis on the group as a regressive displacement of the desire to narcissistically merge with the mother. The Hindu ego is positively constructed from the beginning as an ego of the whole. Once the child sees that all his mothers are one, he detaches from the natural mother, and his self becomes a group self.

The mythology of Krishna is a useful point of entry into the role of multiplicity in shaping the conflicts and resolutions of the Durga complex. In Kakar's interpretation, the mythology of the child Krishna reveals the Hindu woman's infantilization of the male (1978:152–153). The ideal male is seen as a mischievous son, not as a mature and lustful lover. This is the counterpart to the Hindu man's sexual ease with immature girls and prostitutes rather than with a mature wife. For Kakar, the tendency toward an infantilization of the male is not contradicted by the myths of Krishna's sexual sports with the milkmaids (*gopīs*), for in these myths Krishna is but an adolescent while the *gopīs* are full-grown women, the wives of other men. Thus, for Kakar, the sexual element of these myths only confirms the sexualized content of the relationship between mother and son among Hindus.

Kakar's analysis of the Krishna myths concentrates on Yashoda, Krishna's mother, and Radha, the lover of the adolescent Krishna. The other *gopīs* remain in the background. They have no unique role in the psychological processes outlined by Kakar. If pressed, Kakar would undoubtedly speak of the larger group of milkmaids as diffusing the impact of Krishna's relation to his mother. Kakar periodically employs this notion of diffusion, borrowed from Erikson (Boss 1965:72; Erikson 1969:42; Kakar 1978:128–133; 1982b). It is used chiefly, as it is by Erikson himself, to argue that the size of the Hindu joint family prevents a clear focusing and thus resolution of psychological conflicts familiar to us in the West.

I suggest a different approach. The particular role of the *gopīs* and the importance of the opposition between them and Yashoda and Radha must be recognized. The conflict between the *gopīs* and the Yashoda-Radha pair is the counterpart of the conflict between the three goddesses and Santoshi Ma in the film about Santoshi Ma. This conflict represents the struggle between the in-law mothers and the natural mother for the soul of the child. Yashoda and Radha each represent the natural mother, but in Radha's case, where the sexual element is explicit, the connection is obviously not conscious. The conflict between natural and in-law mothers is somewhat less controversial in Krishna mythology than in the film about Santoshi Ma, for here it is portrayed at the more human level of the *gopīs*. Moreover, the struggle between the two kinds of mothers in the Krishna myths is more a gentle, teasing, tugging of conflicting loves than an all-out war. Nonetheless, the conflict is real.

As the opposition between the mothers is played out over the period of Krishna's childhood and budding sexuality, both the mothers and the child move toward a resolution. This is what Kakar misses. The Krishna myths depict a mature movement through the ek-hi phase toward a resolution of the Durga complex. They are not an account of infantilization and regression. It is only possible to see this, however, when the *gopīs* are brought directly into the analysis.

John Hawley, in his extended treatment of the mythology and

poetry of the child Krishna, has spoken at length of what he calls the "battle" between Krishna's mother Yashoda and her fellow *gopīs* (1983:122–136). There are two movements to the battle. At first, Krishna roams through the *gopīs*' homes stealing butter. The *gopīs* then confront Krishna's mother with his thievery and complain that she supervises him poorly. Although she is initially willing to credit the complaints of the *gopīs*, Yashoda soon realizes that their supposedly angry visits are merely excuses to come and see Krishna. Thus she rationalizes Krishna's conduct and ignores their pleas.

Finally, however, pushed to the brink by Krishna's thievery, Yashoda binds her son to a weighty mortar so that he cannot leave home to steal from the *gopīs*. Now the arguments reverse. The *gopīs* come around again, but now they excuse Krishna's conduct and chastise Yashoda for her harshness. Subtly, they imply that they are better mothers to Krishna than Yashoda herself since they have not cruelly bound him and since he seems to prefer their butter (milk) to that of Yashoda.

What these "poems of complaint" are playing with is a battle beneath a battle. Superficially, the debate is about theft and proper punishment. In reality, both the *gopīs* and Yashoda are struggling for access to Krishna. The *gopīs* seem to come to complain. In reality they come to see Krishna. Yashoda seems to punish Krishna by binding him. In reality she wishes to keep him home for herself. It is easy to see that Kakar has picked up on this underlying motivation and identified it with an attempt to infantilize Krishna, to keep him tied down at home. For Krishna, however, true liberation is linked not to independence from either his mother or the rest of the *gopīs* but to finding a way to satisfy all of them as a group. This emerges most clearly in the myths of the adolescent Krishna's sexual sports with Radha and the *gopīs*.

The culminating moment of Krishna's sexual play with the *gopīs* is the great circle dance (*mahā rāslīlā*). John Hawley's study of popular theatrical enactments of this dance is relevant here because it highlights theological issues that must be incorporated into our analysis (1981:155–226). Hawley's study of the dramatic presentation of the dance shows how the transformation of one kind of love, *kām*, into another, *prem*, is a necessary prerequisite to the action of the dance. *Kām* is the lustful, selfish love of ordinary social life, whereas *prem* is a selfless, divine love that flows from bounty and is essentially giving. According to Hawley, the plays are not entirely successful in distinguishing these two forms of love since Krishna's relation to the *gopīs* does sometimes take on the psychological and physical character of ordinary sensuality. Nonetheless, the drama does record an important transformation. Before Krishna will dance with the *gopīs*, they must show a new sort of sensual motivation, one involving a selfless *prem*. As the dance occurs, moreover, the god of ordinary love-lust, Kamdev himself, is defeated and killed by Krishna.

The circle dance itself is presented as the solution to a problem, a problem we are by now familiar with. Krishna and Radha (his chief lover) wish to stand next to one another in the dance. Both realize, however, that this will spark the anger and jealousy of the other *gopīs*. Krishna overcomes the dilemma by using the power of divine illusion to create doubles of himself. Thus, when Krishna dances with the *gopīs*, all are in a circle, and each *gopī* stands beside Krishna himself. From the point of view of Radha, this solution works because she unselfishly supports it. Her support is possible, moreover, because she knows that all of the *gopīs* are ultimately emanations of her divine self. Thus, even when Krishna dances with the others, he is dancing with her. Radha, then, is able to show a generous *prem* for Krishna and to transcend the jealousy of *kām* when she loses her narrow self and recognizes her links with the group.

The great circle dance thus depicts a psychological solution to the emerging incestuous desire of the male child for his mother and to hers for him. Both the child and the mother must realize that the real mother is not, in fact, separate from the in-law mothers. The realization that "all the mothers are one" permits the mother to share the child, and also permits the child to let himself be shared among his various mothers. That is, as the child gives up his selfish but dangerously precocious sexual desire to have his mother all to himself, he gains the capacity to give of himself more safely and freely to all the mothers of the group, including his "own."

The psychic movement of the child toward the group, then, is not a mere multiplication, or even diffusion, of the original incestuous feelings. Once the child is associated with the whole, the power of the incestuous attraction is broken. Thus, there emerges a sublimated satisfaction of the initial, dangerously direct, and exclusive incestuous attraction. This lies in the child's pleasure as the shared plaything of the group. Recall here, for example, the teasing game and other forms of spontaneous group interaction with the child (see above, chapter 4). Recall, too, that according to observers, there is even more spontaneous, playful interaction between a child and the group than between a child and his "own" mother. Even this interaction, however, does not fit our notion of a loving and empathic intimacy. It is precisely the sublimated, relatively desexualized character of this "love" that permits the child to consolidate a "phallus of the whole." That is, his attention is successfully turned from incestuous strivings within the group through a psychic incorporation of and by the group, and he is thus readied for mature sexuality with a woman from outside it.

This notion of the phallus of the whole is compatible with John Hawley's discussion of the links between semen and butter in Krishna mythology (1983:288–307). In Hindu thought, semen is a concentrated form of milk, or butter. Krishna steals and eats the gopīs' butter and later dispenses it back to them in the form of semen. Hawley shows how this process of dispensing semen is a kind of reversal of the myth wherein the world's precious substances are created through the collective action of the gods and demons in churning (like butter) an ocean of milk. Whereas the world's nectar and wealth are created through a concentration by churning, Krishna dispenses precious butterlike liquids with abandon. Moreover, paralleling the myths of Krishna's butter theft are myths wherein Krishna impishly eats a bit of dirt. When his mother forces his mouth open, she is stunned to see the entire universe. Other myths speak of the universe contained in the drool running down Krishna's cheek. These universes within Krishna call to mind the notion of a vast, creative milk ocean inside whose products Krishna dispenses. If Krishna reverses the myth of the milk ocean by dispersing its products, then it must be because he holds that ocean within him.

In short, Krishna internalizes his mothers as a group, here represented by the butter of Yashoda and the gopīs. Having taken the group into himself, Krishna contains, so to speak, a whole world, or a creative ocean of concentrated liquid. Out of this universe within, this creative ocean of concentrated liquid, made productive only through the efforts of a group (the collective churning action of the gods and demons), Krishna is able to freely dispense semen. The consolidation of an ego of the whole in the ek-hi phase thus lays the groundwork for the construction of a phallus of the whole as the outcome of the Durga complex. In other words, the sense, dating from the ek-hi phase, that the group is complex yet fundamentally good (here represented by the necessary cooperation of the gods and demons in churning the ocean of milk) leads to an internalization of the group (here represented by the image, suggested by Hawley's analysis, of the gods and demons churning the milk ocean inside Krishna, or the universe contained in his mouth and drool). The group within, or the consolidated ego of the whole, then leads by way of the Durga complex to a phallus of the whole, the ability to turn an internalization of the group into successful sexual activity with a mature woman who can be brought into the group (here represented by Krishna's dispersal of semen, churned from the milk ocean within, to the *gopīs*).

The notion of a phallus of the whole also illuminates the paradoxically ascetic-erotic character of Shiva mythology (O'Flaherty 1973). Shiva's phallic prowess is tied to the detached character of his sexuality (O'Flaherty 1973:259–267). Indeed, Dimock holds that Shaivite sexual ritual works by way of an inner transformation of greedy desire, or *kām*, into unselfish love, or *prem* (cited in O'Flaherty 1973:261). All this makes sense in light of the link between the Hindu boy's postulated renunciation of selfish, immature phallic ties to the mother and the consequent development of a mature, transformed sexuality oriented toward, and ultimately beyond, the family's maternal group. Moreover, Shiva mythology illustrates the role of the group in this process.

O'Flaherty presents a series of myths in which Shiva erotically cavorts before the wives of the Pine Forest sages, without actually having intercourse with them (1973:178–184). By maintaining his detachment, yet breaking the inner loyalty of the sages' wives for their husbands, Shiva acquires the inner powers of the sages and their wives. In one account, the powers of his rivals are literally absorbed into Shiva's phallus.

In this same group of myths, Shiva's phallus is removed by the angry sages as punishment for his seductive behavior. Yet, when the pure nature of the seduction is revealed (i.e., the fact that Shiva was inwardly detached and not even outwardly engaged in intercourse), then Shiva is compensated for his castration by being granted the boon of eternal worship for his phallus. Shiva is in fact worshiped today in the form of a phallus—or *linga*.)

I think this group of myths depicts the process whereby the young Hindu boy, having moved his erotic attention away from his mother and toward the mothers of the family group, absorbs their collective power in the form of a new maturity, confidence, and, ultimately, potency. While this sensuous immersion in the group of mothers gratifies to a degree the desire to possess these women at the expense of their husbands (the Pine Forest sages), the stance is a psychic solution in that the sexuality involved is indirect. The transformed, sublimated nature of the sexuality in question is depicted by the transformation of Shiva's castrated phallus (following the sages' recognition of Shiva's sexual detachment) into the divine, venerated, cosmos-containing *linga*. Where Shiva's phallus at first absorbs his rivals' powers through erotic competition (but at the price of castration), his phallus eventually gains the powers of his former foes through a collective worship, which comes as a reward for detachment. Thus, the boy's reward for turning direct sexual interest in the mother into indirect, sublimated, sexual interest in the women of the entire group is acceptance and admiration from all the members of the group as well as mature sexual power, absorbed, so to speak, along with the support of the group.[2]

This set of Shiva myths shows how the involvement of the joint family's collective mothers blends with and transforms our familiar oedipal pattern—a pattern of rivalry between two men over a woman. For here such rivalry is overcome by way of a transformed, erotic immersion in the group. The question of male rivalry will be dealt with more fully below. Before concentrating on the role of the father(s), however, more attention must be devoted to the tension between the natural mother and the in-law mothers and to the sexual renunciation this tension prompts in the child.

A pattern of rivalry among mothers can be identified in the mythology of Durga and related goddesses. In Durga mythology, however, the subject matter of mothers and children is far less explicit than in the Krishna myths. Precisely because the reference to human mothers and children is left in protective obscurity, the mythology of Durga is more able than that of Krishna to deal explicitly with the difficult issues of phallic anxiety and danger. Kakar, for example, presents a myth of the Durga type to illustrate his view that Hindu men use psychological self-castration as a defense against maternal seduction:

> The demon Ruru with his army attacked the gods, who sought refuge with Devi. She laughed and an army of goddesses emerged from her mouth. They killed Ruru and his army, but then they were hungry and asked for food. Devi summoned Rudra Pasupati (Shiva by another name) and said, "You have the form of a goat and you smell like a goat. These ladies will eat your flesh or else they will eat everything, even me." Shiva said, "When I pierced the fleeing sacrifice of Daksa, which had taken the form of a goat, I obtained the smell of a goat. But let the goddesses eat that which pregnant women have defiled with their touch, and newborn children and women who cry all the time." Devi refused this disgusting food, and finally Shiva said, "I will give you something never tasted by anyone else: the two balls resembling fruits below my navel. Eat the testicles that hang there and be satisfied." Delighted by this gift, the goddess praised Shiva. (Kakar 1978:98; from O'Flaherty 1973:280)

In this myth, as in the original Durga myth, the male gods are protected from a demon by the goddess. Clearly Kakar has chosen to present this fairly obscure variant of the basic Durga myth because the act of self-castration is unusually explicit. This is how Kakar interprets the myth:

> Here, in spite of commendable efforts to dilute the elements of disgust and dread at the heart of the fantasy by adding such details as the multitude of goddesses, the goat, and so on, . . . [the] maternal threat and the defence of self-castration, are unmistakable although perceived and couched in the rapacious oral imagery of earliest infancy. (Kakar 1978:98)

I think Kakar has dismissed the "multitude of goddesses" too quickly as a mere dilution. This tack enables the psychoanalyst to filter out what is unfamiliar and turn a culturally distinctive whole into a mangled version of Western maturity.

In this myth, Shiva and the demon Ruru each represent aspects of the son. Shiva and the demon also represent the father(s), but this will be discussed below. The slaying of the demon by Devi and her army of goddesses depicts the castration of the child by the mother and the in-law mothers for his incestuous wishes. This is how the child initially interprets, in fantasy, the mother's rebuff as well as the interference by the in-law mothers with his exclusive relationship to his "own" mother. The fear of enforced castration, however, hints at a solution. If the child voluntarily renounces his sexual longings for the natural mother, he can consolidate his place in a loving collectivity.

This explains the role of the army of goddesses in the myth. Their defeat of the demon is, as noted, the perceived castration worked by the in-law mothers through their blocking of an exclusive relation between the immature child and his "own" mother. The threat of these goddesses to destroy Devi herself enacts the jealous battle between the real mother and in-law mothers over the attention of the child. Shiva, the mature child, realizes that he can save both himself and his mother from this jealousy if he will voluntarily renounce his incestuous strivings. Thus Shiva gives the gift of his testicles to the multitude of goddesses. This act and the praise Shiva receives for it depict both a renunciation of infantile sexuality and a sublimated fulfillment of it through the child's consolidation of a secure place within the group. Shiva's castration and the eating of his testicles by the goddess army are thus the parallel to Krishna's sharing of himself (but through *prem* rather than *kām*) with the multitude of *gopīs* in the circle dance. Before Shiva hits upon this solution, however, the goddesses refuse to eat his flesh (that of an impure goat), thus turning aside, once again, the child's incestuous wishes. In explicitly substituting testicles for something that has "the smell of a goat," the myth itself interprets the dual imagery of incestuous desire and castration behind the ritual goat sacrifice of Goddess worship and the identification of the devotee with that sacrifice. In other words, the decapitation and eating of the goat (demon-devotee) in Goddess worship are a complex symbol that embodies the act of incest, the punishment by castration of the incestuous child, the child's renunciation of incest through self-castration, and the sublimated transformation of incestuous sexuality through the sharing of the castrated flesh. The ritually sacrificed goat is both the demon killed by the goddess and the demon-devotee who sacrifices himself. This, then, is how the Durga complex is enacted and resolved.

By focusing on the castration and disregarding the distinction between Devi and the army of goddesses that both emanates from her and threatens her, Kakar is able to interpret the myth as a defensive self-castration in the face of an overbearing maternal presence. The myth, however, is more complex than this, and the distinction between Devi and the army of goddesses is the key to this complexity. Moreover, the myth does portray a solution, but the meaning of symbolic self-castration in Western psychology makes the solution effectively invisible from a traditional psychoanalytic perspective.

This leads us to a consideration of the third key difference between the actual imagery of the Durga complex and the interpretations of that imagery offered by psychoanalysis. Above, we saw that traditional psychoanalytic explanations fail to adequately account for the explicitness and multiplicity of Hindu phallic imagery. Now we turn to the healing or restorative character of this imagery, a quality largely slighted by previous psychoanalytic observers. The myths of the Durga complex do indeed portray development toward a psychological solution. Specifically, nearly every image of self-castration is followed by a restoration of the phallus. This pattern of castration and restoration, however, is either ignored or misinterpreted in traditional psychoanalytic interpretations. The following myth illustrates this pattern of self-castration followed by restoration. It is the myth of Jvala Mukhi, a goddess taking the form of a tongue of flame. The goddess is closely associated with Durga and Santoshi Ma:

> There once was a devotee of the Goddess named Dhyānū Bhagat who lived at the same time as the Mughal Emperor Akbar. Once he was leading a group of pilgrims to the temple of Jvala Mukhi where the Goddess appears in the form of a flame. As the group was passing through Delhi, Akbar summoned Dhyānū to the court, demanding to know who this goddess was and why he worshipped her. Dhyānū replied that she is the all-powerful Goddess who grants wishes to her devotees.
>
> In order to test Dhyānū, Akbar ordered the head of his horse to be cut off and told Dhyānū to have his goddess join the horse's head back to its body.
>
> Dhyānū went to Jvala Mukhi where he prayed day and night to the Goddess, but he got no answer. Finally, in desperation, he cut off his own head and offered it to the Goddess. At that point, the Goddess appeared before him in full splendor, seated on her lion.

She joined his head back to his body and also joined the horse's head back to its body. Then she offered him a boon. He asked that in the future, devotees not be required to go to such extreme lengths to prove their devotion. So, she granted him the boon that from then on, she would accept the offering of a coconut to be equal to that of a head. That is why people today offer coconuts to the Goddess.

(Erndl 1987:125)

In spite of the fact that the symbolic castrations in this myth are clearly healed by the goddess, psychoanalysts tend not to credit or recognize this pattern. When it is dealt with—and that is seldom—the pattern is dismissed as reflecting a peculiar cultural rather than psychological characteristic of Hindu myths: a refusal to let tragic outcomes stand (Kakar 1978:98).[3] Sometimes, moreover, the analysts imply that the son is permitted to keep his penis only on condition that he has shown the willingness to render it useless (Carstairs 1967:160; Kakar 1978:102). Indeed, the very fact of restoration is sometimes downplayed or denied (Goldman 78:363–364).[4] The act of restoration, therefore, is never taken seriously as such. Yet these restorations are pervasive and emphasized. We have encountered them twice before, in the introductory story of the farmer's rock and in the comic book account of Kannappa. In each case, the willingness to kill or mutilate the self results in epiphany and restoration.

My argument is that we need to take these restorations seriously. To my way of thinking, the mythological act of demon decapitation represents the punishment of the child's incestuous wishes by castration. In one way or another, however, these mythological castrations are transformed into self-castrations, which represent not a turn from maleness but a manly sacrifice of infantile incestuous wishes and the willing immersion of self-interest in group interest. The reward for this courageous and noble sacrifice is the reempowerment of the child-man at a more mature level by the group. The phallus is thus restored.

These themes reveal themselves in the myth of the goddess Vaishno Devi. This is the goddess, considered to be a form of Durga, whose cave shrine I was told to visit by the woman I met on the airplane (see above, chapter 1). Many of my informants performed Santoshi Ma's ritual before a picture of Vaishno Devi, considering the difference between the two goddesses to be meaningless. This is Vaishno Devi's central myth:

About 700 years ago, in Hansali village near Katra there lived a Brahman named Sridhar who was a great devotee of the Mother. One day he was performing a *kanyā pūjā* (worship of small girls as manifestations of the Goddess) in order to obtain a son. When Sridhar began to feed the girls, Vaishno Devi in the form of a divine maiden appeared among them. She ordered him to host a grand feast for his village and the surrounding area the following day. He knew that she must be some kind of *shakti* so he went from village to village inviting people to the feast. On the road he met a group of mendicants led by Gorakhnath and invited them as well. Gorakhnath issued a challenge that Sridhar would never be able to satisfy him, his disciple Bhaironath, and his 360 other disciples, as even Indra himself had been unable to satisfy them.

The next day when the guests began to arrive, Sridhar was worried that he would not be able to feed them all, but they all managed to fit into his tiny hut and the divine maiden began to serve everyone food. When she started to serve Bhaironath, he objected to the vegetarian fare, demanding to be served meat and wine. The maiden replied that this is a Brahman's house and that one should accept whatever is offered in a *vaiṣṇava* feast. Bhaironath became angry and tried to grab her, but she was able to read the evil desires in his mind and disappeared.

Bhairo [a common and short form of the name Bhaironath] set out in search of her, stopping at stations along the way (each of which is now a feature of the pilgrimage route). . . .

Bhairo continued to follow her even though she kept telling him to go back. Mahamaya (Great Illusion) was capable of doing whatever she wanted, but Bhairo's desire was also true! Finally, the Goddess entered a beautiful cave on Trikut mountain, posting Langur Vir (a form of Hanuman) at the door as a guard. Bhairo attacked and almost killed him. At that point, Shakti took on the form of a Candi (a fierce form of the goddess) and cut off his head. The head fell into the valley below, while the body remained at the entrance to the cave where it can be seen today as a large boulder. As his head was severed, Bhairo yelled out, "O Adi Shakti (Primeval Energy), O Generous Mother, I am not sorry to meet death, because it is at the hands of the Mother who created the world. O Matesvari (Mother-Lord), forgive me. I was not familiar with this form of yours. Ma, if you don't forgive me, then the coming age will view me as a sinner and castigate my name. A mother can never be a bad mother." Hearing these words again and again, the gracious Mother gave him the boon that after worshipping her, people would also worship him, and he would also attain $mok\d{s}a$ (liberation). If people worshipped at his shrine, their wishes would be fulfilled. A temple was built where Bhairo's head fell, and pilgrims stop there today on their way back from Vaishno Devi's temple.   (Erndl 1989:242–243)

As Kathleen Erndl points out, the myth sets up a contrast between two forms of goddess worship, the pure, vegetarian, devotionalism of Sridhar and the frightening, impure, nonvegetarian, sacrificial devotion of Bhairo (1987:113–114). This opposition is paralleled, according to Erndl, by the difference between the paths of *bhakti* and *tantra*. Erndl notes, however, that these are not irreconcilable sectarian differences. Each approach to the goddess is considered legitimate, and individual devotees can, and do, make use of both.

On the other hand, Erndl presents evidence of the great ambivalence many devotees show toward Bhairo's *tantric* approach to the goddess (1987:120–121,156,268). Some prefer not to visit the Bhairo shrine at all. Others go so far as to deny that Bhairo wanted to rape the goddess at all. This ambivalence makes sense when we see that Bhairo's attempt to rape the goddess represents the acknowledgment of the male child's incestuous wishes. Although Bhairo is transformed by his decapitation into a proper devotee, the relatively undisguised memory of his dangerous wish taints his worship for many. I will now consider this myth from the point of view of the Durga complex.

The opposition between the vegetarian worship of Sridhar and the sacrificial worship of Bhairo parallels the movement from the sacrifice of Dhyānū Bhagat's head in the myth of Jvala Mukhi to the substitution of this by a coconut. These transformations, in turn, are linked to the refusal of the army of goddesses to eat Shiva's goat flesh and their acceptance instead of the "two balls resembling fruits" below his navel (his testicles). Bhairo's and Dhyānū Bhagat's voluntary decapitations (Dhyānū Bhagat's decapitation is voluntary from the start, Bhairo's is voluntary by the end) and Shiva's agreement to offer his goat flesh as a meal, all represent incestuous wishes, punishment for those wishes, and the beginnings of a movement toward transformation through voluntary restraint. Sridhar's vegetarianism, Dhyānū Bhagat's coconuts, and Shiva's fruitlike testicles ultimately also carry the very same meanings. The myths, indeed, maintain this since, for example, the coconut is said to stand for the sacrifice of a head. Yet the movement toward vegetarian offerings illustrates the relative sublimation and transformation of incestuous wishes, and this is why they are accompanied by praise and/ or explicit restorations. This also explains why the transformed offerings are shared out among a group. The incestuous wishes are blocked by the representatives of the group; yet the same group permits a sublimated fulfillment of those wishes.

In the case of the story of Vaishno Devi, we have the same meanings already identified in the myth of Shiva's testicles. In this case, however, the meanings are more clearly teased out into separate strands, and their precise order is changed. In the myth of Shiva's testicles the movement is clearly from the defeat of the demon to the rejection of Shiva's goat-self and toward the solution represented by the group sharing Shiva's "vegetarian" testicles. In other words, the movement is away from childish incestuous wishes and toward their sublimation within a group setting. In the Vaishno Devi myth, the vegetarian solution is attempted but breaks down. The incestuous wishes it seeks to transform break through and must be dealt with anew.

Sridhar represents the mature solution to the incestuous attraction to the mother. He holds a feast in which only pure vegetarian food is offered. He is rewarded for this restraint of his impure appetites when the goddess helps him to accomplish the seemingly impossible. A vast throng of people are able to fit into his tiny hut, and enough food is made to feed them all. Thus, along with the proper restraint of incestuous wishes, the connection to the group emerges. The many guests in Sridhar's tiny hut represent a consolidated ego of the whole. His ability to dispense food to all from his hut is a culinary metaphor for a phallus of the whole.

The *tantric* guru Gorakhnath and Bhairo, his follower, will have none of this. They challenge Sridhar to prove that his way of restraint can satisfy their appetites and those of their followers. The miracle of the hut and the pure food only prompts Bhairo to reveal his unrestrained and impure appetites. His request for meat, followed by the attempted rape of the goddess, confirms that the feast of sacrificial goat meat in goddess worship (as well as the refused meal of Shiva's goat flesh in the testicle myth) are associated with a desire for illegitimate sex. All these examples are particular instances of the link between food and sex so prominent in Hindu mythology (O'Flaherty 1973:279–282).

Bhairo then pursues Vaishno Devi through what are now the landmarks of her pilgrimage, finally trapping her in the famous cave where her image stands today. Vaishno Devi's pilgrims trace this path themselves, as if they were Bhairo chasing the goddess. This is consistent with the identification we have already noted between the devotee and the victim of the goddess. Finally, Bhairo comes close to killing Hanuman (Langur Vir), the protector of the goddess. That is, the child's resurgent incestuous wishes threaten to do away with the effort at mature control represented by Sridhar and Hanuman. At this point, Vaishno Devi fully reveals herself and decapitates Bhairo. The incestuous wishes are met by a fantasied castration. At the moment of punishment, however, a remarkable transformation takes place.

As Bhairo is being decapitated, he realizes his error. He recognizes that what seemed like a young virgin was actually just a hitherto unrecognized aspect of the comprehensive great Mother Goddess. Understanding this, he accepts and even embraces his fate. That is, his enforced castration becomes a voluntary renunciation. Moreover, his request for forgiveness is accompanied by the claim that "a mother can never be a bad mother." This is not a denial of complexity. On the contrary, it embodies the central insight of the ek-hi phase that the mother who frustrates is not different from the mother who satisfies. Having successfully passed through this phase, the child uses its insight to accept the castration of the Durga complex and to transform it thereby into a key to the restoration of a mature phallic sexuality. This restoration is represented here by the erection of a shrine at the site where Bhairo's severed head falls, the attainment by Bhairo of *mokṣa* (liberation), and the power of Bhairo to grant the wishes of his devotees. The solution parallels that seen above when Shiva's castrated phallus gains worship as the *liṅga*. The parallel also makes the castration imagery at stake explicit.

Now we are in a position to better understand the contrast between the *bhaktic* and *tantric* modes of worship represented by Sridhar and Bhairo. The relation parallels the contrast between the story of Santoshi Ma presented in the printed pamphlet and her story as presented on film. The *tantric* approach emphasizes meat sacrifice, acts of physical mutilation, and controlled, symbolic sexual action (Gold 1987:174–176; Erndl 1987:87–91,120–121,156,268,302; Kinsley 1982:20,55,60–63; Padoux 1986:278–279). These forms of worship all directly raise the exciting but dangerous incestuous underpinning of Goddess worship even as they ultimately reject it. Approaching the Goddess through pure vegetarian devotionalism involves the same struggle. The offering of a coconut instead of a goat, for example, is still mythologically connected to the symbolism of the Durga complex. This purer approach, however, keeps incestuous desires fairly disguised and places the stress on the psychic solution.

In the discussion of the ek-hi phase, we saw that the film and written story about Santoshi Ma each play upon the same set of psychic conflicts, ek-hi conflicts. In the case of the film, however, the conflicts are closer to the surface. They are both more exciting and more dangerous. The ambivalent status of film in a Hindu context permits a clearer expression of the myth's underlying conflicts while still allowing devotees to downplay these conflicts in the setting of ordinary worship. This accounts for the success of the film. In a similar way, worship of the Goddess through blood sacrifice and various *tantric* practices remains an accepted, yet controversial, ritual form. As Hindus acknowledge, the paths of *tantra* and *bhakti* lead to the same insights. Depending on the nature and strength of a devotee's own psychic conflicts at a given point, however, a particular path will be more healing. It would be fascinating to analyze individual Hindus from the standpoint of their particular resolutions of ek-hi and Durga issues and then relate these resolutions to their shifting choices of modes of worship.

I have identified three important aspects of Durga imagery the psychoanalytic view of Hindu goddesses fails to adequately account for: its explicitness, its multiplicity, and its depiction of psychic resolution in the form of phallic restoration. Attention must now be shifted to key differences in the child-rearing situations in East and West that account for the distinctive character of Durga imagery. The first of these differences has already been discussed. Hindu mothering is multiple mothering. The importance of this is reflected in the split between the natural and in-law mothers and the resulting impact of this split on the imagery of the Goddess. The second key difference between Hindu and Western child rearing is the nature and timing of the male child's shift from female to male caretakers.

Both Carstairs and Kakar speak of a kind of second birth for the male child. This is the time when he is moved from the sleeping quarters of the women to the area of the men of the joint family. Now the child passes his day very differently than before. With little preparation, he is now subject to adult male standards of social restraint and decorum. Gone are the days of physical indulgence, playfulness, and gentle teasing. As noted, the psychoanalysts treat this shift as traumatic. Early overindulgence is now complicated by a precipitous withdrawal of gratification. What is worse, the distant nature of the father-son relationship prevents the new situation from creating a positive male identification capable of softening the blow of the loss of the mother. The results, according to the psychoanalysts, are oral fixation and deep oedipal hostility, which are defended against by a negative oedipal stance.

Kakar places the male child's exit from the world of women at the age of about four or five (1978:126). While there is good evidence to support this, there is also evidence that the move can take place even later. Luschinsky, for example, places the boy's transition to the men's quarters at ages six, seven, or eight (1962:258). Clearly, then, even from Kakar's perspective, most of the classic oedipal period of the West (ages three through five) is in India spent among women. Of course, even in the early years, the male child will have contacts with his father, uncles, and grandfather. As Carstairs points out, moreover, from a fairly early age there will have been occasions for the witnessing of parental intercourse (1967:66,158–159). As might be expected, however, Carstairs treats these contacts, particularly the witnessing of the primal scene, as further sources of trauma for a child deprived of a clear opportunity to identify with a benign and friendly father.

I take a different approach. In particular, from my point of view, the male child's incestuous strivings are played out, especially at the start, not in a triangle of father, mother, and son but in a triangle of in-law mothers, natural mother, and son. Because psychoanalysts have overlooked the way in which the work of the ek-hi phase, and of the Durga complex after it, breaks the male child's immature attachment to his mother, the movement out of the women's quarters has appeared to them more traumatic than it is. The lateness and rapidity of the boy's shift to the men's quarters does not set him up for shock and disappointment. On the contrary, the shift comes only after the power of incestuous strivings has been broken and an ego of the whole consolidated. The sense of nesting within the whole can then be transferred to the men. The distance of the natural father in this context, therefore, is the proper counterpart of the mother's own restraint before the representatives of the group. The ongoing construction of the child's ego is facilitated by his placement within a larger group of men. By focusing on the individual father instead of the group, the analysts see only a breakdown of our familiar path of development. In fact, we are faced with a movement along an alternative path.

I argue that the male child's reaction to the father and other male relatives may be understood as the transfer of a psychological mode already developed through interactions with the various mothers in the Durga complex. For example, the pattern of self-castration followed by phallic restoration is first worked out vis-à-vis the mother and in-law mothers and is later applied to the father. We see this in the story of Kannappa where a phallic sacrifice and restoration, paralleling that found in Goddess worship, are played out in front of Shiva.

This pattern is also preserved in the son's everyday respect behavior toward the father. The son "abases" himself by touching the father's feet. This is followed, however, by the father raising up the son. This latter gesture, a vital part of Hindu respect behavior, is far less often noted by Western observers than the initial act of submission. Here again we have a kind of symbolic self-castration. It must be understood, however, not as the submission of one individual to another but as the symbolic immersion of an individual in a group represented by a senior member. Only this insight makes such behavior (intolerable to a Westerner concerned with his dignity as an individual) possible. The raising up of the son by the father, then, affirms the initial insight into the importance of the group. The seeming act of abasement is not a loss of self-respect but a gaining of the power of the group. He who loses his false self by falling is raised up, empowered by the representative of the whole. As we saw with Dhyānū Bhagat and the goddess, the head that is cut off is restored and for the same reason—the individual is able to satisfy through a sacrifice of self to the group desires that brought pain and danger when sought alone.

It is clear, then, that the pattern behind these mythic and ritual castrations and restorations parallels the central insight of Hindu philosophy. The abandonment of a narrow ego frees one to see one's links with the larger collectivity of Being. In place of the pain and inevitable loss of individual existence, a deathless participation in something beyond any single soul is achieved. This philosophical stance is not rooted in a regressive slide into infantile narcissism. Rather, it is the furthest extension of the characteristically Hindu movement out of infantile selfishness and toward maturity. It represents the final stage in the consolidation of an ego of the whole. What was first played out among mothers and then among fathers is finally applied to existence itself.

The position taken here in no way excludes the notion that the Hindu child experiences a primary narcissism, i.e., an early state in which boundaries between the self and the world are unformed. No doubt, as Freud himself maintained, this early state contributes to the character of Hindu mysticism (Freud 1961b:11–15). Nonetheless, I argue that the Hindu experience of unity with Being is more complex than this. This fact has remained hidden until now because from the perspective of our Western individualism both primary narcissism and the Hindu child's mature sense of immersion in the family group seem alike in that each lacks our notion of clear individual boundaries. Thus, psychoanalysts have explained the Hindu sense of immersion in the group as a mere extension and displacement of an early, unresolved narcissistic union with the mother.

This position misses the way in which the subtle and unfinalized frustrations engineered by the Hindu mother during feeding (see above, chapter 4) prompt the child to separate from her and consolidate thereby a new and more mature sense of immersion in the group. In a similar fashion, our characteristically Western process of individuation depends on complex transformations of an early narcissism. For example, the achievement of a mature Western sense of a separate self depends on an introjective identification with loved objects. For it is only when there is a conviction that the qualities of a beloved parent have been taken in and taken on that the child feels able to function independently (Freud 1961b:74–76,

Segal 1964:11–23). Yet this very process of identification—the process that makes our Western individualism possible—is a mature transformation of the early absence of clear boundaries between mother and child. That is, the process by which a child comes to feel that he has become "just like" his parents draws on the early sense that there are no firm or fixed boundaries between the self and other objects. Thus, Freud saw relatively mature processes, such as identification and object-love, as late transformations of an early narcissism (Fenichel 1945:84; Freud 1961b:65,76–79, 1963:69; Laplanche and Pontalis 1973:206,256).

Similarly, then, the Hindu sense of being immersed in a continuous, unbounded group is a complex and mature transformation of an early, primary narcissism. It is not, therefore, evidence of a problematic failure to transcend that early state. Our Western individualism has simply prevented us from grasping the distinction between immature, primary narcissism and the distinctive vicissitudes of narcissism in a Hindu context. Thus, the Hindu philosopher's sense that a transcendence of self is the key to happiness and maturity can be seen as the fruit of a cultural self-analysis, so to speak, rather than as a seductive call to regression. Whereas in the West we draw on early narcissism to construct identifications that link a child to his family even while permitting the individual to function independently, Hindus draw upon early narcissism to nest persons in a kind of group ego even as this process detaches these persons from their natural mothers and fathers.

Let us return, then, to the problem of the father's role. There is another sense, briefly noted above, in which the basic patterns played out among the various mothers in the resolution of the Durga complex are later transferred to the boy's relations with men. The father's emotional distance from his son, so often treated as pathogenic by psychoanalytic observers, might now be seen, on the analogy of the mother's pause before the mother-in-law, as a necessary prerequisite to the young boy's ability to turn his attention to the larger group and so to consolidate his self within it.

May we say, then, that the Durga complex is the end of the story? Does the role of the father simply fit into the patterns established in the years before the transition away from child rearing by a group of women? I cannot give a definitive answer to this question. Although I am confident that this transfer effect is operative, it is also true that my own investigations have focused on the imagery of the Goddess. There are clusters of Hindu myths, particularly those concerned with Shiva and the great Hindu epics, that on examination may well yield a third stage or pattern. Such a pattern would feature relations between the son, father, mother, and the larger group and would retain enough of a distinct character to deserve treatment under a different name, perhaps a Shiva or Rama complex. The epic of Rama, in particular, is suggestive in this regard. It features a direct conflict between Rama and a demon who has kidnapped his wife. This ten-headed demon, moreover, calls to mind the role of a group of men in blocking access to a woman. Here, then, the rivalry between males in a group mode is the dominant strain in the myth.[5]

Leaving open a possible place in the system for a later, male-oriented complex, I attempt to show here that such a notion may be superfluous. For the idea of a Durga complex already prefigures and even incorporates and transforms elements of male rivalry familiar to us under the heading of the Oedipus complex. Consider, first, a myth that may well point to a period of development following on the early Durga complex—a period involving the exposure of the son to the world of men. The myth is the famous account of the birth of Ganesh (Courtright 1985:41–90; Dimmitt and van Buitenen 1978:179–185).

> Ganesh was created by Parvati from the dirt of her body to be her servant and guard. Having created him, Parvati stationed him outside her bath with orders to let no one in without her permission. Shiva soon arrived and sought entrance, which was barred by Ganesh. Shiva called Ganesh a fool for trying to bar him from his own home, but Ganesh had never met his own father and therefore did not know him. In the battle that followed, Ganesh defeated Shiva's servants, forcing Shiva to cut off Ganesh's head. While Shiva was sorry for this, Parvati was furious. She threatened to destroy the whole world, including the gods, in her anger. Shiva, therefore, had his servants cut off the head of the first creature they encountered, an elephant with one tusk. This head was fastened onto Ganesh and life put back into him. Shiva made him the doorkeeper of the world and lord over auspicious beginnings.

This myth has what appear to be classic oedipal overtones. The son guards his mother's bath and is beheaded by the father in punishment. What I find interesting is the notion, stressed in the myth, that Ganesh does not know Shiva. The idea that Ganesh was created by his mother alone and that he reacts in ignorance to his father's approach suggests the difficult adjustment of the male child, previously cared for by women, to a life among men, one of whom has a special claim on his mother.

In this myth there is also a castration and restoration. This pattern, in fact, is embodied in Ganesh's elephant head. With its single tusk and phallic trunk, it betokens at the same time phallic sacrifice and consequent reempowerment. While the head sacrifice is not overtly voluntary, Ganesh is often, although not always, considered a celibate deity. Ganesh's shifts between celibate and married states embody the paradox of the phallic trunk and missing tusk. Moreover, many versions of the myth of Ganesh's birth make his submission to Shiva more explicit (Courtright 1985:74–90). In some variants, for example, once Ganesh sees Shiva begin to strike with his axe, he calmly accepts mutilation, knowing that the divine axe of Shiva must never miss its mark. While direct rivalry between father and son is on the surface of this myth, then, it is also possible to recognize the distinctive Hindu themes that make the application of strictly oedipal analysis improper. Like his father Shiva, Ganesh is both ascetic and erotic; with his single tusk and long trunk he is at once castrated and hyper-phallic.[6] While the myths of Shiva and Ganesh may be rooted in a period of male-to-male interaction and competition following the son's departure from the world of women, the phallic self-sacrifice and restoration they embody follow the pattern established in the resolution of the early Durga complex.

It must be emphasized that the Durga complex itself, and Durga mythology in particular, does incorporate the father and his rivalry with the son. This, in fact, is one of the strongest arguments in favor of the decisive nature of the stage of development out of which the Durga myths grow. The relation to the father is first paradigmatically worked out in a Durga context.

I have already argued that the demons slain by Durga and associated goddesses represent the son. This is true at both the ek-hi and Durga levels. In the ek-hi phase, the demon represents the anger of the child at the withdrawal of the mother's ministrations, in particular her withdrawal in the presence of the in-law mothers. In the Durga complex this pattern is played out again but now in a phallic mode. The symbolism of the demon is complex, however. The demon is not only the son, he is also the father.

This emerges clearly in the Krishna myths that, as I have argued, are a transformation of the myths of Durga and related goddesses. In the dramatization of Krishna's circle dance discussed above, for example, the god of desire, Kamdev, takes on a role that parallels that of the demon in Durga mythology (Hawley 1981:155–226). He represents selfish lust—the kind of love the *gopīs* have for the husbands whom they have left to be with Krishna. In the dramatic performance of this myth recorded by Hawley, Kamdev is portrayed as a mature, fully mustached man while Krishna is still a young adolescent. Just prior to the dance, *prem's* triumph and the abandonment of *kām* are marked by Kamdev's defeat and death before Krishna. Thus, while Krishna's dance with the *gopīs* embodies the rejection of immature sexuality and the discovery of a new kind of sexual empowerment through a transcendence of jealous and selfish division within the group, it also represents a victory over the father in the battle for the mother's affections. A young boy defeats a mature man (Kamdev) and wins the *gopīs* away from their conventionally lustful (Kamdev-like) husbands.

I argue that the demon in Durga mythology plays a similar role to that of Kamdev in the drama of Krishna. Carstairs, in fact, makes a similar point. As noted, he sees the feasting on the meat of the sacrificial goat as an alliance between the mother and child against the defeated father (1967:165–166). The goddess's rejection of the demon's desire for marriage and sex leaves her alone, so to speak, with the devotee (son). This, however, is but one side of the matter. At a more mature level, it is not the demon but the gods under attack by the demon, the gods whom Durga protects, who represent the male adults of the family. In the myth of Durga, after the gods have created Durga for the sake of defeating the demon, they stand aside from the action. Yet the gods are present both in the background and in the fact that Durga's own weapons are the borrowed weapons of the gods (Dimmitt and van Buitenen 1978:234–235; Kinsley 1986:97; O'Flaherty 1975:247).

From this point of view, the rejection of the demon's sexual advances and his subsequent beheading represent the mother's pushing aside of the child (demon) in favor of the father(s) (gods). The gods who stand in the background of the Durga myth might be seen as both an early acknowledgment by the child of limited contacts between the father and mother and as a record of the relatively late awareness, after the movement to the men's quarters, of the men's role in relation to the mother.

In the drama of Krishna's circle dance, Kamdev and the gopīs' husbands are not merely replaced by Krishna. On the contrary, Krishna abandons the way of lust and founds a new type of generous love. In Durga mythology, too, the father as the symbolic demon is not merely finished off, leaving the devotee alone with his "mother." On the contrary, from a second and more mature perspective on the myth the son, this time replacing the father as the demon, is redeemed from lust by a transformative phallic sacrifice and restoration. Thus, the slaying of the demon embodies at once the triumph of the son over the father, the son's punishment, and the son's ultimate transfiguration by a turning of punishment into voluntary sacrifice. The son, then, abandons his rivalry with the father and exclusive attachment to the mother on the model of his earlier reconciliations with the in-law mothers.

As an expression of this resolution, the devotee's willingness to identify with the demon and mutilate his own body before the Goddess is rewarded by the divine power of Goddess possession these acts of mutilation are said to manifest. The point of the ceremonial mutilations, in other words, is not simply guilt, punishment, or castration. Rather, what is stressed is the devotee's ability to endure mutilation without pain or lasting physical damage through an ecstatic merger with the Goddess. Thus the sacrifice, if made voluntarily and in a spirit of devotion, yields both phallic restoration and a fusion with the Goddess.

The fusion of possession in the worship of the Goddess represents the ongoing consolidation of an ego of the whole. The devotee rests within the Goddess and she inside of him (Freed and Freed 1962:260–261). Undoubtedly, at a certain level, this merger gratifies the sensual desire for the natural mother. In its fullest expression, however, possession is something more. The Goddess herself, for example, is the creation of the gods and carries their weapons. Moreover, most devotees are possessed by more than one goddess or by both gods and goddesses (Erndl 1984:11–14, 1987:282; Freed and Freed 1962:261). Thus the phallic sacrifice yields a merger with the entire group—natural mother, in-law mothers, father, and other male relatives. The ecstasy of this fusion moves the child beyond the selfish desire for the natural mother, offering both a reduction of danger and a more sublime level of pleasure in return for a withdrawal of infantile desires and rivalries. It is this final movement of the mythic and ritual pattern that individual-oriented analyses like those of Carstairs and Kakar miss.

The issue of Goddess possession returns us to the question of homosexual impulses. Recall that both Carstairs and Kakar read the motif of self-castration as an indication of feminine identification. According to both psychoanalysts, this identification serves as a defensive stance at both the pre-oedipal and oedipal levels. Kakar and others have used the ritual possession of Hindu males by Durga and related goddesses as key evidence for this argument (Kakar 1978:102; Obeyesekere 1981:154–159; Spratt 1966:237). To my way of thinking, however, these psychoanalysts are making the mistake of attributing to possession behavior the inner meaning it would have in the West. The notion of the Durga complex casts such female identification in a different light.

The mutual encompassment of the male worshiper and Durga, his being taken up into her and her resting within him, enacts a psychological solution. The link is not so much an identification with the mother as a fusing into the group. In this case the group-as-Goddess is represented by Durga, a goddess who contains many other goddesses and who bears in her multiple arms the weapons of the gods. The female tone, so to speak, of the group-as-Goddess is consistent with the tone of the child's actual social context when he first makes the breakthrough into the group and away from an incestuous focus on his mother as an individual. His transformative sacrifice of both the infantile wish for the mother and his anger and rivalry with the in-law mothers and the father(s) is enacted by the symbolic castrations and restorations that accompany the act of possession.

From this perspective, the female identification present in Goddess possession does not reflect a negative oedipal stance with consequent homosexual implications. This is because the solution represented by containment in (and of) a group embodied in a woman is transferred by the male child onto the group of men he eventually enters. The way for this transfer is prepared in the early Durga complex when the boy child is chiefly among women, and it is carried out in the later Durga complex as the presence of men takes on importance for the child. This is why the fathers of the group are represented in the Durga myth both as fatherly weapon givers and as one aspect of the demon.

This same explanation applies to the male worshiper's frequent taking of the *gopīs'* role in his attitude toward Krishna. Both Carstairs and Kakar emphasize this ritual stance in their discussion of the Hindu male's feminine identification and subtle homosexual trend. The *gopīs'* ecstatic dance with Krishna is the counterpart of ecstatic possession by Durga. It represents not the son mimicking the female position in relation to the father but the child at the moment of his break from exclusive attachment to a single mother (Radha), celebrating his discovery of a mature pleasure in the merger with the group. Again, the fact that the merger with the group at this vital stage means a merger with women does not sexually cripple the male child. This is because the link with women, as a group, is not a defensive stance but a movement away from infantile desires. It therefore prepares the way for a later immersion in a group dominated by men.

Both Carstairs and Kakar point to the sexual threat represented by a Hindu man's wife as evidence for the retreat from a mature oedipal resolution. From the perspective of the Durga complex, however, this issue can be seen in a new light. For the male child, the direction of psychological resolution takes him away from an exclusive attachment to one woman. This is the rationale not only behind the mother's careful distance from the child among the in-law mothers but also for her refusal to "spoil" the child by accompanying her physical ministrations with overmuch attention, praise, or mirroring (Maduro 1976:166–167; Minturn and Hitchcock 1966:119–121; Mencher 1963:62; Poffenberger 1981:83; see also above, chapters 3 and 4). This same pattern is then transferred onto relations between the adult husband and wife, who are more sexual than romantic partners. Bennett's discussion of the potential danger of family partition posed by the in-marrying wife shows how the structure of the kinship system elaborates and reinforces the early lesson that too much emphasis on a relationship to one woman is dangerous (Bennett 1983).

It is true, however, that a Hindu husband can successfully relate to a single wife. Yet he does so, above all, by seeing in her an embodiment of the group. Through her, after all, he fulfills his duty to the group—strengthening it with the addition of children and forming an alliance with other families through his marriage. The perception of the wife as an extension or embodiment of the group, set up in the unconscious mind by the successful resolution of the Durga complex, is what makes understandable the Hindu willingness to accept a marriage arranged by the senior members of the group, even one involving little or no contact between husband and wife prior to the wedding. The principle and practice of arranged marriage, so puzzling to Westerners, is extended by the many rules of restraint barring direct contact between a young husband and wife in the presence of senior family members (Mandelbaum 1970:74–79). These rules repeat the effect, at a much later stage of life, of the rules limiting contact between a mother and her "own" child. They are not so harsh a restraint as they appear from a Western perspective, however, because for a traditional Hindu, mature satisfaction is centered on life within a group, not—as in the West—on an intimate relationship with another individual.

Although the wife, from the mature perspective, then, is the representative of the group, this very fact must be emphasized by an ongoing system of restraint. From this point of view, a movement toward greater emotional intimacy with and exclusive interest in the wife represents not a developmental advance for which the man is unprepared but a regressive pull maturity obliges him to resist. It is an error, then, to judge the emotional growth of Hindus by the standards of the peculiarly Western pattern of romantic love. Our notion of love is the logical outcome of the pattern of one-to-one intimacy between parent and child that motivates our transcendence of infantile pleasures. So too, the Hindu relationship between husband and wife enacts among adults the pattern of renunciation of individual connection in favor of a merger with the group, which moves the Hindu child through the stages of infantile sexuality. If Hindu men speak of the seductive dangers of wives and if brief affairs and visits to prostitutes are not treated as romantic betrayals, this is neither surprising nor evidence for a failure to achieve a proper oedipal outcome. The true nature and extent of marital fidelity in India is as yet relatively unstudied. It would be a mistake, however, for future students to distort their efforts by using Western romantic love and its psychological underpinnings as their standard.

The notion of the Durga complex also permits a new understanding of the Hindu man's concern with semen loss. The idea that an excessive preoccupation with sex results in semen loss has long been linked by psychoanalytically oriented observers to the threat evoked by the wife as stand-in for the mother of childhood (Carstairs 1967:159; Kakar 1978:94–95). As noted, the traditional psychoanalytic view is that the failure to detach from the mother provokes a defensive regression into infantile dependence and/or feminine identification. Thus adult sex with a mature woman is seen as threatening. In fact, however, the successful resolution of the Durga complex requires of a man a mature transcendence of excessive emotional entanglement with a single partner. Since the sacrifice of such entanglement yields both a fusion with the group and a sense that one contains the group, failure to sacrifice an exclusive bond would reverse the process. That is, an excessive entanglement with one woman would make it impossible for a man to hold the group inside him. It would cause the group to leak out, so to speak. This accounts, for example, for the notion that sex with an older woman drains the body of semen and makes its replenishment impossible (Daniel 1984:169). Connection to an older woman calls to mind the exclusive, selfish, and dangerous (*kām*-like) connection to the mother, which precedes the generous *prem*-based connection to the group— a link that makes multiplication and bounty possible. Examples of such multiplication and bounty are Krishna's creation of multiple selves during the circle dance and Sridhar's feast for the masses in his tiny hut. Indeed, the popular notion that one drop of semen is a precious distillation of many drops of blood (Boss 1965:76; Carstairs 1967:83–84) conveys a sense that the potency of an individual flows from and expresses the power of a larger group.

In my discussion of the Durga complex I have already noted that the consolidation of an ego of the whole is paralleled by the construction of a phallus of the whole. This is symbolized by Krishna, whose ability to satisfy Yashoda and Radha as well as the *gopīs* as a whole gathers their collective butter inside of him and turns it into dispensable semen. The pattern here is also conveyed in the metaphor, suggested by Hawley's analysis, that Krishna contains a universe within, or a giant ocean of milk that is churned in order to produce semen. For a man to preserve this ocean within, he must paradoxically, like Krishna, share himself out to the larger group.

Thus, when Hindu men caution that excessive preoccupation with sex or with a wife results in a damaging loss of semen, they convey the idea that an ego and phallus of the whole depend for their construction on a relative freedom from attachment to any one individual. This would be true in an actual case of impotence, where an early failure to detach from the mother and move toward the group would likely be at work. Thoughts of semen loss could also be a healthy concern, however, for those who are not impotent. The interest in semen loss is an internal parallel, so to speak, to the rules limiting contact between a young married couple in the joint family. As noted, these rules are not neurotic defenses but bulwarks of healthy egos of the whole. They trace the Hindu path to maturity—a loosening of individual bonds for the sake of fusion with a group.

There is another reason why the Hindu notion of semen loss strikes the Western observer as regressive. The imagery seems extreme—a remnant, perhaps, of primary process thinking. I have already argued that Western individualism yields a concern for sexual privacy that partly explains the absence of such publicly explicit discourse over sexual issues in this culture. There is more at work than this, however. The imagery of semen loss raises a problem that is the counterpart of the one seen in the comic book story of Kannappa—the explicit nature of Hindu images of castration. What is the source of this explicitness?

Edmund Leach long ago challenged psychoanalytic interpretations of South Asian symbolism with the observation that phallic symbolism in this part of the world is explicit rather than unconscious. Obeyesekere has countered Leach by arguing that although the symbolism is explicit, its psychological meaning remains unconscious (Leach 1967:91–93; Obeyesekere 1981:18–21). Obeyesekere accounts for the explicitness by calling it the product of a cultural idiom of expression. I think this begs the question of the origin of such an idiom. Moreover, as noted, psychoanalytic explanations of Hindu images of semen loss and castration are able to handle the problem of explicitness by frankly seeing in them a reflection of pathology. If this is mistaken, however, and we are not confronted by pathology, another explanation is required.

The answer, I think, lies in the analysis of the Durga complex. From this point of view, the symbolism of castration at the most mature level is not a denial of sexuality but a transformative sacrifice that signals the abandonment of infantile attachments. This, in turn, suggests that in the Hindu case a distinctive defensive pattern is at work. We might call it renunciation and contrast it with the more characteristically Western defense of repression.

I agree with Obeyesekere that even some of the most explicit and seemingly obvious symbolic connections are in fact unconscious for the vast majority of informants (Obeyesekere 1981:18–21). For example, even though Kannappa takes out his eyes to repair the bleeding eye of a ritual phallus, the eye sacrifice may not be regarded as a symbolic castration by Hindus themselves. It must be added that the deepest meaning of the symbolic castration, the child's renunciation of his sexual desire for the natural mother, also remains unconscious. Nonetheless, the form the defense against the infantile background takes is different in India than in the West. The symbolism, rather than being driven entirely underground, is openly acknowledged. The acknowledgment's purpose, however, is to permit the explicit renunciation of infantile pleasure.

The origin of the difference between the defenses of repression and renunciation must be in the characteristic modes of child rearing discussed in chapters 3 and 4. That is, in the West the child is simply forbidden certain pleasures. The breast is withheld, defecation at will is interfered with, the mother's physical presence is withheld, and masturbation and nakedness are discouraged. The child, deprived by force of such pleasures, must then with maturity begin to repress even his craving for them, his very memory of them. In return, he clings to the sublimated pleasures his beloved parents hold out to him in recompense for their insistence on maturity.

In Hindu India, on the other hand, the pleasures of infantile sexuality are not overtly withheld. Rather, the relative emotional distance of the parents, their focusing of interest and emotion on the group itself, prompts the child to spontaneously turn infantile pleasure aside for the sake of inclusion in the group. In this instance, the child may more easily retain a memory of the pleasures abandoned as they were always made freely available. What is decisive, however, is the act of sacrifice, and this is what the mythic and ritual recollections of childhood pleasures consistently prompt the devotee to reenact. That the matter does involve unconscious conflict is affirmed by the controversial nature of the most explicit symbolic acts. Animal sacrifice and the polluting consumption of the sacrificial meat, the *tantric* mutilation of body parts, or ritual intercourse in which the seed is withheld, all bring back the infantile underpinnings of Hindu symbolism so clearly that, in spite of the renunciations they embody, a breakthrough of infantile pleasure always threatens. That is why these ritual actions are often disguised or performed in secret under a cloud of disapproval (Bharati 1975:279–299; Erndl 1987:87–91,120–121,156,268; Kinsley 1982:20,55,60–63; Pocock 1973:49). Thus, beneath the explicit symbolism the dialectic of desire and defense is evident. In this case, however, psychic conflict takes on a culturally distinctive shape in the form of the defense of renunciation.

A final point must be made in connection with the Durga complex. It concerns the reasons for Goddess worship in India. Why is it that in the Judeo-Christian West Goddess worship is not present? Even the worship of Mary in the Catholic tradition, while important, is not at the center of theological concern. Why, on the other hand, is Goddess worship so important a part of Hinduism? The notion of the Durga complex suggests a possible answer. The Hindu child's sojourn in the world of women lasts longer than it does in the West. Moreover, due to the general separation of the male and female worlds in India, males are relatively unavailable during the early years even as subsidiary caretakers. For these reasons, all of the most crucial stages of infantile sexuality are played out in a predominantly female environment. I have argued that this leads neither to faulty male gender identification nor to pathology of a broader sort. On the other hand, this situation does make the Hindu emphasis on the Goddess comprehensible. In worshipping the Goddess, Hindus recapitulate and reinforce their successful developmental journey through the world of women.

Having completed the discussion of the Durga complex, some reflections on the significance of the argument presented here are in order. Superficially, I have strayed from Santoshi Ma. In fact, however, it is impossible to discuss the Goddess without discussing Santoshi Ma and vice-versa. The identities of Santoshi Ma and goddesses such as Durga and Vaishno Devi are merged by informants. Therefore, what is said of one necessarily applies to the others.

Moreover, properly understood, Santoshi Ma is not really an individual goddess who merges with others but a momentary glimpse of a Goddess whose unity is prior and fundamental. This unity is borne out by the structural link between my analysis of Santoshi Ma's myths and the myths of other goddesses. Although the symbolic meanings of these myths are not always identical, some stressing ek-hi issues and others Durga complex issues, the two levels interpenetrate. Each developmental stage, moreover, follows a related pattern, involving the unification of natural mother and in-law mothers. A full understanding of the importance of this split and its ultimate overcoming is the final fruit of the lesson I learned in my initial groping after Santoshi Ma's identity. Once I took seriously the idea that all the goddesses are one and put this insight at the center of the analysis rather than in the background, the way was opened for a transformation of the traditional individualist-psychoanalytic understanding of the Hindu Goddess.

The system of interpretation outlined here is in an important sense provisional. Clearly, a great deal of future research on Hindu child rearing remains to be done. This is so because the limited number of studies now available are structured by traditional, individualist psychological theory. While another way of looking at the data culled by these studies has been offered here, primary research from a nonindividualist theoretical perspective is urgently needed.

The reader will also have noted that my discussion of the Durga complex, unlike my treatment of the ek-hi phase, is centered on the male rather than the female developmental struggle. After the ek-hi phase the male and female paths diverge markedly since for the boy the natural mother comes to be the object of phallic desire. Even in the ek-hi phase, however, differences between male and female development no doubt exist. The female experience of Hindu development, an experience that culminates in the consolidation of feminine gender identity, thus remains to be explicated. The most important reason for this hiatus in the model is that current psychoanalytic discussions of Hindu development are also limited to the male perspective when dealing with the later psychosexual stages. Since my work is a kind of reworking of these classic approaches, material on the female developmental path has been less available and therefore less susceptible to rethinking. However, I am able to redress this imbalance to a degree below. In the chapter on Indian clinical psychoanalysis, I consider two case studies of Hindu women (see also note 5, chapter 8).

There is another area into which the theoretical approach taken above needs to be extended. In my treatment of the ek-hi phase I have concentrated on ego (i.e., ego of the whole) issues. Unlike my treatment of the Durga complex, where the problem of phallic sexuality came to the fore, my discussion of conflicts on the pre-Durga level has not focused on infantile sexuality. Yet issues of oral and anal sexuality are closely bound up with the conflicts of the ek-hi phase, and these areas deserve concentrated attention. In particular, I think that a reworked notion of Hindu orality and anality will shed considerable light on Hindu concepts of purity and pollution and on the system of hierarchy associated with these concepts.

Having acknowledged the provisional nature of the approach to Hindu culture presented here, I must make the case for its fundamental legitimacy. I have offered a systematic and nearly comprehensive reinterpretation of the analyses of Hindu culture made by Carstairs, Kakar, and several other psychoanalytically oriented observers. My work is based on the literature on Indian child rearing, the Hindu system of myth and ritual (and current anthropological interpretations of that system) as well as on my own field research on the myth and cult of Santoshi Ma and other Hindu goddesses. In this respect, since their data are of the same order, my argument rests on no less substantial a foundation than do those of Carstairs and Kakar. In fact, as I have attempted to show, the approach offered above gives considerable weight to aspects of Hindu child rearing and mythology underplayed or ignored by psychoanalytic observers. Whatever the need for future research or theoretical revision, then, the approach outlined here calls for careful consideration. If nothing else, it shows that a new sort of psychoanalytic interpretation of other cultures is at least possible. It is possible, in other words, to preserve the fundamentals of depth psychology, notions such as psychic conflict, the unconscious, and infantile sexuality, while still breaking in a fundamental way with the Western individualist assumptions embedded in contemporary psychoanalytic anthropology.

Chapter 7

Clinical Psychoanalysis in India: Toward a New Reading

What can our reshaped psychology of Hindu culture tell us about clinical psychoanalytic work in India? This question may seem to put the cart before the horse. After all, Freud moved from clinical case histories to an understanding of culture and not from cultural phenomena toward patient treatment. On this model, many analysts continue to prefer that psychoanalyses of culture begin from a basis in clinical casework. Behind this preference lies the view that myth and ritual, being divorced from the life histories and free associations of individual patients, permit only a secondary sort of access to the unconscious. In this perspective, studies of child-rearing practices are of merely tertiary importance because they appear to tell us more about behavior than about the inner representation of behavior.

From my perspective, however, neither case histories nor more obviously cultural materials ought to be privileged as modes of psychoanalytic inquiry.[1] Certainly, psychoanalysis was created as a way of understanding the distress of individual psychiatric patients, and psychoanalytic technique and insight are particularly suited to this context. To this day, however, the focus of analysis on individual patients has deflected our attention from the cultural assumptions built into psychoanalytic theory as well as from the shared cultural characteristics of psychoanalytic patients. I am not arguing that the hidden cultural aspects of psychoanalysis must necessarily be purged from the theory. However, I do think the cultural dimension of psychoanalysis ought to be recognized so that it can be more clearly thought out and especially so that it may be modified when applied to non-Western contexts.

Case histories, as opposed to more obviously cultural symbols and behaviors, have their own characteristic advantages and disadvantages as pathways to psychoanalytic insight. The study of individual patients is particularly suited to revealing pathology. That is, case histories provide excellent access to the conflicts that underlie the seeming unity of everyday life and thought. If, as I have argued, myth and ritual actually point toward culturally characteristic paths of psychic resolution, then for that very reason distressed patients can highlight unconscious conflict more easily than can collective representations. Conversely, however, clinical reports are often less suited to help us understand how unconscious conflict is characteristically structured and resolved in a given culture than are collective cultural "texts."

In the matter of child-rearing practices, it is true that outward observation does not grant transparent access to inner meaning and representation. However, by juxtaposing child-rearing practices with myth and ritual, a picture of the inner meaning of development can be built up.

Nor must myth and ritual be subordinated to clinical material as a route to the unconscious. At the close of the last chapter I argued that the explicit symbolism of Hindu myth and ritual is not simply a cover for deeper symbolic meanings. I did point out an unconscious level behind the symbolism, but I also argued that the relative explicitness of Hindu collective representations is tied to a culturally characteristic defensive structure based on renunciation rather than on repression. This process of renunciation permits symbolic gratification to lie relatively close to the surface so that it can be overtly sacrificed. Thus, the character of the defensive process underlying

Hindu myth and ritual can be said to provide clearer access to the unconscious than the more roundabout, repression-based symbolism characteristic of Western collective representations. This tends to mitigate the absence of free associations and patient histories. It can even be argued that the explicitness of myth and ritual elevate them above much traditional clinical material as routes of access to the unconscious.

Moreover, a comprehensive and contextual study of myth and child-rearing practices offers us a counterpart to clinical associations and patient histories. The same sort of patterns and correspondences that build conviction on the clinical level operate at the cultural level when diverse myths, rituals, and socialization practices are juxtaposed. In effect, the many permutations of underlying patterns found in diverse myths, rituals, and child-rearing practices act as functional equivalents of individual associations and personal developmental histories. They confirm, deny, modify, and enrich initial and isolated symbolic interpretations.

Also, a genuinely contextual study begins to approach myth and ritual in much the same way as a clinician would. For example, we saw above that my informants' personal ambivalence about the dispute scenes in the film about Santoshi Ma were central clues to lines of conflict expressed within the myth and ritual of the goddess.

The issue of preferences for a given type of psychoanalytic data, however, comes fully into focus only when we consider the problem of constructing or shaping a psychoanalysis appropriate to a non-Western culture. As long as the problem is filling in gaps or making minor modifications in an established theoretical paradigm, the argument over the advantages and disadvantages of different types of data can play itself out on traditional grounds. However, the real question is: How do we construct a culturally sensitive theory of psychoanalysis? At this point, the special relevance of child-rearing observations and data from myth and ritual becomes more clear.

To this it might be objected that Freud himself constructed a broad theory primarily out of clinical material. Why cannot the same thing be done for another culture? In principle, I think it is possible to generate an Indian psychoanalysis from clinical material. It is not, however, the only way, or necessarily the best way, to culturally reshape the theory. To understand this, we must first realize that Freud's own theory is built on an unacknowledged cultural foundation, and this gap in awareness is tied to the theory's origins in clinical practice.

In the chapters above, I have discussed aspects of psychoanalytic theory that have unrecognized cultural roots. An individualist focus on the one-to-one love relationship is built into the gratification/frustration model of child rearing and is closely connected with the notion of repression. This dimension of the theory is taken to be natural rather than cultural, and as such it has not been marked for theoretical discussion or even been clearly recognized as a cluster of related ideas.

Were an imaginary "Indian Freud" to have developed an analogous, clinically based theory, that theory would also have a parallel and unacknowledged cultural dimension. This imaginary Hindu Indian psychoanalysis might have included a detailed discussion of renunciation and of the tension between the natural mother and the in-law mothers without realizing the cultural basis of these phenomena. From the point of view of such a theory, Western behavior would appear in a distorted perspective. Perhaps Western parents would be chided for their overt punishments and their precipitous, forced withdrawals of pleasure from the child—actions that make sense only in light of child rearing based on the love-repression dynamic. Indeed, Hindus today actually do misunderstand and condemn Western parenting because of the "no's" and punishments central to its functioning (Nichter and Nichter 1987:71,72–73).

As long as we remain in the clinical setting and in the society that has given birth to the theory of treatment, the problem of cultural bias can be held at bay. In practical terms, if a healer and patient are part of the same social world, the treatment is unaffected by the fact that implicit cultural elements of the theory are taken to be natural. As soon as we try to bridge two cultures with the same theory, however, the implicit cultural issues are forced to the surface. Or rather, these issues ought to be allowed to surface. For the alternative is, and has been, an inappropriate and distorting imposition of cultural assumptions.

For this reason, then, the traditional preference of psychoanalysis for clinical material cannot govern our effort to reshape psychoanalytic theory. Precisely because the theory is being stretched to accommodate conditions in widely diverse cultures, data and phenomena whose importance have heretofore been underplayed even in a Western context must of necessity take a leading role in our work. A cultural reshaping of psychoanalytic theory requires explicit attention to the conduct and principles underlying socialization in a given culture and draws our attention to collective representation as an essential window onto the subjective underpinnings of this socialization behavior.

Even the special advantage of clinical material—the insight it gives us into conflict and pathology—is available to us only from the perspective of a broader, socially based theory of normal development. This connection is also brought to the surface by the attempt to stretch psychoanalytic theory across diverse cultures. In the West, the cultural norms that inform psychoanalytic notions of health can remain generally implicit. This is why psychoanalysis has long been able to focus on pathology—its theory of normality was already present, primarily in the form of unspoken cultural assumptions. As soon as the theory is brought to another culture, however, its implicit Western norms pose a problem for our evaluation of clinical material.

Thus, before interpreting clinical data from India, I have attended to collective symbolism and behavior. This attention has made it possible to formulate a developmental norm according to which individual Indian pathology can be understood. In fact, all pathology is ultimately social rather than individual. A particular person's conflicts are a misfiring or breakdown along a culturally distinctive path of psychological development. The nature of psychological conflict itself, in other words, is actually constituted by the patterns and principles of development in a given culture. If we do not specify these developmental principles for Hindu India, then Hindu Indian patients will be judged, or misjudged, according to Western processes and norms. Thus, in bringing the implicit problem of norms to the surface, the application of psychoanalytic theory to diverse cultures prompts us to devote special attention to extraclinical, explicitly cultural material.

However, I do not want to exaggerate the importance of either child-rearing observations or collective cultural texts. It is true that these materials offer us special advantages if our goal is to make explicit the cultural characteristics of developmental psychology. And this is the goal an extension of psychoanalysis to other cultures ought to highlight. On the other hand, it must not be forgotten that the clinical setting does give us access to culture and must be expected to do so. Since I argue that culture is not distinct from the psyche but rather pervades it, the treatment of Hindu Indian patients would have to reflect and exemplify the very processes we have examined by way of socialization and myth.

Recall that I granted, in principle, the possible existence of an "Indian Freud." This hypothetical Indian thinker, drawing on his implicit cultural knowledge, could create a clinically based theory— a theory that could reconstruct from the mental life of Indian sufferers the patterns and principles of Hindu child development. It is not that a connection between distinctively Hindu developmental processes and clinical material cannot be made. Rather, the problem is that the unspoken cultural assumptions in psychoanalytic theory are Western, and unless they are made explicit, we will remain unable to recognize the various indications of a singularly Hindu psychology that are now only hinted at in Indian clinical work. Likewise, as noted, an exclusively clinical theory created in India would risk taking Hindu cultural assumptions as natural givens and would thereby distort our view of non-Indian cultures. Thus, the cross-cultural problem serves to highlight, not to deny, the implicit cultural dimension of clinical work. Therefore, overtly cultural data, like myth and ritual, while particularly useful for my purposes, do not replace or exclude the value of clinical material for the construction of a cultural psychoanalysis. Ultimately, the clinical situation is a cultural situation.

It must also be said that attention to more overtly cultural material brings no guarantee of theoretical reformation. After all, there has already been psychoanalytic field observation of family life in India, and no understanding of the process of renunciation or of the complex interactions between the natural mother and the in-law mothers has emerged from this. Ultimately, priority in the generation of a theory goes to the social and cultural roots of knowledge and not to the source of our data. If some new process is recognized in familiar material—whether that material is clinical or ethnographic—then this is because social conditions have changed in such a way as to encourage us to recognize (or construct) such a pattern. The contemporary crisis of Western individualism probably has more to do with opening a new understanding of the role of the group in the Indian psyche than does any special access to the psyche provided by either anthropological observation or clinical psychoanalysis. In any case, there are certainly no valid grounds for insisting that a psychoanalytic theory of Hindu culture grant unique priority to clinical data.

Before moving to a direct examination of Indian psychoanalytic case histories, I need to confront a second general issue raised by a concern with the clinical setting. The reader will have noticed that in the course of discussing the status of clinical data, I have employed the term *pathology*. This interest in pathology may seem out of place given my earlier critique of conventional psychoanalytic interpretation. After all, I have argued that a central problem with psychoanalytic views of India has been their tendency to overlook distinctly Hindu modes of psychic resolution. These Hindu paths to maturity have been distorted through the lens of Western psychological categories into lurid versions of familiar Western pathologies.

However, my point will have been misunderstood if it is taken to mean that pathology is absent from the Hindu Indian scene. On the contrary, the fact that there is a distinctly Hindu path of psychic resolution necessarily means that there are distinctly Hindu forms of failure to transit that path. While the notion of cultural difference does permit a critique of unduly pathologizing universal schemes, the culture concept inevitably also generates a multiplicity of more appropriately conceptualized pathologies.

The word *norm* is closely linked to the idea of culture. To have a culture is to have a cultural norm, and the existence of a norm necessarily entails an abnormal. Of course, there may be a lack of shared cultural assumptions in a given society, putting various norms in competition with one another. Even here, however, we confront not the absence of normality but multiple models thereof.

In the contemporary postmodern West a principled antagonism to norms of all sorts is growing—an attitude that in itself constitutes a kind of norm. From the postmodern perspective, any notion of pathology is problematic. This position has the advantage of tolerance, but it also serves to undercut positive as well as negative valuations. It therefore tends toward relativism and paralysis. Whatever the advantages and disadvantages of this contemporary perspective, however, it is quite alien to the Hindu Indian context, where a relatively powerful and deep consensus on fundamental values persists.

Of course it can be argued that profound cultural differences are present on the Hindu Indian scene. Diversities of caste, class, gender, and urban versus rural settings may be thought to crosscut and complicate any simple notion of a broad Hindu normality/pathology dichotomy. There is something to be said for this view, particularly with regard to highly Westernized sectors of the urban elite. On the other hand, the lesson of our encounter with Santoshi Ma was the persisting depth and breadth of Hindu cultural notions of the self. Whereas contemporary theorists were quick to identify Santoshi Ma as an indication of increased diversity in the social-structural and cultural content of Hinduism, Santoshi Ma seems instead to affirm the power that deep-rooted Hindu principles of identity and relationship continue to hold across a wide spectrum of social situations (Kurtz 1990:103–295).

For this reason I continue to speak of pathology when addressing cases of those who have made only halting progress in their transit of the path toward Hindu maturity outlined in the preceding chapters. If the word continues to grate, this indicates the distance between our postmodern situation and the relative consensus on underlying values to be found throughout most of Hindu society.

In keeping with this, it ought to be noted that Hindus themselves have distinct ideas about mental pathology—notions that flow from cultural and psychological norms. Deborah Bhattacharyya, for example, has given us a detailed study of the Bengali notion of *pagalami* and contrasts *pagalami* with its counterpart or cousin, the Western idea of madness (Bhattacharyya 1986). June McDaniel, in turn, has drawn our attention to the paradoxical relationship between what she calls secular or ordinary madness and what is understood in Bengal as the divine madness of ecstatic saints (McDaniel 1989).

Without undertaking a detailed analysis, I note here that the psychoanalytic approach outlined above may well shed light on the problems raised by Bhattacharyya and McDaniel. For example, ordinary Bengali madness is said to be rooted in desire, greed, frustration, and disappointment. Such madness is characterized by an instability of mental state. Divine madness, on the other hand, transcends these angry, grasping impulses, achieving thereby a stable, continuous vision of the multiformed Goddess (McDaniel 1989:146,250,286).

The distinction between ordinary and divine madness is said by Bengalis to parallel the transition from *kām* to *prem* (from selfish love to spiritual, generous love) and as such can be linked to the child's movement—outlined in the preceding chapters—from the natural mother to the larger group of mothers (McDaniel 1989:286). From this perspective, if the greedy desire for the natural mother is never abandoned, the sufferer is torn between regression toward merger and the impossibility of sustaining this dangerous state. Unstable, so-called secular madness is the result. On the other hand, if the immature tie to the mother is broken, a divine madness of merger can be experienced on the stable and mature level of connection with the collective mothers, i.e., the multiformed Goddess.

The divinely mad ascetics studied by McDaniel tend to have suffered an important parental loss or series of losses in childhood. And this connection between ascetic madness and childhood loss is also made by Hindus themselves (McDaniel 1989:9,12,34,62–63,70,75,250). I think these ascetics are forced to work harder than the typical Hindu to achieve what is essentially a heightened form of the classic Hindu developmental solution. The early losses suffered by these ecstatics could have driven them backward into "real" madness, but instead these holy men were able to surmount the regressive pull of unfulfilled infantile desire by way of an intense and explicit focus on the classic Hindu developmental solution. To overcome the loss of loved ones, there is a renunciatory movement toward merger with the group, i.e., the broader circle of family or, when the family is unavailable, toward the religious community and the collectivity of deities who represent the mature family group. Despite, or rather, because of the fact that this movement by ascetics toward the group solution is experienced at the cost of great personal conflict, it is recognized, paradoxically, as paradigmatic of psychological growth. Overcoming the regressive pull of early parental loss, the ascetic shows Hindus the way to escape the lesser but still painful losses and frustrations experienced by everyone in early childhood. The solution, exemplified by the ecstatic's merger with the collective gods, is voluntary renunciation of infantile connection in favor of a merger with the group.[2]

By making explicit the conception of pathology necessarily implicit in our reshaped developmental framework, it is possible to acknowledge and to interpret indigenous notions of the normal and pathological, for example, the Hindu distinction between ordinary madness and divine madness.

The by now familiar interplay between the natural mother and the in-law mothers is at the core of my proposed reading of psychoanalytic case histories from India. My suggestion is that many psychoanalytic patients in India are caught, in one way or another, at the transition point between the natural mother and the in-law mothers. Either their mothers failed to execute the push toward the group, or the members of the group neglected to pull the child away from the mother and toward themselves. Often, some combination of these factors may be at work.

I am not a clinician. What I offer here is a reading of published psychoanalytic case histories from India—a reading that highlights indications of the natural mother/in-law mother dynamic. I can do no more than point in the direction of this issue, for the analyses in question were conducted with the classic triangular focus on the nuclear family as their theoretical background. While suggestive evidence for the phenomena that interest me can be uncovered in the case reports, that evidence remains limited and unsystematic since it was not explored by the reporting clinicians.

If the natural mother/in-law mother dynamic has the fundamental significance for Hindu development I have attributed to it, one might reasonably ask whether clinical work in India that is based on traditional psychoanalytic principles could have any validity or therapeutic effect at all. A reading of various case histories has persuaded me, however, that much insight and healing has come from the practice of traditional Indian psychoanalysis. Certainly, I intend to argue that attention to the dynamic between the natural mother and the in-law mothers would prompt advantageous modifications in theory and technique. Nonetheless, I am convinced that Indian psychoanalysis works up to a point. This in itself constitutes a theoretical problem.

I think Indian psychoanalysis works because the central predicament of many of its patients is a fairly close cousin of the familiar psychoanalytic dilemma. More often than not, the patient's tie to the mother has not been broken. Unfortunately, however, clinicians have too often traced the excessive closeness of Indian psychoanalytic patients to their mothers to the close physical contact characteristic of Hindu child rearing, prompting the conclusion that Hindu Indian mothers in general are dangerously close to their children.

I have already shown that the physical closeness favored by Hindu mothers is actually part of a complex and culturally distinctive process for distancing the child from its primary connection. This process depends on a degree of emotional detachment on the part of the mother, whose restraint in combination with a complex intervention by the in-law mothers (and later, the fathers) prompts the child to voluntarily move toward the center of mature group life.

What Indian psychoanalysts seem to encounter are cases where this process has misfired. The separation from the mother has not occurred, and the analysis is able to make progress by bringing this fact to consciousness and working it through to the point where a degree of movement toward maturity is possible. The difficulty is that the involvement of the in-law mothers in all this is unrecognized.

Often, the role of the in-law mothers is overlooked because the very problem with the patient is that a larger group of women was *not* present in order to help draw the child away from the mother. Thus, the in-law mothers seem not to appear in the patient's associations. In other cases, the role of the family's several women is simply assimilated by the analyst to that of the mother, and signs of the patient's interest in these women are therefore interpreted as further evidence of the unresolved attachment to the mother. In fact, however, the patient's feelings about these in-law mothers may be indications of an incipient movement toward maturity. In other cases, hostility from the in-law mothers may short-circuit the process of detachment from the mother even where the natural mother is not disposed to cling to the child.

All this implies that psychoanalysis with Hindu Indian patients could benefit from attention to the natural mother/in-law mother dynamic. At present, there is too much focus on the seductive emotional presence of the mother. This is a real enough factor in the lives of many patients and is of course recognized to be pathogenic by the analysts. Nonetheless, the current theory allows too little awareness of the difference between the pathogenically close mothers of patients and the culturally distinctive pattern of distancing that characterizes normal Indian mothering. As a result, genetic reconstruction and working through overlooks the role played by the absence or failures of in-law mothers as well as the incipient signs of health that can be found in the patient's interest in nonmaternal female (and later in nonpaternal male) caretakers.

One final consideration is in order before turning to the case histories. It is legitimate to note that the individualism built into psychoanalysis inheres not only in the theory but also in the fundamental principles of analytic technique. Kakar himself has written at some length on the difficulty of adapting the psychoanalytic setting with its requirement of psychological-mindedness and its emphasis on autonomy to India, where healing tends to focus on family groups, healers exercise authority more than they promote autonomy, and the emphasis is on instruction rather than on dialogue or introspection (Kakar 1985). No doubt these problems account for the peripheral status and limited reach of psychoanalytic practice in India.

Perhaps the presence of psychoanalytic practitioners in India is possible only because of the increasing Westernization of the urban elite, from which the vast majority of psychoanalytic patients are drawn (Kakar 1985:446; Roland 1988:55–71). Here, if anywhere in India, a degree of departure from traditional nonindividualist notions of the self can be found. On the other hand, it is striking how pervasive the traditional emphasis on groups often is even in the most Westernized setting. Thus, I offer my model of the Hindu psyche as an ideal type drawn from the characteristic setting of the joint family in traditional, rural India. While this ideal type may no longer be entirely applicable to all patients who would visit an Indian psychoanalyst, I argue that focusing on multiple caretakers is far more productive of insight even in the urban and modern setting than has heretofore been recognized.

Having set the scene with a discussion of both the significance of case history for theory and the problem of normality and pathology and having sketched the outlines of a possible alternative approach to Indian psychoanalytic practice, I proceed to a closer examination of five clinical case histories. The first three of these cases are Kakar's published accounts of psychoanalyses with male Indian patients (Kakar 1979, 1980, 1989, 1990a, 1990b:129–140). These reports provide a good opportunity to explore the clinical implications of my critique of Kakar's overall approach. The last two case histories, one reported by B. K. Ramanujam and one by Alan Roland, describe the treatment of female patients (Ramanujam 1986:78–82; Roland 1988:154–174). An examination of these cases will enable us to show that the dichotomy between the natural mother and the in-law mothers affects women as well as men, and it will provide at least a bit of balance to the focus on men necessitated by my earlier rethinking of work by Carstairs and Kakar. Following consideration of these five case histories, I close the chapter with some reflections on the work of Girindrasekhar Bose, the first Indian psychoanalyst and founder of the Indian Psychoanalytic Society (Bose 1949; Kakar 1990a; Sinha 1966).

Case One: Mr. D.

The story of D. was published by Kakar in 1979 under the title "A Case of Depression." This article followed by a year the appearance of *The Inner World*, Kakar's programmatic treatment of Hindu Indian culture and personality. The case of D. clearly is an ideal-typical clinical exemplification of the cultural psychology presented in *The Inner World*. This is Kakar's longest and most detailed case report. The material is presented with admirable clarity. We are moved by D.'s suffering and heartened by the very significant and hard-won improvement that is clearly the result of his analytic work with Kakar.

D. entered analysis severely depressed, having broken off an arranged marriage because of doubt of his sexual potency. A diligent and successful student and engineer, the collapse of the engagement had made him apathetic about work, putting his job in danger. D. complained of a harsh and authoritarian father who had broken the blissful early closeness between D. and his mother when D. was about four or five. At that time, the father had argued frequently with D.'s mother and beat both mother and child. A kindly servant who had offered some compensatory affection during this painful period soon drew the child D. into a homosexual relationship. Much later, in adolescence, a move to live without his parents in an uncle's family again brought misfortune, as the older cousins forced D. into passive homosexual relations and publicly branded him as a passive homosexual at school.

Success at his studies provided D. with a route to some stability and satisfaction. It drew him away from his unhappy rural and small town homes and into an urban university setting. D.'s progress at the university, however, was marred by a breakdown just before one of his crucial final examinations. This breakdown passed, and D. moved on to a good job as an engineer. However, D.'s subsequent veto of an arranged marriage because of doubts about his sexual potency precipitated a more serious depressive apathy that endangered his career. Moreover, in the aftermath of the engagement's collapse, D. actually had incestuous intercourse with his younger sister, an act for which he felt quite guilty. All this brought him into analysis with Kakar.

Through analysis, D. began to uncover the ambivalence toward his mother hidden beneath his memories of an early paradise. In retrospect he could recall the way his mother had mocked his movement toward adulthood by making unflattering comparisons between him and his father. In effect, D.'s mother had infantilized him so as to keep him tied to her in her battles with the father. Increasingly, D. could recall that the early cries of his mother behind closed doors were the result of sexual pleasure rather than of beating. D. also recalled that many punishments at the hands of his father were actually instigated by his mother.

These memories freed up a lost current of affection and admiration for the father. Underneath D.'s conscious oedipal hostility, there was hidden a passive homosexual trend. D.'s early identification with his mother had prompted a passive sexual yearning for the father, a child's way of seeking out a tie that might actually draw him away from the mother's embrace and encourage a mature masculine identification. However, the father's lack of availability and the servant's selfish sexual abuse had left D. unconsciously frozen in this emotional state. In light of this, it was discovered that the first breakdown at college had been prompted by hidden homosexual yearning for a new roommate, who had arrived just before the exams.

As a result of the analysis, D. was eventually able to marry and enjoy a satisfying sexual relationship with his wife. Periodic retrogression under stress provided the occasion for more analytic working through, and D. emerged with a strengthened marriage and very significant career advancement.

The story of D. really does provide a textbook case illustrating Kakar's general theory of the Hindu Indian psyche. We have an overly close mother who seductively engulfs her son as a counter against the father. The tight bond to the mother is challenged by the father only when the son is around four or five years old. The trauma of this late intervention by the father leaves searing memories, flavored by oedipal bitterness. Underneath this, moreover, we find the defensive identification with the mother and passive homosexual longing for the father—a longing that is never securely overcome because the father remains emotionally unavailable. The result is an inner self-hatred, a sense of being castrated (experienced as an insecurity about sexual potency), and a consequent instability of the marital tie.

In *The Inner World*, Kakar seems to have D. in mind when he refers to patients whose vivid, painful memories of the second birth are central to character formation (Kakar 1978:132–133). The *second birth*, as we recall, is Kakar's expression for the time when the boy leaves the intimate and indulgent embrace of the mother and is pushed, with little preparation, into the demanding world of men (Kakar 1978:126–133). At the conclusion of chapter 4, I suggested that patients for whom the second birth is traumatic may be significant more as departures from the Hindu Indian norm than as slightly exaggerated examples of a typical Indian developmental path. In other words, I argued that patients traumatized by the second birth would be those who had not been properly ushered through the precrackdown phase of early childhood—those whose attachment to the natural mother had not been broken by the intervention of the in-law mothers prior to the advent of adult male demands. I think that D. represents just such a case.

Consider Kakar's reconstruction of D.'s earliest years:

A Brahmin by caste, D. hails from a village in Bihar. His fifty year old father is a police inspector in charge of the village *thana*. Both his grand-fathers were poor farmers. D. is the eldest son and spent the first three years of his life with his mother at the home of his maternal grand-father. His memories of this period are hazy but wrapped in the golden glow of a "lost paradise." He remembers being made much of by his mother and his grandparents since he was the only child in this household. His father, who was at that time a police constable in a different village, visited the family only occasionally.

When he was three years old, D. and his mother moved to the father's house. His memories of this period, from three to five years, as they gradually emerge in analysis, are quite sharp. D. was very unhappy at having to share his mother with his stranger father.

(Kakar 1979:62)

This account makes it evident that D. could not have been exposed to the detaching pull of the in-law mothers in the typical Hindu Indian fashion. First of all, when his father was away, D. and his mother lived with *her* parents rather than at the paternal home. This is unusual. In the paternal home, the normal main residence of a Hindu Indian bride (even when her husband is away), all the rules of restraint on own parents are at work. On the other hand, in the mother's home, generally encountered only on short visits, these restraints are not in place. Since D.'s mother would not have had to restrain herself with the child before in-laws during the crucial first three years, the grandparents' fussing over the child would have reinforced rather than countered and replaced the attentions of the mother, and this all the more so since D. was at that time an only child.

The unusual nature of D.'s early childhood would only have been compounded by the move to his father's home after age three. There, because of the absence of normal distancing imposed by the in-law mothers over the first three years, the father's intervention really would have been experienced as traumatic.[3] Moreover, during his early adolescence, D. was forced to leave both parents and live in the home of his uncle and cousins. That his older cousins took advantage of him sexually at this point may have been made more possible precisely because D. was shy, withdrawn, and unused to life in a joint family setting. Also, D. would have lacked the presence of his own parents, who, in the typical model, would have insured that D. suffered no disadvantage in treatment at the hands of his cousins, aunts, or uncles.

Thus, while D. clearly did experience a traumatic loss of an early maternal indulgence, the conditions of that trauma were highly atypical. Living as an only child in the maternal rather than paternal household for the first three years meant that the push away from the natural mother and the pull toward the in-law mothers could not work. On the contrary, the attention of *maternal* grandparents would reinforce, rather than defuse, the tie to the mother. The later shift to the world of the father therefore lacked the traditional preparation and was complicated still further when in early adolescence an unprepared D. lived with in-laws without the protective and reassuring presence of his natural parents. D. never really had a chance to experience the complex and necessary tensions between natural and in-law parents. He lived either with his mother without paternal in-laws (in early childhood) or with in-laws without his mother and father (in early adolescence). Therefore, D.'s problems are not, as Kakar treats them, a slight exaggeration of the typical Hindu Indian pattern. Rather, D.'s difficulties stem from the fact that in his case the typical mechanisms of Hindu socialization were never put in place.

The case of D. not only presents the clearest clinical illustration of the thesis of *The Inner World*, but it also provides the central clinical vignette for a later article by Kakar on the relationship between Hindu fathers and sons (Kakar 1982b). In that article, Kakar recapitulates his notion of a traumatic second birth. This time, however, he places a bit more emphasis on the presence of in-law parents and on the existence of restraints on relations between a child and its own parents.

Kakar's focus is more on the mother's brothers-in-law and father-in-law than on what I have called the in-law mothers. Thus there is no sense of the early and beneficial effects of multiple mothering on the child. Indeed, the whole phenomenon of multiple parenting seems to be identified by Kakar with the traumatic second birth around the fifth year, whereas the involvement of the in-law mothers actually begins long before this.

Kakar's real concern is with the restraint shown by the father in his attentions to the child in the presence of the paternal grandfather and uncles in the joint family. This is said to result not in a breaking and resolution of rivalry, but in the diffusion of oedipal hostility over the larger group of men. More seriously, the Hindu boy's desperate need for an identification with a father capable of countering the overwhelming presence of the mother is said to be frustrated by the restraint imposed on the father by the group.

From this perspective, Hindu customs of restraint on "own" parents are intrinsically pathogenic rather than adaptive along a distinctive Indian developmental path. Because Kakar's theory is focused on individual identification rather than on an ego of the whole, the periodic withdrawal of the father can only seem to confuse and frustrate the child. Indeed, Kakar's individualism results in a concern about paternal inconsistency that exactly parallels Carstairs' strictures against the care by the Hindu mother, who withdraws from the child in the presence of the mother-in-law. Thus Kakar speaks of:

> Bewildering, contradictory messages of simultaneous love and restraint, emanating from . . . father. . . . [The Indian boy] does not have that necessary conviction that his father is a dependable constant to learn from, be loved by, and emulate.
>
> (Kakar 1982b:422–423)

For Kakar, D.'s problems are rooted in an absence of the reliable father—an absence related to the general pattern of restraint by the Hindu father in the group of family men. In fact, however, D.'s problems originate in the absence of the in-law mothers, who could have prompted in D. a renunciation of his mother and, according to this model, could have prepared D. to immerse himself in a group of restrained "fathers." If anything, D.'s natural father, because of his isolating job, is notable for functioning away from the family and thus outside a group of men. In the context of a joint family, D.'s father's restrained but consistent and protective influence could have enabled D. to take a secure place as a member of the group.

Case Two: Mr. K.

The story of K. is presented by Kakar in a paper entitled "Observations on the 'Oedipal Alliance' in a Patient with a Narcissistic

Personality Disorder" (Kakar 1980). This piece is only a few pages long and makes no attempt to fully set forth K.'s history or treatment. Rather, Kakar gives us enough general information about K. to illustrate a central point concerning the oedipal alliance. Kakar stresses the way in which the analytic relationship serves to fulfill K.'s deep need for a supportive male who can help him to free himself from emotional domination by a sexually threatening mother. As we have seen, both the sexually dominating mother and the remote, emotionally unavailable father are central to Kakar's general picture of Hindu family life. Indeed, as with D., Kakar uses the case of K. to illustrate his 1982 article on the problems posed by the emotional distance between Indian fathers and sons (Kakar 1982b).

K. is a forty-year-old lecturer in philosophy at the university. He came to Kakar tormented by severe anxiety and obsessive ideas about castrating and blinding himself. While nominally deferent to Kakar, K. would hold forth during sessions as though lecturing a class, placing Kakar in the position of an appreciative but uninvolved audience. Gradually, K. came to idealize Kakar, bringing him into his grandiose world. Eventually, however, K. took tentative steps toward the notion of a genuine alliance in which the analyst represented a distinct and powerful male presence who could provide a point of escape from the overpowering seductiveness of the mother and of women generally.

K.'s immediate problems (the anxiety and ideas of castration and blinding) were rooted in his recent friendship with a divorced female colleague. She wished the relationship to become sexual. K. was sorely tempted but also guilty and anxious about the prospect of leaving his wife and children. Behind this, moreover, lay a powerful childhood precedent.

K.'s mother was at once overprotective and self-involved. Generally withdrawn, living in her own fantasy world, she also encouraged sexual advances by the young K. As they lay together, she would pretend to sleep while K. rubbed his penis against her thighs until ejaculating in his pants. Although she pretended to be passive at such times, K.'s mother would lock the doors against the father's possible entry. She even hinted to K. that he should satisfy her more directly. Meanwhile, K.'s father generally kept his distance from his two sons (K. being the oldest), considering the upbringing of children to be the proper concern of a woman.

K.'s narcissism, his initial refusal to bring Kakar into his world as anything other than a peripheral and appreciative audience, replayed his mother's distance and self-involvement. Beneath the guise of the confident and self-absorbed lecturer, however, lay the guilt and fear of a small boy, terrified and helpless in the face of his mother's seductive presence. Thus, the sexual promptings of K.'s female colleague had set off his problems. Once the analysis had gone into these deeper issues, K. began to see Kakar as the father who had never really been available to him. The analyst now became the man who could help K. to separate from his seductive mother.

As noted, Kakar uses a brief vignette from the case of K. (along with a longer excerpt from the case of D.) to illustrate his 1982 article on Indian fathers and sons. Immediately after presenting the vignette on K.'s search for an oedipal alliance, Kakar makes the following general comments:

> Identification ... requires that over the years the father be constantly available to his son, a criterion fundamentally at odds with the rationale and structure of the Indian extended family. For the strength and cohesion of the extended family depend on a certain emotional diffusion; it is essential that nuclear cells do not build up within the family, or at the very least, that these cells do not involve intense emotional loyalties that potentially exclude other family members and their interests.
>
> Thus the principles of Indian family life demand that a father be restrained in the presence of his own son and divide his interest and support equally among his own and his brother's sons.
>
> (Kakar 1982b:422)

The difficulty here is that the case of K. does not really exemplify this situation. At least as Kakar describes it, there is no indication of anything but a mother, father, and a younger brother in K.'s family. What is striking about K.'s family is that it represents extended family principles displaced into a dysfunctional nuclear family context.

The distance of K.'s father might have worked had it been nested in the context of in-law mothers, uncles, and grandfathers. The notion of K.'s father that women bring up young children makes sense if we understand that it is really the in-law mothers, rather than the father, who first draw the child away from its natural mother. Indeed, Kakar fails to note the contradiction between his statement that Indian norms forbid intense emotional loyalties between nuclear cells and his picture of *normal* Indian mothering as seductive and emotionally overwhelming. The problem with K. is not a childhood lived amidst the Indian extended family. The problem with K. is that he was *not* in such a family and therefore was allowed to form precisely the sort of "nuclear cell" with his mother the Hindu joint family discourages. Indeed, the seductiveness of K.'s mother alternated with an emotional distance. This distance would have provided precisely the opening needed by the group to draw K. away from a too close maternal entanglement if only the group had been present.

The Hindu father's distance makes sense only if we understand that identification with an individual is not the goal of Hindu development. Rather, the goal is immersion within a group, in which no individual connections are permitted to dominate. This pattern is not an extension of the early tie to the mother. Rather, it is a culturally distinctive way of breaking the tie to the mother. Thus, according to the model of the tension between the natural mother and the in-law mothers, the father's restraint works because there are other men around as well. The boy, already distanced from his natural mother by the in-law mothers, blends into this group without excessive individual entanglements. His father's special role— the positive converse of paternal restraint—is to ensure that his son's uncles and cousins form no special alliances that would disadvantage the boy (a process that misfired in the adolescence of D.). The case of K., then, does not illustrate the psychological pitfalls of the Hindu Indian extended family. On the contrary, this case illustrates the problems attendant on the breakdown of that traditional family structure.

Case Three: Mr. M.

The case of M. has been reprinted in several publications by Kakar (1989, 1990a, 1990b:129–140). It is the least detailed of his published cases, being less a record of treatment than a brief sketch of a fragment of an analysis interwoven with intriguing thoughts on

Hindu myth and on the history of psychoanalysis in India. Consequently, even more than in the cases above, I will simply be able to point in the direction of new ways of considering the issues involved.

In this case, moreover, the limitations on the data are bound up with the theoretical issues in question, for Kakar attempts to show that M. is dangerously immersed in his family's maternal world—a world consisting of four women. These are M.'s mother, paternal grandmother, father's brother's wife, and his father's unmarried sister. However, precisely because Kakar treats these in-law mothers as extensions of the natural mother, he quickly drops any discussion of them and concentrates on M.'s mother. There is no real exploration of the actions of women other than the natural mother and no consideration of any tensions or interactions between the natural mother and the other women of the family.

Instead, we learn that M. has many memories of holding his erect penis against the buttocks of his sleeping mother—always fearful that she may wake up, notice his forbidden touch, and turn to confront him. On crowded buses M. has the compulsion to rub against middle-aged women whose backs are turned to him. Likewise, when having sex with his wife, the most exciting position for M. is to approach her from behind when she is half asleep. Indeed, when his wife is fully awake and enthusiastically facing him for sex, premature ejaculation and precipitous loss of erection can result.

It seems to me quite possible that here, as with the case of K., we might be facing a situation where the natural mother actually encouraged this sort of sexual tie. M.'s fear of the mother turning toward him and of her glance of recognition may not only be a secret conflicted wish but also a frightening memory of a real event. Or, M.'s fear of the mother turning to face him may be a deeper recognition on his part of the many and subtle ways in which she kept him to herself rather than pushing him toward the group. In other words, the maternal closeness here may be a misfiring of the typical Indian pattern and not, as Kakar presents it, an archetype of that pattern.

If this is true, then some of the tidbits we are given about M.'s nonmaternal female caretakers may take on a new significance. In Kakar's presentation, these women simply reinforce M.'s dangerous closeness to his mother. Undoubtedly, if his mother neglected to push M. toward the group, the family's other women would indeed have been experienced as agents of an overwhelming maternal presence. On the other hand, Kakar may have overlooked signs of M.'s interest in nonmaternal women that may actually indicate a desire on his part to move away from his mother. For example:

> One of . . . [M.'s] earliest recollections is of a woman who used to pull at the penises of the little boys playing out in the street. M. never felt afraid when the woman grabbed at his own penis. In fact, he rather liked it, reassured that he had a penis at all or at least enough of one for the woman to acknowledge its existence.
>
> (Kakar 1990b:133)

This recollection is striking because it features a woman who does aggressively and sexually face M. and yet whose presence is reassuring. While Kakar simply treats it under the rubric of "the omnipresence of women" in M.'s life, I see it as a token of his yearning for the "pull" (literally) of the in-law mothers. The Nichters report the same practice in South India:

> Not uncommonly, older, non-Brahman women would walk up to Simeon, pull on his penis, pretend to eat it, and say, "Um, a chili pepper, it's so good to eat." (Nichter and Nichter 1987:75)

This practice fits with others examined in chapter 4. Such practices involve patterns of attention and teasing by the group that have the effect of drawing a child away from the mother. The sexual element in such practices is not dangerous, precisely because it is detached from a close personal relationship, is spread out over a group, and is deployed *against* the tie of the boy to his mother.

There are other signs of M.'s yearning for the saving presence of the in-law mothers. For example, M. has a fantasy of a jungle tribe that hangs the bodies of its dead, unclothed, on trees. M. imagines himself coming at night upon a beautiful, naked dead woman of the tribe and copulating with her. As he does so, other tribe members are eating parts of the hanging corpses. Kakar tends to interpret this imagery as an incestuous wish extended over the larger maternal group. Certainly the incestuous element is there. On the other hand, I think we can uncover a deeper layer.

The beautiful woman is a corpse, one of a number of corpses in the process of being eaten by the group. I think this indicates that underneath M.'s incestuous desire there lies the hope that the group will rid him of his overbearing mother, killing and eating her, so to speak. The image brings to mind the myth of Shiva's testicles and the army of goddesses, analyzed in chapter 6. Recall that in that myth, without Shiva's sexual sacrifice, without his voluntary turn away from incest, the group of goddesses threatened to consume and destroy even Devi (the natural mother) herself. In effect, M. is wishing for such a group action against his mother in order that he be saved from his own incestuous desires. Interestingly, this fantasy of a group or tribe comes to M. on a crowded bus, the same setting in which he is wont to brush against the backsides of middle-aged women. One might guess that for M. the crowd not only offers a cover for his activities but also provides him with the comforting sense of a check against his impulses taking him too far. How much can he really do sexually with a crowd all around? Thus, M.'s symptomatic acting out contains not only the incestuous wish but also the desire for a group counteraction of that wish.

Kakar is certainly aware of M.'s desire for relief from his dangerous tie to the mother, but Kakar associates this trend in M. solely with the potentially saving, but sadly limited, presence of the father. This is in keeping with Kakar's interest in what he calls the oedipal alliance with the father and in the difficulty of sustaining that alliance in the Hindu family context. Yet my interpretation of the comforting memory of the woman who pulls little boys' penises as well as of the tribe who may save M. from incest by consuming his mother would indicate much room for an examination of the role of M.'s in-law mothers not simply as reinforcers of the overwhelming maternal presence but as potential alternatives to it. Clearly, in M.'s case, the pull away from the natural mother misfired, probably because she never pushed her son toward the group, but perhaps also because the in-law mothers did less than they might have to draw M. away. In any case, the problem of this tension between the natural and in-law mothers needs analytic reconstruction and working through, something that cannot take place as long as all the family's women are indiscriminately treated under the broad rubric of "the maternal feminine."

Case Four: Ms. R.

The case of Ms. R. is presented by the Indian psychoanalyst B. K. Ramanujam (1986:78–82). R. was born as the first grandchild of a traditional and very prosperous extended Hindu family. All the members of the extended family, with the exception of R.'s father, were successful professional people. In early adolescence, R.'s parents moved away with her to set up their own household. At this time, however, the continued professional limitations of R.'s father forced her mother to study and work outside the home. A woman working to support the family was most unusual in this social circle, and R.'s mother undertook the task only out of necessity.

Against her traditional parents' wishes, R. was determined to attend college and eventually did so. She continually turned down offers of advantageous arranged marriages in favor of living the untraditional, Westernized lifestyle of her college friends. In important ways, however, R. herself remained traditional, neither fully understanding nor fully participating in the new social and sexual mores current on her college campus. She assumed that her first involvement with a man at college would eventuate in marriage. When it did not, she developed a series of psychosomatic symptoms and completed the academic year only with difficulty.

After college, R.'s persistent rejection of marriage arrangements brought all proposals to a halt. She continued to adopt the unconventional lifestyle of the modernized elite at least superficially and soon developed a platonic friendship with a man of a different caste. She began to feel love for him and assumed they would marry. Her parents reluctantly consented to this since her earlier series of refusals had now made an arranged marriage within their established social and caste network untenable. When confronted, however, Ms. R.'s friend made it clear that he did not wish to marry.

This hit R. very hard. She locked herself into her room at home and closed all the windows. She received food from her family but beyond that had only minimal contact with them. This went on for months, accompanied by depression and self-destructive thoughts. At this point, Ramanujam was brought in. Following her work with Ramanujam, R. was able to reidentify with some of her parents' values while still maintaining her integrity. She married a man of her own choosing, but the marriage was also approved of by both families, and the wedding was traditional.

Clearly, R.'s difficulties were rooted in part in the complexities of negotiating the profound and painful changes at work in a modernizing India. Nonetheless, according to Ramanujam, there was also a deeper psychological source for R.'s conflicts. During much of the time that R. was growing up in her parents' extended family, her mother was the only daughter-in-law of the household. The mother-in-law of the house was difficult and demanding, and Ramanujam notes indications that R.'s mother may have tried too hard to please her harsh mother-in-law by constantly doing household chores. This took R.'s mother away from her much of the time. When her parents broke away to form their own family in R.'s early adolescence, R. looked forward to greater intimacy with her mother. However, as a result of the father's continued professional failure, R.'s mother was forced to leave the house in order to earn the family a living. This further separation from her mother built up resentment in R., which led to her ostentatious rejection of her parents' values along with their several marriage arrangements. On the other hand, beneath her resentment, R. wished to be included in the traditional family and could therefore never fully comprehend or give herself over to the mores of the Westernized college elite.

I think there is much to be said for Ramanujam's understanding of R.'s situation. Certainly, his work with her had beneficial effects. On the other hand, I think there is more at stake here than an unresolved attachment to the mother. The nature and extent of R.'s unresolved tie to her mother only makes sense when we bring in the tension between the tie to the natural mother and that to the in-law mothers.

It is not unusual for a young Indian mother, as the daughter-in-law of the house, to be drawn away from her child by chores. Often, a family's in-law mothers actually spend more time with the child than the natural mother. R.'s problem may be less her mother's early absence than the failure of the in-law mothers to adequately take the mother's place. Also, the extent to which R.'s mother was taken away by excessive chores may itself have been due to certain tensions with the in-law mothers—tensions about which Ramanujam tells us little. Ramanujam does let us know that there were many caretakers in R.'s extended family, but their exact relation or status is not specified. Thus we must ask why these caretakers did not draw R. fully enough into the group to moderate the pain of her mother's absence. I suspect that the answer to this question lies with the financial problems of R.'s father.

The situation in R.'s family bears some resemblance to that of the family depicted in the story of Santoshi Ma. In that story, the brother who does not work in the fields is resented by the extended family group. This resentment is directed not only at him but also at his wife. At first the tensions are expressed secretly and subtly, but eventually the dispute breaks into the open, with family partition as the end result. Something like this may well have occurred with R.'s family.

Ramanujam emphasizes that the nonearning status of R.'s father did not prevent him from obtaining a favorable marriage. But this is not surprising as R.'s family was respected and successful, and R.'s father was still young at the time of marriage. As the years went by without appreciable earnings by R.'s father, however, it seems likely that his family's resentment would have grown. R.'s mother would be under pressure to do more than her share of work simply to show that she and her husband were contributing something to the larger family. Thus, the particularly difficult, fearful, and demanding stance of the mother-in-law probably reflected her underlying dissatisfaction with having to carry the weight of R. and her parents.

Unfortunately, R. would have suffered under such conditions. Not only would her mother have been often away at chores, but the mother-in-law and other caretakers in the family would have done relatively little to draw R. into their pleasing company. On the contrary, stinting R. of their presence may well have been a subtle way to send out the message to R.'s parents that they were not really wanted. Quite possibly the situation was an adult replay of the process of renunciation outlined in chapter 4. Rather than overtly withholding money and benefits from R.'s parents, the group may have provided honor and goods, but only slowly and with subtle messages of reproach. The goal of this would have been to prompt R.'s family to shape up, either by earning more or by voluntarily leaving the joint family.

Of course, all of this is speculative reconstruction. The point is, however, that such central issues are not discussed by Ramanujam. Despite his overt statements about the importance of the extended family in the Hindu context, Ramanujam's focus remains on the nuclear triangle. He never tells us, for example, just why R.'s extended family broke up and what long-term tensions preceded that break. In sum, while R. may have been pained by her distance from her mother, we need to see why that distance was never compensated for and, indeed, how R.'s distance from her mother may have even been heightened by the actions of the in-law mothers.

I do not mean to imply that the in-law mothers hold the entire key to this case. For example, there is a clear sense in which R.'s determination to defy her parents in matters of marriage and education expresses a paradoxical positive identification with her mother. After all, her mother left R. in order to work, first in the traditional joint household and later in the untraditional modern work force. Going to college was a way of experiencing the closeness of identification with a working mother. At the same time, by going to college and spurning traditional marriages, R. could hurl a reproach at her mother, who actually did not want her daughter to follow in her footsteps. By taking the college route, the daughter could effectively say, "Alright, I'll be modern and work, just like you. You won't like what I do any more than I like what you do." Also, R.'s identifying with her mother's reluctant modernity was a reproach to her unsuccessful father since it highlighted her mother's having had to work, despite their family's traditional role ideals. (See the conclusion of chapter 9 for a discussion of the conflict between mothering and career in Indian and American women.)

In one form or another, Ramanujam brings out many of these triangular issues, but he misses the way in which this nuclear family situation is nested within and profoundly influenced by the tensions within the joint family. Had R.'s father enjoyed greater career success, her early separation from her mother because of demands by resentful in-laws would likely have been less pronounced. Also, such separation as is inevitable and necessary in the joint family would have been eased through a smooth incorporation of R. into the larger group represented by the in-law mothers. Equipped with a theory about all this, a clinician would be more inclined to recognize and draw out early key memories related to the group. For example, we can imagine that R. might have some very important memories about her interactions with her paternal grandmother or aunts (the in-law mothers) when her mother was off doing chores. Clearly, analysis of that period could open a way to further healing for R. and patients like her.

Case Five: Shakuntala

The case of Shakuntala is the most detailed of the patient histories presented by Alan Roland in his book *In Search of Self in India and Japan* (Roland 1988). Shakuntala, who is in her late twenties, lectures in the humanities in Bombay. The central conflict in her life is whether to give in to pressure from her mother and accept an arranged marriage, or whether to continue her long-term affair with Kumar, the husband of a close friend and a man some fifteen years her senior. Roland also notes a third possible route, which offers almost as much conflict as the other two. Shakuntala's maternal aunt is a well respected holy woman and the head of an ashram (a religious hermitage). Shakuntala deeply respects this aunt and spends much time in meditation. Her aunt, perhaps seeing in Shakuntala a successor, pressures Shakuntala either to marry or to renounce the world and join her at the ashram. Shakuntala's mother would oppose this.

Roland traces the childhood roots of Shakuntala's conflict over marriage. Before Shakuntala's birth, an older and only son of the family tragically died in a fall from a window. This depressed Shakuntala's mother, who, in any case, shows a long-term tendency to depression. In light of the loss of the first son, Shakuntala's family lavished unusual attention on her. Much of this attention was withdrawn a year and a half later when another son was born. Shakuntala responded by shifting her interest from her mother to her father, who was quite the opposite of the stereotypically distant Indian disciplinarian. Shakuntala's father remained deeply and overtly attached to her and set very few limits on her actions.

In a sense, Shakuntala's acceptance of an arranged marriage would represent a reconciliation and identification with her depressed mother. Shakuntala's mother makes this difficult, however, by directly tying Shakuntala's willingness to marry to her (the mother's) whole happiness in life. For Shakuntala to undertake an arranged marriage would thus be to accept the notion that her own unmarried state is at the root of her mother's depression. Alternatively, for Shakuntala to remain single would be to reproach her mother for her depression and neglect, both in the present and in the past.

Shakuntala's affair with Kumar, as Roland makes abundantly clear, has roots in her incestuous tie to her father. Clearly, an affair with an older man, the husband of Shakuntala's close friend, has incestuous overtones. Shakuntala's feelings about the affair focus on how special it makes her feel but also betray much guilt. Both of these elements, of course, are key markers of the incestuous tie. Clearly, then, although Shakuntala's bond to her father was able to ease her away from the disappointment with her mother, it raised as many problems as it solved.

Roland has relatively little to say about the unconscious developmental sources of Shakuntala's conflict over the role of meditation and world renunciation in her life. He does dispute the classical Freudian notion that Shakuntala's meditation practices are regressive and pathological. Indeed, Roland argues that Shakuntala's ability to devote herself to disciplined meditation actually increases as some of her unconscious conflicts are resolved. On the other hand, the meditative trend in Shakuntala's life is not directly traced by Roland to her childhood situation. Roland does relate Shakuntala's keeping her meditation secret from her "modern" friends to what he calls the "private self" of Hinduism. This notion of the private self, however, has no clear developmental grounding. In Roland's system, the idea of a private self seems to function to counterbalance the pathological implications of the prolonged period of symbiosis said to be characteristic of Hindu childhood. In effect, by putting forward the view that Hindus maintain a hidden or private self, Roland preserves the classic psychoanalytic idea that individuality is the antidote to symbiosis.

My suggestion, however, is that Shakuntala's meditation can be linked to her efforts at a group-oriented developmental resolution. Shakuntala's devotion to meditation and her consideration of a life at the ashram represent attempts to renounce her unconscious ties to her mother and father by way of a psychic movement toward immersion in the actual and symbolic extended family.

Roland never gives us a clear account of Shakuntala's larger family. This is a problem with all of our Indian psychoanalytic case histories, and something I think needs to change. It appears, however, that Shakuntala was raised by an essentially nuclear family with grandparents, aunts, uncles, and cousins on the father's side either nonexistent or living elsewhere for most of her childhood. On her mother's side, however, there were a number of aunts, uncles, and cousins, many of whom had a powerful impact both on Shakuntala's life and on her associations, dreams, and transference reactions in psychoanalysis. Given the patrilineal kinship system of North India, however, these maternal relatives did not live in Shakuntala's home.

As noted, Shakuntala's favorite aunt—her mother's sister who eventually came to head an ashram—exercised an influence on Shakuntala second only to that of Shakuntala's mother and father. Despite the fact that Shakuntala persistently refused marriages arranged for her by her parents, she had once agreed to marry her first cousin, the son of her favorite aunt. This match was the idea of the aunt herself but was vetoed by Shakuntala's father because North Indian Hindu kinship norms forbid such cousin marriages.

Shakuntala's interest in this marriage to her first cousin certainly betrays the incestuous wish that emerged in her relationship to Kumar. On the other hand, I think Shakuntala's acceptance of this proposal was also an attempt to move further away from her parents and toward the closest substitute for the paternal extended family that was available to her—the home of her maternal aunt. Had Shakuntala had paternal aunts, uncles, and cousins present at home, they may well have been able to ease the transition away from her mother after the birth of her younger brother while also blocking the excessive and subtly incestuous tie to the father. Indeed, this is a case where the father's need to show restraint with an own child in the joint family context would have been a great developmental advantage.

Shakuntala's ongoing tie to her religious aunt bespeaks her desire to escape from a dangerous nuclear family configuration. Indeed, I think in the Hindu context the very practice of meditation represents a healthy technique of detachment from one-to-one bonds that facilitates the lifelong Hindu developmental focus on movement toward a collectively oriented consciousness. Roland is right to respect the practice of meditation in Shakuntala's life and in Hindu culture generally. Yet his picture of Hindu development fails to expose the culturally distinctive psychological roots of such practices.

In the course of his discussion of Shakuntala's long-running affair with Kumar, Roland makes an acute observation on the conduct of Veena, Kumar's wife and Shakuntala's close friend. Veena does not know of the affair between Kumar and Shakuntala, but she still senses the threat from Shakuntala's closeness to her family. Thus she acts in a very subtle and characteristically Hindu way to distance her family from Shakuntala. Veena continues to enthusiastically invite Shakuntala to visit, but quietly Veena tells Kumar that Shakuntala has lost interest in them. Rather than actually reduce her invitations, Veena hopes that she can create enough distance between Shakuntala and Kumar to prompt Kumar, or better yet Shakuntala herself, to moderate or end the relationship.

Roland identifies this tactic with the Hindu Indian capacity for nonverbal empathy—getting messages across without having to state them outright. I think Roland shows a good eye for culturally specific patterns here, but to my way of thinking the theoretical framework remains too Western. For Roland, the Indian focus is on nonverbal empathy derived from an early, intense symbiosis. Thus, in Roland's understanding, this general, symbiotically based capacity for nonverbal empathy just happens here to be utilized as part of an effort to subtly break off a relationship. From my point of view, however, the move to distance overly close relations is at the core of the cultural phenomenon here. By stretching the Western notion of empathy to cover the Indian situation, Roland misses the fact that Hindus have their own way of breaking the early symbiotic tie. Hindus are not so much specialists at empathic symbiosis as they are practitioners of a culturally specific way of *countering* symbiosis—a process I call renunciation.

In renunciation, the Hindu child is prompted to voluntarily forgo immature incestuous ties in favor of a movement toward the group. The group aspect of renunciation remains hidden, however, as long as these distinctively Indian processes are understood by way of concepts, such as nonverbal empathy and private self, that are only slightly modified versions of classic psychoanalytic notions. These concepts either make Hindus seem more enmeshed in symbiosis than Westerners, or they posit ways of circumventing symbiosis that are simply vague variations on Western solutions. From the standpoint of the renunciation concept, however, we can develop a comprehensive theory that will permit us to understand culturally distinctive phenomena that Roland does at least partially recognize (such as Shakuntala's meditation and Veena's subtle separation tactics) and then to link these patterns to culturally distinctive phenomena Roland overlooks (such as the importance of Shakuntala's extended maternal family in both her external life and in her analytic dreams, associations, and transference reactions).

Let me illustrate this through a consideration of one of Shakuntala's dreams. Here is Shakuntala's narration of the dream, followed by Roland's account of her associations:

"The first part is vague, seemingly with Kumar and possibly Veena, who seems to have turned into my mother at some point. Then, their four children are going into a cart, the cart swaying from side to side like a see-saw, the children going in and out of some square structures. Kumar's oldest daughter (the second oldest child) falls out of the cart and is run over by a truck. I see it and cry out, then I come running over crying out Uma, Uma (the name of her deity) and I pick up the bloody child. Kumar suddenly turns into her uncle, and her mother (originally Veena in the dream) has to go to the toilet. Someone offers her some cool melon juice. Others there seem rather unconcerned about the child, who is taken to the hospital, where an aunt (the uncle's wife) pulls on the tongue of the child and says she will live. The girl is all right."

In her associations, the uncle is someone who likes Shakuntala a great deal and feels she is very spiritually advanced and above this world. Shakuntala feels she definitely isn't above this world, though she has had some intense spiritual experiences. Her associations to the daughter who was run over are that she is a sickly girl whom Kumar is concerned about, and she is not an overly good-looking girl as yet. Shakuntala feels that this daughter is overly in love with Kumar, and has many compulsive, cleaning rituals around the house, which Shakuntala feels might be due to guilt.

(Roland 1988:161–162)

There was no time left in this session to obtain further associations to the dream. Roland goes on to interpret for us, however, that Shakuntala was struggling with her incestuous love for Kumar, with Kumar representing Shakuntala's father in the dream and Veena (Kumar's wife) transforming into and representing Shakuntala's mother. I think Roland is right about the incestuous roots of this dream. In addition, however, I think the dream pushes through the anxiety over incest and retaliation and moves toward a solution involving the extended family.

In the dream, Kumar and Veena's children ride the cart, swaying from side to side and moving in and out of square structures until the oldest daughter (the second oldest child) falls from the cart and is run over by a truck. Certainly, the swaying and movement of the cart as well as the fall and truck accident stand for incestuous sex between Kumar and the injured daughter, i.e., Shakuntala and her father. In addition, however, I think the fall and truck accident represent the deadly fall of Shakuntala's older brother. In the dream, the second oldest child, the daughter (i.e., the symbolic child Shakuntala and not her older brother) is the victim of the accident and is thus the center of attention and concern. When Shakuntala sees the stricken child (her young self) in the dream, she calls out to her mother goddess for help. Here, Shakuntala is trying to give her mother a chance to undo the pain of the early abandonment of Shakuntala in favor of Shakuntala's younger brother and in favor of the depressive memory of her older, dead brother. In the dream, then, the problem is how to retain the caring attention of her mother while still having sex with the father. So far, the situation seems classically oedipal, but the dream is not over.

After the accident in the dream, Kumar turns into an uncle while Veena, who has turned into Shakuntala's mother, leaves to go to the toilet. At one level, I think the uncle here continues to represent Shakuntala's father. After symbolic incestuous sex, Shakuntala is left alone with her father (the "uncle") and is abandoned by her mother, who goes to the toilet. The mother going to the toilet here probably represents the childhood image (emphasized in the work of Melanie Klein 1975a, 1975b, 1975c) of feces used as symbolic weapons of retaliatory anger (in this case the retaliation is for Shakuntala's incest with the father). The mother's going to the toilet may also represent a birth image, which is often anal in childhood

(Dundes 1972). In other words, Shakuntala envisions her mother's giving anal birth to her younger brother as a kind of retaliation for Shakuntala's incestuous interest in the father.

At another level, however, I think the uncle in the dream represents the men of Shakuntala's real and wished for extended family. If Shakuntala could only play out her incestuous wishes in a transformed and sublimated way on male uncles and cousins, then she might avoid the wrath and abandonment of her mother. I think this sort of solution is indicated by the end of the dream, where an aunt, the uncle's wife, examines the injured child in the hospital and confirms that she will live. The aunt here represents Shakuntala's maternal aunt(s), who helped to make up for her problems with her mother. Yet I think the caring aunt in the dream also stands for Shakuntala's mother as she could be if only Shakuntala could deflect her sexual desire away from her father and toward real or symbolic uncles. This would effectively transform Shakuntala's mother into an "aunt"—i.e., just another member of the larger group and not Shakuntala's special rival. Thus, in the dream Shakuntala plays out her incestuous wish, encounters the anxiety of maternal retaliation, and moves toward the solution of shifting her passions to the extended family. This would allow some satisfaction of sexual desires without totally alienating the women of the family, particularly the mother. Indeed, this solution would unite Shakuntala and her mother but now as members of the larger group. Had Shakuntala actually been able to live out this extended family solution in childhood rather than merely dream about it later she might have been more prepared for her adult sexual relationships.

Shakuntala's associations to the dream uncle fit nicely with this interpretation. Shakuntala recalls this man as someone who likes her and who feels she is spiritually advanced and above this world. Shakuntala, however, feels that she is definitely not above this world although she has been trying to move in that direction through her spiritual practices. The uncle, therefore, represents the possibility that Shakuntala might be able to detach herself through the process I call renunciation from her incestuous desires, something she has been trying to do through meditation and otherwise but without full success.

Finally, I think we can say that the aunt at the end of this dream, who examines the injured child in the hospital and declares that she will live, represents Roland himself. Roland is Shakuntala's doctor—her hope for health and maturity. Appropriately, he is associated with the extended family relatives, whose actual presence in Shakuntala's parental home could have done for Shakuntala what Roland does now, namely, draw her away from intense nuclear ties. Also, Shakuntala feels particularly comfortable with Roland because he does not condemn her for her affair with Kumar. Thus, Roland is represented by an aunt, who tolerates in the dream and could have tolerated in Shakuntala's childhood a more mature and transformed, if still subtly incestuous, tie to her husband, an uncle.

My approach to this dream can be confirmed and extended by an examination of another of Shakuntala's dreams. This second dream plays a central role in Roland's presentation of Shakuntala's case. Here is Shakuntala's narration:

> "Kumar drops off his youngest son at my flat and takes me in his car to a place with a large lawn and trees. We are about to kiss when a policeman comes over and insists we get out. I said 'This is absurd, Kumar is simply my *māmān* (maternal uncle),' but the policeman insists Kumar return tomorrow at 5 P.M. I am very uneasy."
>
> (Roland 1988:168)

Shakuntala associates the large lawn and trees with her childhood home. Five P.M. reminds her of the time of her analytic sessions, and her uneasiness about time reminds her that she recently spent a couple of unaccounted hours with Kumar, about which Veena may become suspicious.

Roland concentrates on these associations and again interprets the incestuous triangle at the base of the dream. Shakuntala is alone with a symbolic father and about to kiss when she is stopped by the maternal police. Roland then relates this childhood situation to the transference, Roland himself being the policeman who breaks up the incestuous tryst and who insists on a return to the next analytic session at 5 P.M. Roland sees Shakuntala struggling with an image of him as the punitive maternal superego. Shakuntala's recent efforts to get Roland to appear at her school are seen as an attempt to make him into a helpful person and thus to offset the punitive, unconsciously maternal, policeman image of the dream. Roland concludes from all this that Shakuntala's case supports the notion that the Oedipus complex is universal (Roland 1988:169).

I think Roland glosses too quickly over the appearance of the *māmān* (maternal uncle) in this dream. In describing Shakuntala's associations to the dream, Roland says:

> The *māmān* or maternal uncle represents a usual niece-uncle romantic attachment, but she never had such an involvement with her *māmāns*. This was clearly a diversionary tactic in the dream.
>
> (Roland 1988:168)

Roland means that Shakuntala calls Kumar her *māmān* in the dream simply to divert the policeman (the maternal superego—analyst) from attention to her incestuous desires. I think there is more to it, however. Shakuntala's associations indicate that she regrets not having had the kind of harmless romantic attachment to her *māmāns* in her youth that could have drawn her away from her father. I think she also wishes for a larger paternal extended family, which could have played the same role. Following up on this line of interpretation, I think that Roland himself represents not only the punitive maternal superego but also the more moderate maternal aunt superego. Shakuntala's efforts to turn Roland into a helpful visitor to her school are an effort to counteract her punitive maternal superego by transforming Roland into a tolerant and helpful aunt—exactly the role played by the "doctor" aunt at the end of the first dream we examined.

In my view, then, Shakuntala's case does not argue for the universality of the Oedipus complex. While Shakuntala does participate in an incestuous triangular dynamic, this dynamic is nested in a more complex mental context involving multiple figures from the extended family. Indeed, Shakuntala's problem is that extended family figures capable of breaking and transforming her incestuous attachments are even more profoundly present in her dreams and transference reactions than they were in her actual childhood. Roland, however, continues to treat extended family members either as doubles of the parents or as targets of displaced feelings toward the parents rather than as potential and complex counterweights to the parental tie. Yet, it seems to me that Shakuntala's case only confirms the suggestion, made in the preceding chapters, that a universalist oedipal theory deflects our attention from the culturally distinctive factors in development created by the normative presence of multiple caretakers. We know, for example, that an analyst would not hesitate to highlight and interpret a boy's yearning for a father who could help him to break an incestuous tie to his mother. Kakar's notion of the need for an Indian oedipal alliance leads him to make just such interpretations (Kakar 1980, 1982b). Why should we in the Indian context not also recognize as fundamental a patient's unconscious yearning for the extended family relations who characteristically can and do help Hindu Indian children to break their childhood attachments via the culturally distinctive process of renunciation? Until the notion of a universal Oedipus complex is abandoned, however, we shall continue to overlook, dismiss, or misinterpret evidence of the fundamental psychological importance of nonnuclear relatives in non-Western cultures. To make this theoretical shift, however, there is no need to forsake the idea of incestuous or retaliatory wishes and fears involving the real parents. We need only be open to the complex way in which these conflicts are reshaped by their being placed into the framework of broader group processes.

Some further and final reflection on our five Indian clinical histories is now in order. In each of these cases I have pointed to ways in which the presence (or absence) of extended family members combines with and transforms the meaning of interactions within the nuclear triangle. Even the absence of extranuclear relatives is significant in the Indian case because the normative Hindu mode of child rearing is geared to work by way of multiple caretakers. Thus, the physical closeness combined with emotional distance favored, for example, by the mother of Kakar's patient K. becomes particularly dangerous precisely because the normal group context of this physical closeness is absent.

In the normal Indian pattern, as sketched out in the preceding chapters, the controlled physical closeness of the mother combines with an emotional distance to provide an opening through which the group can pull the child toward itself. Moreover, the group not only exploits the opening between mother and child but also helps ensure that appropriate maternal distancing, both physical and emotional, will take place to begin with. Clearly, K.'s mother, while creating some emotional distance between herself and the child, let her physical contact take on an intrusive seductiveness that far outstripped even the normal Indian degree of contact. The presence of the group would very likely have prevented this.

The problem with Kakar's theoretical approach to this case and others is that the absence or misfiring of the normative, group-oriented process of Hindu development is mistakenly regarded as a typical or near-typical instance of Hindu psychological growth. Kakar notes that his patients' mothers are too close to them physically and that the fathers are too distant to prevent the damaging seduction. This is then attributed to the fact that in the traditional model the Hindu mother is in close physical contact with the child while the father is restrained by rules concerning own parent contact.

What Kakar fails to note is that the own parent restrictions also create distance between the mother and her child and that this affective gap is normally the centerpiece of a complex maternal push of the child toward the waiting in-law mothers. When the process works correctly, the natural mother's ambiguous availability combines with the lure of the group and prompts the child to a voluntary renunciation of his infantile attachments. This entire system, however, is effectively invisible to Kakar, who sees only its modern, nuclear malfunction—and this through the lens of individualist, Western psychoanalytic theory. Kakar's theory of traditional Hindu socialization is thus constructed from a viewpoint destined to filter out the group dimension essential to its operation. The result is a picture of pervasive pathology. Of course, the pathological implications of the theory are supposed to be countered by Kakar's notion that Hindu culture somehow approves of or supports symbiosis and relationship. However, Kakar's underlying focus on pathogenic maternal seduction continually returns to undercut this. In contradistinction to this, my point is that Hindu culture does *not* promote or support prolonged symbiosis. There *is* a focus on relationships in groups, but this acts as a culturally distinctive counterbalance to excessive emotional connection and not as an exemplification or continuation of such a connection.

Most of the cases we have examined are characterized by the absence of the extended family relations necessary to the operation of traditional Hindu socialization. The patients in these cases, like most Indian psychoanalytic patients, are highly educated members of the urban upper middle classes. This would seem to suggest that psychological problems emerge after the transition away from traditional family structures but before principles of socialization appropriate to more nuclear family structures are in place. On the other hand, even in the traditional rural setting, there must be many instances where for one reason or another a child suffers because of limitations on the number and type of available caretakers.

Nonetheless, the case of Ms. R., as presented by Ramanujam, provides a useful balance to our other clinical examples. Here, despite the issues of modernity in work habits and sexual mores, the central tensions seem to flow from what must be a very typical source of psychological pain and dysfunction in the traditional system. Ms. R. seems to have suffered because of the struggle of the adults around her as her extended family cracked and split apart. The similarity of Ms. R.'s case to the classic depiction of joint family tension in the story about Santoshi Ma has already been noted. Ms. R. was probably a "victim" of renunciation. That is, poor treatment of the child R. by her in-law mothers may well have been part of the way in which her parents were prompted to "voluntarily" withdraw from the larger family. This does not mean, however, that the normative process of renunciation, as played out between the natural mother, the child, and the group in a relatively stable joint family, is pathogenic. It simply means that when renunciation, or any other cultural-psychological process, is the medium of a war between adults, children will suffer. The important point is not that developmental breakdown or pathology are entirely absent from Hindu development. The point is, rather, that such breakdowns have culturally distinct causes and characteristics.

I hope that my reading of psychoanalytic case histories from India has served to suggest new areas into which investigation can be pushed. Clearly, however, I have only been able to point out possible avenues of approach. After all, clinical reports currently give short shrift to precisely the figures, processes, and conflicts that most interest me. Only a clinician influenced by the point of view put forth here could present a thorough analysis of the interplay between multiple figures in a Hindu joint family as it affects a patient. For example, a detailed clinical analysis of the male child's response to early shifts from the natural mother to the in-law mothers and the linking of this to renunciatory self-castration imagery has yet to be undertaken. These issues, of course, focused much of my above discussion of the Durga complex.

The problem of self-castration calls to mind the clinical and theoretical issues raised by Girindrasekhar Bose, who founded the Indian Psychoanalytic Society (Sinha 1966) in 1922. Throughout his career, Bose carried on an extensive correspondence with Freud, the central issue of which was the meaning of castration imagery encountered in the analyses of Indian patients (Sinha 1966). Bose did not deny the appearance of castration ideas in his Hindu patients. Indeed, he noted that such images were encountered frequently, either directly or through symbolic substitutes. He also acknowledged that castration threats were extremely common in Hindu childhood. Yet Bose argued that castration fears were not fundamental to his Hindu Indian patients in the way they were to European patients. For Bose, the castration idea was grounded in an even more basic one—the desire to become a woman, and Bose noted that this desire to be a woman was more easily brought to the surface in his Indian male patients than in his European ones. Bose further argued that the intense European dread of castration was chiefly a defense against the wish to be a woman (Bose 1949).

In his later work, Kakar consciously returns to his Indian predecessor's ideas (Kakar 1989, 1990a, 1990b:129–140). For example, Kakar notes in his own patients a relative fluidity of gender identification. Kakar explains this, however, by referring back to his fundamental idea of the sexually overwhelming Hindu Indian mother. For Kakar, her presence in childhood and the defensive self-castration she allegedly prompts in her son makes sense of Bose's point about the relatively free play of castration images and mixed gender identity in Hindu analytic patients.

I take another approach. As detailed at some length in the chapters above, I lay out the fundamental factors behind the ubiquity and openness of Hindu castration imagery. Self-castration imagery in India works as part of the process of renunciation and helps to move the male child away from his incestuous tie to the mother. Self-castration imagery, therefore, is not rooted in a defensive demasculinization before the sexually overwhelming mother. On the contrary, Hindu imagery of self-castration, representing the voluntary sacrifice of the incestuous tie to the natural mother, allows the boy to move toward the group of in-law mothers. Thus, Bose easily found an association between the wish to be a woman and

Hindu castration imagery because the Indian boy originally sacrifices his incestuous sexuality in order to become part of a group of *women*—the in-law mothers.

Bose's implication that the castration anxiety characteristically central to the analyses of Western patients is merely a defense against the deeper wish to be female is thus a case of reverse ethnocentrism by an "Indian Freud" (Bose 1949:231,237). This is a clinically based cultural bias of the type I discussed at the beginning of this chapter. In Western patients, castration anxiety leads to masculinity by prompting a turn away from the mother and a corresponding identification with the father. Because there are no in-law mothers and no process of renunciation, the wish to be a woman in the West really would take the boy back toward his infantile relation to the mother. In India, however, a subtly prompted self-castration, i.e., "voluntary" abandonment of incestuous desire for the mother, paradoxically makes a boy *more* masculine by associating him not with his mother but with a group of women. The important point is that these women are different from his natural mother and that the boy's movement toward this female group sets the precedent for his later immersion in the male group.

My point about renunciation as a defensive process is also relevant here (see the conclusion of chapter 6). Renunciation allows the imagery of infantile sexuality to remain relatively explicit. This is because health for Hindus consists less in a repression of infantile sexuality than in its deliberate sacrifice. This process not only helps explain the explicitness of Hindu myth and ritual, it also helps explain why Bose's Hindu clients had both more access to castration imagery and less anxiety connected with it than did his Western patients. This does not mean that Westerners are therefore excessively repressed. Rather, Westerners use repression while Hindus use renunciation. Each process is distinct, and neither is an inferior version of the other. Again, note that our careful early attention to the larger cultural context of development has enabled us to circumvent the ethnocentrism built into *both* Western and Eastern clinical theories.

Unfortunately, Bose's case reports tend to be brief, and they are particularly thin on accounts of the family background of the patient. This prevents me from reanalyzing Bose's fascinating material on explicit castration imagery from the standpoint of the natural mother/in-law mother dynamic. However, I am convinced from Bose's work as well as from the case histories already examined that the theoretical framework I have presented can make a contribution to the ongoing enterprise of psychoanalysis in India. Clearly, even in the most modern of Indian settings, from which the vast majority of Indian psychoanalytic patients come, the extended family continues to be an important factor in child development through its presence and/or its absence.

However, there is probably a sense in which the most interesting and complex connections between multiple Hindu parenting and the unconscious take place in relatively traditional and rural joint family contexts, where the influence of Indian clinical psychoanalysis is limited or nonexistent. Thus, psychoanalytically informed anthropological field studies of individual Hindus represent another avenue by which to reach a quasi-clinical understanding of the processes I have been outlining. This is the sort of study for which Gananath Obeyesekere is justly famous, and in the following chapter I begin with a critique and reinterpretation of Obeyesekere's recent work. This will include a rethinking of the life and times of Abdin, Obeyesekere's most detailed informant case study.

Chapter 8

South Asia and Beyond:
Obeyesekere and Spiro

The reshaped psychoanalytic theory I have presented here can illuminate development in many cultures, not just in Hindu India. It is not my object, however, to use the ek-hi phase or Durga complex to analyze non-Hindu societies. This would repeat the mistake of imposing one culture's norms on another. Instead, I wish to make the principles of my analysis more explicit. How has it been possible to reshape psychoanalytic theory to match the unique conditions of Hindu Indian culture and how can a set of analogous reshapings adapt psychoanalytic theory to other cultural settings? In this and the following chapter I hope to make some headway toward answering these questions.

Up to this point, an examination of the work of other psychoanalytic anthropologists has helped me to construct a systematic approach. I have thus drawn upon the writings of particular theorists as the occasion warranted. Now, however, I want to undertake a more concentrated and direct critique of some recent and important work in theoretical psychoanalytic anthropology. This will help us make the transition from Hindu Indian material to a broader comparative perspective.

Obeyesekere

Gananath Obeyesekere's recent book, *The Work of Culture* (1990), is an important meditation on the theoretical and comparative issues raised by the psychoanalysis of South Asian culture. In that book Obeyesekere unites his earlier psychoanalytic work on Buddhism and Hinduism in the complex religious milieu of Sri Lanka (1981, 1984) with a close consideration of Hindu psychology throughout India itself. All this, moreover, is made the object of a careful and important attempt to liberate comparative psychoanalytic theory from cultural bias. My own view is that Obeyesekere does not finally succeed in breaking with psychoanalytic universalism. However, Obeyesekere's book is valuable for its very thoughtful efforts to move in this direction.

A critique of *The Work of Culture*, then, should begin to clarify what is distinctive in the approach I am offering.[1] A critical reading of Obeyesekere's Hindu psychology will permit a quick, contrastive replaying of my own views. Moreover, a rethinking of Obeyesekere's remarkable informant case study will help clarify the links between my conceptualization of Hindu developmental psychology and the standpoint outlined in my chapter on Indian clinical work. Finally, a critique of Obeyesekere's broader theoretical framework, particularly in its comparative dimension, will prepare us for the examination of work by Melford Spiro that forms the second half of this chapter.

Obeyesekere's purpose in *The Work of Culture* is to preserve psychoanalytic insight while at the same time adjusting psychoanalytic theory to the particularities of South Asian culture. This intention leads to much that is of value. Obeyesekere's focus on the progressive rather than merely regressive character of cultural symbols is welcome. His related attention to degrees of psychological remove from underlying conflict yields valuable comparisons between different strands of ritual and myth. In other words, Obeyesekere shows us the subtle ways in which a common set of psychological conflicts can be played out, in more or less mature fashion, in a given ritual or even in a given ritual practitioner. This helps move us beyond simple, homogenizing symbolic analysis.

In my discussion of the Durga complex, for example, I noted that similar underlying conflicts could be played out either through controversial and conflicted *tantric* rites or through a set of related but less disturbing symbols. I suggested that it would be interesting to compare the psychological backgrounds of those who prefer one set of rituals to another. In many ways, Obeyesekere begins to carry out this sort of work, and for this we are greatly in his debt.

Nonetheless, from my point of view, Obeyesekere never really breaks away, as he says he intends to, from classical Freudian theory (1990:xx–xxi). The theoretical strategy of *The Work of Culture* is the same in all its essentials as that adopted by Kakar in *The Inner World*. Indeed, at critical points in his argument Obeyesekere draws directly on Kakar (Obeyesekere 1990:32,64–65,66,83).[2]

Rather than offer us a genuine reshaping of psychoanalytic theory, Obeyesekere highlights aspects of the classical theory he finds applicable to South Asia, and he discards other elements of the theory as culture-bound (1990:xx). When even the relevant aspects of psychoanalytic theory imply pathology in South Asian culture, Obeyesekere, like Kakar, has recourse to the notion of a cultural idiom of expression or a separate level of cultural support (e.g., 1990:66–67). This cultural support for a characteristic type of psychological stance is said to redeem the emotional conflict in question from pathology. Yet the psychological roots of the cultural idiom remain a mystery. Cultural support thus serves merely as an explanatory escape valve, permitting universalist psychoanalytic explanations to remain in place while seeming to moderate the pathological implications of that theory. Nonetheless, because basic psychoanalytic theory is never really modified, its pathological implications return, despite Obeyesekere's best efforts to banish them.[3]

For example, Obeyesekere explicitly identifies the Hindu oedipal configuration as the negative Oedipus complex of Freud (1990:75–105). As with Carstairs and Kakar, there is said to be a homosexually based submission to the father leading to adult fears of impotence. Moreover, the related symbiotic identification with the mother is never overcome, and thus the dichotomy between wife and whore can never be reconciled (1990:30–31,75–105). The grounding of the Hindu negative Oedipus complex is the alleged sexual seduction of the Hindu boy by his mother based on the symbiosis between them (1990:32,64–65,81–85). In depicting all this, Obeyesekere relies directly on Kakar. According to Obeyesekere, this pattern of socialization in turn is rooted in the Hindu cultural emphasis on close group activity within the joint family and caste (1990:81–85).

Because it is supported by group-oriented cultural values, the negative oedipal configuration is said by Obeyesekere to be normal and appropriate to the Hindu context (1990:81–88). But what prevents us from returning to the classical position and viewing this group-orientation as itself the product of a dangerous, unresolved maternal symbiosis as well as of a pathological negative oedipal stance? Indeed, despite himself, Obeyesekere does effectively return to such a pathologizing position.

On the issue of psyche and culture, Obeyesekere draws inspiration from Wittgenstein's notion of "family resemblance" (1990:xx–xxi, 89–103)—a position reminiscent of my discussion above of a "cousinship" between the nuclear complexes in different cultures. The problem is that Obeyesekere never really follows up his broader theoretical goal with a real reworking of the underlying psychological framework. Whereas Obeyesekere argues that the players in the Hindu nuclear complex potentially involve a wide range of family members, he never brings what I call the in-law mothers directly into his theory. Instead, the felicitous notion of "degrees of symbolic remove" from underlying conflicts is made to explain more than it really can.

For Obeyesekere, "the work of culture" draws us toward a greater and greater degree of remove from underlying conflict. Thus, Obeyesekere focuses on the progressive character of collective cultural symbolism. Yet this notion preserves the artificial dichotomy between psychology and culture—a dichotomy Obeyesekere claims to be subverting (1990:24). All movement toward resolution is put onto the cultural level while the underlying, universal theory of psychological conflict, which focuses on pathology, is preserved. In other words, Obeyesekere argues that while Hindus may have a negative Oedipus complex, Hindu cultural support works to transform it in a healthy direction (1990:81–88). In my view, however, a real subversion of artificial distinctions between psyche and culture would show how the same movement toward resolution takes place at both levels. This in turn would demand a genuine cultural reshaping of the underlying psychological theory.

By putting the movement toward collective resolution entirely onto a distinct cultural level, Obeyesekere misses the chance to incorporate the notion of a group-oriented resolution directly into the theory of early psychological development in Hindus. I have argued above that there is a distinctive and group-oriented Hindu path to early psychological resolution. This reshaped theory of the Hindu psyche is linked in a circle of causation to the conscious Hindu cultural emphasis on the group. We miss all this, however, if we confine our interest in the group to a separate cultural level— a level that somehow mitigates the impact of conflicts that are pathological in their individualist Western context (e.g., the negative Oedipus complex). It is not that the Hindu cultural preference for groups makes the negative Oedipus complex acceptable. Rather, this Hindu cultural norm is a clue to the fact that something very different from the positive *or* negative Oedipus complex is going on in early Hindu psychological development.

Let me give an example here of how these difficulties in Obeyesekere's theoretical approach are reflected in his analysis of myth and ritual. Obeyesekere offers an extended and insightful analysis of the myth and ritual of the Hindu goddess Pattini (1990:28–40). At the climax of that myth, Pattini actually tears off one of her breasts and hurls it into a town, destroying the wicked residents within it.

The curious thing about Obeyesekere's analysis of the Pattini myth and ritual is the radical distinction he creates between two aspects of the myth's symbolic meaning. On the one hand, Obeyesekere shows that at the psychological level the myth and ritual revolve around unconscious conflicts over impotence, castration, and the wife/whore dichotomy. Obeyesekere then traces these unconscious conflicts to maternal symbiosis and the negative Oedipus complex (1990:30–33,75–105). On the other hand, Obeyesekere identifies a second level of symbolic meaning centering on conscious cultural ideas about kingly and divine justice. According to Obeyesekere, these conscious cultural themes about justice "have nothing to do with the core psychological conflict" (1990:33).

Obeyesekere then goes on to discuss the climactic moment of the myth—Pattini's ripping out of her own breast and her use of it as a terrible, destructive weapon. For Obeyesekere, this tearing out of the breast is a complex equivalent of castration (1990:36–39). As Obeyesekere notes, however, the myth does not end with Pattini's great sacrifice. After her furious and painful assault on the wicked city, Pattini's compassion is restored by the community of cowherds. The members of the cowherds' community achieve this by rubbing cooling butter on the burning wound left by Pattini's sacrifice of her breast (Obeyesekere 1990:38).

It is important that Obeyesekere sees no unconscious psychological significance in the myth's touching denouement. For Obeyesekere, the healing of Pattini's terrible wound by a group of compassionate cowherds responds only to the conscious, cultural sense that justice demands some consolation or recompense for Pattini's great sacrifice. Moreover, as noted, Obeyesekere has said that this concern for kingly and divine justice has "nothing to do with the core psychological conflict" depicted in the myth, i.e., the conflict involving castration and the negative Oedipus complex (1990:33).

I cannot agree with Obeyesekere here. Indeed, in the preceding chapters I have laid out a culturally distinctive path of psychic resolution in which a central theme is the healing and restoration of self-castration by an association between the sacrificer and the group. To my mind, the healing and calming action of the community of cowherds toward Pattini represents this same theme and thus reveals a vital aspect of the myth's unconscious meaning.

Unfortunately, by confining the myth's concern with healing to the adult, conscious, and collective level, Obeyesekere effectively walls off his core psychological conflicts from serious rethinking. What we get instead is a rehashing of classic Freudian theory, the most pathological elements of which (the negative Oedipus complex) are identified with the South Asian case. These pathological themes, moreover, are now separated from the modes of resolution (namely, positive oedipal ones) to which they are connected in the West, and no real alternative form of resolution is available as a replacement. However much cultural approval for the negative Oedipus complex is detected, there is no real theoretical explanation of how the pathology built into the classical picture of this psychological stance is overcome. What is needed, then, is a reading of the conscious and progressive level of the myth that will allow a reconstruction of the culturally distinctive pattern of psychological resolution that is the myth's unconscious source. Without such a theoretical reshaping, the tendency of the underlying universal psychology to pathologize non-Western cultures is bound to reassert itself.

These theoretical difficulties in Obeyesekere's approach can be seen in the fascinating case history of Abdin at the beginning of the book (Obeyesekere 1990:3–24). Abdin hangs his body on hooks in the temple of the god Kataragama. He also practices rites of bodily mutilation and possession in worship of the goddess Kali. Obeyesekere presents this exciting case study with great insight and sensitivity. He successfully shows how Abdin's personal history of conflict, particularly with his father, has written itself into both his ritual activity and his pattern of work. In a striking and fascinating episode, Obeyesekere shows how Abdin undergoes a psychogenic paralysis rooted in guilt when he temporarily abandons his ritual hanging on hooks after the death of his father. Obeyesekere was able to understand the roots of the paralysis and encouraged Abdin to worship again in Kataragama's temple as a way of coming to terms with the loss of his father. When Abdin did so, his paralysis lifted.

Obeyesekere contrasts the relatively regressive character of Abdin's ritual activity and personal life with the more progressive character of the ideal-typical female ascetics in his study (1990:11–15,19–23,68). For Obeyesekere, the decisive difference is that the female ascetics eventually transcend their conflicted episodes of demon attack and move toward an adaptive ritual stance. Abdin, on the other hand, is struck by symptomatic paralysis when he gives up his ritual. For Obeyesekere, this contrast is emblematic of the difference between the potentially progressive or regressive character of ritual.

I think Obeyesekere successfully shows that there is a significant difference between Abdin's level of conflict and the level of conflict of the typical female ascetic. On the other hand, Obeyesekere tends to underplay significant progressive aspects of Abdin's worship and life, and I think this is because Obeyesekere has no real theoretical way of grasping the psychologically progressive character of Hindu rituals of body mutilation. Obeyesekere interprets such ritual in classic Freudian terms whereas I have argued above that castration symbolism in Hinduism is a way station on a culturally distinctive path toward psychic resolution. Without this notion of early psychic resolution by way of symbolic castration, Obeyesekere's view of Abdin remains unduly pathologizing. Although Obeyesekere grants that rituals of body mutilation, like all rituals, must have a progressive potential (1990:14), his lack of an adequate psychological theory makes him overlook this potential when it is actualized in Abdin's case. On the other hand, Obeyesekere is able to adapt traditional psychoanalytic notions of mourning to the basic pattern of female ascetic ritual, and this makes it easier for him to conceptualize the progressive character of their practice (1990:11).

It is true that when Abdin temporarily gave up his hanging on hooks, a symptom was substituted for a symbol—Abdin was paralyzed. For Obeyesekere, this is decisive proof of the regressive character of Abdin's ritual activity. However, Obeyesekere records, but greatly minimizes, a clear movement of Abdin toward psychological resolution. After the paralysis incident, Abdin's worship of Kataragama continued, his paralysis disappeared, and his hanging on hooks became only occasional (1990:10). Moreover, for the first time, Abdin was able to steadily work at an occupation (1990:11). With great insight Obeyesekere attributes Abdin's less compulsive practice of hanging on hooks to Obeyesekere's own role as a kind of de facto analyst/father—and I think correctly so (1990:232). Yet Obeyesekere keeps his analytic emphasis on Abdin's fall into paralysis and minimizes Abdin's later move toward moderation in his ritual and occupational stability. I think this is because a focus on Abdin's progressive movement would bring to the surface the possible role the rites of bodily mutilation may have played in Abdin's improvement, and Obeyesekere has no real way of conceptualizing this.

The fact that Abdin practices Hinduism although born a Muslim significantly complicates the situation. Bracketing this problem, however, I want to give an example of how my notion of a group-based movement toward psychic resolution in Hinduism might shed light on case histories of this general type. (For Abdin's history, see Obeyesekere 1990:3–11.)

Abdin's father had two wives, one of whom was infertile and the other of whom had many children. Abdin was given as an infant to the infertile wife. When Abdin was four, the two wives quarreled, and Abdin's adoptive mother left the house, taking Abdin with her. Abdin began his body mutilation rites in worship of the goddess Kali when he returned as an adult to live near the home of his father and "second mother." Obeyesekere sees this return to the natal family as reactivating Abdin's puzzlement over his identity. This puzzlement, Obeyesekere says, aggravates the deeper problem—Abdin's unresolved identification with his adoptive mother. This feminine identification has led to psychic impotence. According to Obeyesekere, Abdin's confusions of identity prompt him to strongly repudiate his masculinity through symbolic castration before the goddess who possesses him. Abdin thus regressively retreats from conflict by embracing his feminine identification and receives ritual power in exchange.

In Obeyesekere's view, Abdin's "second mother" (technically his natural mother) is important only insofar as she further aggravates Abdin's confused failure to break the identification with his adoptive mother. From my viewpoint, however, Abdin's worship of Kali can be understood as an attempt to draw himself away from the mother with whom he has been isolated for years by worshiping a symbolic in-law mother (i.e., Kali). That is, Abdin is attempting a psychological reconciliation with his larger family, to whose location he has just returned, through the worship of a goddess who often (as I have shown above) represents the break from the natural mother in favor of an immersion in the larger family group. Thus, contrary to Obeyesekere, Abdin's symbolic castrations are actually an attempt to regain his masculinity rather than representing a repudiation of it. In the Hindu pattern I outlined above, symbolic castration and identification with Kali represent a repudiation of the incestuous tie to the "real" mother in favor of a sublimated movement toward the other mothers and eventually toward the family's group of fathers. Abdin's early shift of mothers as well as his expulsion from the larger household and the consequent isolation with a single mother mean that the group solution is available to him only tenuously and only after long personal and ritual "work." Nonetheless, Abdin's heavily conflicted situation must not blind us to the essentially progressive nature of his ritual activity. In worshiping Kali, Abdin is actually attempting a psychological movement away from his "main" mother and toward a more mature participation in the larger family group. This makes Abdin more, and not less, masculine and helps account for the positive changes in Abdin that Obeyesekere fleetingly reports but greatly underplays.

A final illustration of the difficulties in Obeyesekere's approach can be found in his brief comparison of South Asian material with Gilbert Herdt's extraordinary ethnography of the Sambia of New Guinea (Herdt 1981, 1987, Herdt and Stoller 1990; Obeyesekere 1990:61). The Sambia practice a form of ritualized homosexuality in which young male initiates for years confine their sexual activity to male-male fellatio. The interesting thing about this practice is that the ingestion of semen is conceptualized as the foundation of masculinity and not as its contradiction. After the years of initiation have passed, Sambia men move on to marriage and sexual relations with women, which are understood as an age-appropriate further development of masculinity.

As in the Hindu case, then, something we might traditionally view as contrary to the development of masculinity (castration symbolism in rituals of body mutilation or homosexual fellatio) actually seems to encourage masculinity according to a culturally specific model. Obeyesekere, however, cannot reshape the classic psychoanalytic view enough to account for these diverse cultural paths to masculinity. As a consequence, despite his emphasis on progressivity, he falls back into the pathologization of entire cultures.

Obeyesekere notes that both the Sambia and the South Asians are concerned with semen loss. However, the South Asian concern is generally displaced onto symbolic substitutes. So, for example, a Hindu might try to eat or drink certain foods in order to build up stores of semen. The Sambia, however, actually ingest semen in fellatio, and for Obeyesekere this makes Sambia ritual more clearly regressive than South Asian ritual. That is, the literalness of the sexual symbolism means that Sambia ritual is only barely removed from the underlying and dangerous psychic conflict, and for Obeyesekere this is the mark of regression and pathology (1990:12–15,68).

As noted, however, Obeyesekere's concept of symbolic remove, valuable as it is, is made to explain too much. The notion of symbolic remove from underlying conflicts depends on there already being a good psychological theory of the conflicts themselves. But because Obeyesekere's psychological theory is still essentially that of Western psychoanalysis, the nature of psychic conflict outside the West is misunderstood, and cultures are left to be compared according to a universal standard of explicitness that is bound to mark out some cultures as more regressive than others. That is, because Obeyesekere's underlying theory of psychological conflict is held essentially constant across cultures, psychological variation begins to be conceived of simply in terms of greater or lesser degrees of regressive explicitness. However much he might resist the implications of this scheme, the fact is that Obeyesekere's use of a universal notion of regression forces him to subtly pathologize the symbolically explicit Sambia in relation to South Asians in just the way psychoanalysis has traditionally pathologized South Asians in relation to the West. That is to say, by classifying the Sambia as symbolically regressive, Obeyesekere identifies the entire culture with a symbolic mode (regression) clearly treated as pathological in the body of his analysis (1990:12–15,68).

My analysis of renunciation as a culturally distinctive form of defense (see especially the conclusion of chapter 6) gives some indication of a way out of this dilemma. In my view, Hindu myths are explicit compared to Western cultural symbolism not because they are dangerously close to the underlying conflicts but because psychological conflict in India is actually structured differently than in the West. In the West, infantile desires are repudiated and forgotten for the sake of a caretaker's loving demands. In India, infantile desires are recalled and overtly sacrificed for the sake of full and honored participation in the life of a group.

I think the explicitness of the Sambia case in comparison to the South Asian material may be explainable in terms of the culturally distinctive shape of conflict in Melanesia. In an analysis of Malinowski's Melanesian material, I have identified a distinctive psychological pattern I call *polysexualization* (Kurtz 1991). In polysexualization, infantile desires are overcome through a collective seduction of the child into more mature forms of pleasure. The Sambia practice of collective fellatio as a way of pulling initiates out of incestuous attachments and toward a later state of heterosexual marriage can thus be seen as an enactment of polysexualization. Rather than being regressive, such concrete group seduction is actually a culturally distinctive strategy for promoting developmental progression.

Thus, in place of Obeyesekere's universal category of regression, which cannot help but make some cultures seem more regressive and thus more pathological than others, I propose a scheme based on fundamentally different types of psychological conflict and resolution. In Obeyesekere's scheme variation is by degree, and thus some cultures are advantaged over others. In my scheme, variation is by type, and each culture therefore possesses its own appropriate path to maturity. While some of these culturally distinctive developmental patterns may make underlying conflict more explicit, they are not, for that reason, more regressed. I do think that regression is a useful concept for identifying degrees of symbolic remove from underlying conflict. For me, however, the notion of regression only makes sense against the background of a given developmental theory. Thus, the concept of regression must be deployed as a tool for analyzing conflicts *within* a given culture's unique path of development. Comparisons of entire cultures on a universal scale of regression cannot substitute for a careful and very basic reshaping of psychoanalytic concepts as we move from culture to culture. In the absence of such reshaping, any given culture will appear to be a regressed version of the culture whose developmental theory implicitly controls the comparison. While Obeyesekere may not set out to adopt such a universalist comparative method, I fear he ends up doing so. From my point of view, the test of broadly cross-cultural comparison reveals the limitations of Obeyesekere's theoretical framework. Despite his protestations to the contrary, Obeyesekere's approach continues to be dogged by the liabilities of psychoanalytic universalism.

Spiro

The problem of universalism and pathology in comparative psychoanalytic anthropology is posed with particular clarity by the work of Melford Spiro. The great value of Spiro's work is its unashamed universalism. While Obeyesekere's overt push against the limitations of orthodoxy stimulates us, universalism remains as a relatively hidden and distorting undercurrent in his writings. With Spiro, on the other hand, a frank defense of "dated" universalism is fortified by a mind thoroughly schooled in the best of contemporary anthropology.

Spiro's work is nothing if not polemical. His book *Oedipus in the Trobriands* (1982) is a cutting, relentlessly logical attack on the great anthropologist Malinowski, who presented what is widely recognized to be the first, most extensive, and most persuasive case for cultural variation in the unconscious. Spiro attempts a thorough rebuttal of Malinowski's psychoanalytic relativism, using Malinowski's own detailed ethnography to build a universalist case. Then, in the concluding chapter of *Oedipus in the Trobriands* (1982:144–180), Spiro broadens his perspective. Drawing on the lessons of the Trobriand material, Spiro introduces a set of general arguments in defense of the universality of the Oedipus complex. I shall now examine these arguments more closely. My critique, I hope, will be understood not as narrow disputatiousness but as a tribute to the power and significance of the case that Spiro has mounted on behalf of the universalist view. Spiro's brilliant and tenacious polemic demands and deserves a serious answer.[4] My response to Spiro, moreover, should prepare the way for a positive statement of my own comparative perspective in the following chapter.

As noted, Spiro reanalyzes Malinowski's classic Trobriand Island data in order to show that the Oedipus complex is universal. Malinowski (1985, 1987) had argued that Trobriand males rather than being incestuously attracted to their mothers and aggressively rivalrous with their fathers were actually attached to their sisters and aggressively disposed toward their maternal uncles. Spiro attempts to show, however, that the Trobriand sister and mother's brother simply act as symbolic representatives of the mother and father, respectively. This symbolic displacement is necessary, Spiro argues, because the Trobriand Oedipus complex is stronger and thus more repressed than is the Oedipus complex of people in the West.

Spiro's technique of comparison, like that of psychoanalytic anthropologists generally, is quantitative rather than qualitative. Unlike Malinowski, he sees not a variety of psychological complexes across cultures, each different in type, but one fundamental complex, varied only in strength or degree of repression. Clearly, my notions of a Hindu ek-hi phase and Durga complex come much closer to Malinowski's view than they do to Spiro's. However, my approach shares elements of both Spiro's and Malinowski's cross-cultural psychologies, but it combines these elements into a unique, systematic perspective. In order to clarify this, let us consider Spiro's comparative method in some detail.

In the final theoretical chapter of *Oedipus in the Trobriands*, Spiro allows for three kinds of cross-cultural variability in the expression of the Oedipus complex—variability in structure, intensity, and outcome. Variability in intensity is a major theme of Spiro's preceding analysis of Malinowski's data. Spiro therefore limits his concluding remarks to the questions of structure and outcome. Similarly, I have already addressed the question of variability by intensity in the body of this study, arguing, for example, that the early Hindu mother-child relationship cannot simply be characterized as an extreme form of narcissism and that, consequently, Goddess imagery cannot simply be interpreted as evidence of an unusually powerful mother fixation. Thus, in contrast to Spiro, I have shown the dangers of treating psychological variation across cultures as variation of degree rather than of kind. Like Spiro, then, I focus my discussion in this chapter on psychological variation in both structure and outcome.

By *variability in structure* Spiro means that the members of the oedipal triangle may, theoretically, vary across cultures. Rather than a triangle between a boy and his biological parents, for example, we may find a triangle involving a boy, his sister, and his mother's brother. This position, which is argued by Malinowski for the Trobriand Islands, is rejected by Spiro on empirical rather than theoretical grounds. Spiro does not hesitate to concede that the oedipal triangle is grounded in sociology rather than biology. Variability in membership and in social relationships within the household might indeed be expected to produce divergent objects of sexual and aggressive wishes among children across cultures. According to Spiro, however, such variability in the structure of the oedipal triangle is not to be found empirically. Spiro then explains this lack of variability by the fact that biological mothers and fathers are the key agents of socialization in the Trobriand Islands and elsewhere.

Thus, while Spiro finds diversity of structure possible in theory, it appears to him to be absent in fact. This is a neat yet questionable resolution of a paradox. Perhaps this finding is due not to universal features of household composition or child-rearing techniques but to the fact that variability is from the outset conceived of merely as a variability of membership in the classic oedipal triangle. Even Malinowski preserves the notion of a triangle, simply substituting the sister and mother's brother for the mother and father. If, however, variability in structure is taken to refer to something beyond mere shifts in the membership of a universal triangle, then the way is open to recognize the real sources of cross-cultural difference in the structure of the psyche.

In his final chapter, Spiro argues at length and, I think, persuasively for the universality of an incestuous attachment between mother and son. He further argues that the role of the father as consort of the mother must inevitably arouse aggressive feelings of rivalry from the incestuously attached son. Given all this, Spiro asks, how could the Oedipus complex possibly *not* be universal? I think my work on the Hindu psyche provides an answer to this question. I do not cast doubt on the idea of an incestuous attachment between mother and son; my work, in fact, is premised on the existence of this attachment and on the corresponding need to break it. Furthermore, I allow for feelings of rivalrous hostility from the son toward the father, which are seen very clearly, for example, in the myth of Ganesh, who loses his head while trying to keep his father out of his mother's bath. Nonetheless, in Hindu India the incestuous attachment between son and mother and the rivalrous hostility between son and father are set in a unique social-psychological context, one that takes us far beyond a mere triangle and that entails not merely differences in the number or nature of the triangle's members but differences in fundamental principles of interaction.

In my discussion of the Durga complex, I noted that contact with the father is relatively limited during the oedipal period (from the third to early in the sixth year), the time when the heightening of genital sexuality brings to the fore the male child's incestuous attachment to the mother in a phallic mode. In traditional Hindu India, the main barrier between the child and his mother at this time is not the father but the in-law mothers. These women, moreover, are not primarily rivals of the child for the love of the mother. Rather, they are rivals of the mother for the love of the child.

As in the classic Oedipus complex, the child does experience the efforts of the in-law mothers to break his singular attachment to the mother as an attempt at castration. Since he wants the mother with his newly discovered penis, the customary distancing between mother and child demanded by the in-law mothers is interpreted as a threat to that same penis. Yet the perceived attempt at castration stems more from the jealous love of would-be mothers for the child than from the rivalrous claim of another man upon the mother. This was seen in the myth where the many goddesses that spring from the mouth of Durga threaten to turn on the goddess herself until they are placated by the gift of Shiva's "vegetarian" testicles.

The myth of Krishna's dance with the gopīs is also pertinent here. The problem for Krishna is how to sport with Radha without arousing the jealousy of the other gopīs. The solution involves a multiplication of his self until he can be a companion to all the gopīs as well as a transformation of simple lust into a more divine sort of love. Thus, again, the Hindu pattern is to break the incestuous attachment to the mother by interposing not a rival of the child for the mother but a group of rivals of the mother for the child. This in turn entails a different resolution altogether from that found in the Oedipus complex. The Hindu son gives up his immature genital attachment to the mother in return for the more sublime satisfaction of being immersed in a group of mothers. Moreover, the boy child's renunciation of incestuous genital strivings for the mother, followed by his more mature immersion in a group of mothers, is symbolized as a voluntary castration followed by a phallic restoration. This symbolic pattern is not a record of unresolved pathology but the signpost of a culturally unique path of developmental advance.

The Hindu boy's entrance into the world of men, which follows the early, phallic phase of the Durga complex, is irrevocably shaped by the early outcome of the Durga complex. While the father does represent a more classically "oedipal" rival of the son for the sexual attention of the mother, a great deal of the son's incestuous attachment to the mother has already been broken by the interaction with the in-law mothers during the resolution of the early Durga complex. This, then, sets the tone for the son's response to the father in the late Durga phase. His rivalrous hostility is resolved by a sexual renunciation—a self-castration—followed by a phallic restoration in the context of his immersion in the group of men that follows the model of his earlier relations with the family's collective mothers.

Thus, even though my model retains the classical notion of an incestuous attachment to the mother and a rivalrous hostility to the father (to which Spiro also adheres), each of these stances are radically transformed by the larger social-psychological context in which they are embedded. Attention to this context, moreover, is possible only if we conceive of structural variation as involving more than a mere variation in the membership of a universal triangle. This means that attention must be turned to the interactions at the level of the group rather than exclusively to those between individuals. It also means that the basic processes and principles of personal interaction by which early attachments and rivalries are transcended must be considered variable *in kind* across cultures.

Clearly, Spiro's notion of structural variation conforms to his general practice of quantitative comparison. This is so because Spiro finds no structural variation at all in practice and because he allows in theory only for a shifting membership in the classical oedipal triangle. There is no place in Spiro's scheme for a fundamentally different kind of psychological complex. This adherence to a quantitative rather than a qualitative comparative method also holds true for Spiro's concept of variation by outcome in the cross-cultural manifestations of the Oedipus complex.

Spiro allows for three possible oedipal outcomes: the extinction of oedipal wishes, the repression of the Oedipus complex, and the incomplete repression of the complex. One of these three alternatives is said to be the dominant outcome in a given culture. While he does not say so explicitly, these three outcomes appear to be ranked according to their relative degree of health, with the extinction of the Oedipus complex representing both the most desirable outcome and the one most characteristic of Western cultures. I shall shortly turn to the problem raised by this value orientation. Right now I want to look further into Spiro's substantive notion of the three possible outcomes.

By *extinction* of oedipal wishes Spiro appears to mean a resolution of the Oedipus complex on Freud's classic model; that is, the boy identifies with the father by seeking out a woman who represents for him what his mother was to his father. This enables the boy to surrender his incestuous attachment to the mother and the consequent rivalry with the father. *Repression* as an outcome, on the other hand, means that the wish for the mother and consequent rivalry with the father are never really abandoned. They are simply pushed underground, emerging in the form of neurotic symptoms. While Spiro appears to reserve the outcome of extinction for Western society, he never assigns the outcome of full repression to any one society or group of societies. Although he speaks as though some societies do belong to this category, the only examples he gives involve societies he had elsewhere assigned to the other category of outcome, that of *incomplete repression*. Spiro devotes most of his attention to the outcome of incomplete repression to which, in practice, he seems to assign the vast majority of non-Western cultures.

Hindu India, in fact, is the first example cited by Spiro of a culture in which incomplete repression is the dominant outcome. Spiro uses Manisha Roy's assertion that the Hindu mother and son remain "highly cathected libidinal objects [for] . . . a lifetime" as evidence for his conclusion that the Hindu boy's attachment to the mother is neither fully abandoned nor fully repressed (Spiro 1982:166; Roy 1975:125). My treatment of this issue, however, suggests a different reading.

It is true, as Roy points out, that the Hindu mother remains a factor in her son's life far into his adulthood. In the joint family, she influences his important decisions and, especially in the early years of the son's marriage, his contact with his mother is less regulated by formal restrictions than his contact with his wife. Nevertheless, none of this need indicate an insufficiently repressed oedipal attachment. As we know, the resolution of the Durga complex enacts a destruction of early incestuous attachments, and this is a developmental process neither Roy nor Spiro take into account. Moreover, as noted above, the resolution of the Durga complex results in an ego of the whole that is at its symbolic root feminine. However, because this ego is composed not of a defensive negative oedipal identification but of a mature immersion in a group, the Hindu man's relative ease with his mother does not indicate a failure to break free from infantile attachments. Rather, this ease with the mother in the joint family ratifies his successful transcendence of an infantile attachment to her by way of a mature movement toward the group of mothers. Just as the young child learns to accept the fundamental goodness and ultimate authority of the mother-in-law (i.e., his paternal grandmother), the purest representative of the group itself, so the adult son subordinates his attachment to his wife to his respect for and acceptance of the ministrations of the new head of the joint family's women, his mother. Ironically, then, the man is able to be close to his mother precisely because he *did* move away from her as a child. Her importance for him derives as much from the way she sums up the group in her seniority as from the ancient connections of motherhood.

The difficulty with Roy's analysis of the Hindu family (1972) is that it uses the Western model of romantic love as its touchstone. For Roy, whose work was initiated under Spiro's supervision, the emotional contours of the Hindu family are decisively shaped by the wife's frustrated desire for a close romantic attachment to the husband. For example, according to Roy, a husband's closeness to his mother disappoints the wife and at first draws her closer to her husband's younger brother and later to a guru. Thus Roy continually refers to the joint family system as "aggravating" an already problematic attachment between the son and the mother (1972: 120,167). The contrast with my own approach is clear. Where Roy treats the emotional demands of the joint family as a separate layer of "social custom" intruding clumsily on universal psychological requirements (1972:120), I have tried to draw the group directly into the process of psychological development. Only by thus uniting an analysis artificially divided into social and psychological components can we overcome the tendency to see only pathology outside the West. Only by uniting the social and psychological levels can alternative pathways toward psychological resolution be conceptualized.[5]

This discussion of Roy and of Spiro's use of her work anticipates a critique of Spiro's central point about societies in which the Oedipus complex is incompletely repressed. In cases of incomplete repression, Spiro asserts that important "social and cultural" consequences arise. These consequences entail the emergence of institutions capable of accomplishing the work individual psyches cannot achieve of their own accord. In other words, when individuals cannot adequately repress their incestuous wishes and consequent aggressive rivalry, society must do it for them.

This is how Spiro explains customs like the separation of children from the parental household to live, for example, as in the Trobriands, in small "bachelors' huts" (1982:106–109). This is also how Spiro explains the widespread practice of painful initiation rites for children and adolescents (1982:167–171). For Spiro, these practices are society's way of filling in for the individual's incomplete repression of the Oedipus complex. For example, the separation of a male child from the household takes him further away from a situation of incestuous temptation for his mother and consequent rivalry with his father. Painful initiation rites, often involving cuts to the body and even directly to the penis, strengthen castration anxiety and thus heighten repression.

Most often, Spiro speaks of these social practices as heightening repression or simply physically removing a boy from temptation. On occasion, however, Spiro hints that these social practices might actually promote the extinction of oedipal wishes (1982:169). On this score, however, he is ambiguous and makes no concrete assertions. I think that Spiro is prevented from following out this line of thought by his adherence to an artificial distinction between the psychological and social levels.

By assuming a universal psychological complex, Spiro makes it impossible to envisage any form of psychic resolution other than that known in the West. All cultural differences are thus conceptualized as varying degrees of incompleteness in the repression or extinction of oedipal desires. This is the quantitative comparative method in its purest form. With a universal psychological underpinning thus established, undeniable variation in social or cultural institutions is taken as a kind of external aggravation (as with Roy) or support of some general process. While Spiro sometimes speaks as though social institutions promote psychic *resolutions* rather than merely support or reinforce universal psychological processes, he fails to follow out this line of thought. This is because such speculation would raise the possibility of many roads to psychic resolution, and Spiro is reluctant to introduce any serious modification in psychological theory per se.

I suggest that institutions such as the separation of the child from the parents and puberty rites do indeed promote psychic resolutions. Yet these are not resolutions of our Oedipus complex but of a wide variety of culturally varied complexes. Moreover, such cultural practices are only late and relatively visible examples of a social shaping of the psyche that is active from the earliest period of infancy. So, for example, while Carstairs and Kakar (like Spiro on the separation of the male child from the Trobriand household) treat the movement of the Hindu boy child from the women's quarters to the men's as an effort to break his incestuous attachment to the mother, they do not see that the pattern of group mothering found in the women's quarters begins this process and thereby shapes the pattern of psychic resolution that will occur later in the men's quarters. Thus, both Carstairs and Kakar exaggerate the traumatic impact of the rapid shift in the child's social setting. Where I see an early, gradual, and consistent movement toward maturity through the resolution of issues of the ek-hi phase and then of the Durga complex, they see a failure to break from the mother counteracted too harshly and too late by a traumatic movement into the world of men.

In an analysis of the Trobriand material set forth elsewhere (Kurtz 1991), I offer a similar reinterpretation of Spiro's point about the separation of the male child from the household. Where Spiro sees a social custom intervening at a late date to move the boy away from a mother to whom he is overly attached, I see a late example of movement toward psychic resolution that follows a pattern set in infancy. Spiro misses the unique cultural shape of the Trobriand psyche and exaggerates its pathological nature because he insists on distinguishing a prior universal psychology from social customs that merely intervene late in order to push and pull the psyche without ever mixing with and transforming it.

Inevitably, Spiro's universalism makes other cultures appear as less successful copies of our own. Unlike early psychoanalytic anthropologists, however, Spiro is relatively circumspect about this implication of his work. All too often, contemporary psychoanalytic anthropologists simply refrain from explicitly elaborating the value implications of their cross-cultural comparisons as though it were possible thereby to remove those implications. Spiro's way of understanding the universality of the Oedipus complex clearly implies that only Western culture is able to resolve or extinguish it. Other cultures, therefore, whether they are locked into full or incomplete repression, must be judged neurotic by comparison with ourselves. It may be objected that Spiro's emphasis on the use of social and cultural institutions to mitigate incomplete repression implies a way out of pathology. Yet this is not the case.

Spiro quite explicitly treats the need to construct elaborate initiation rites in order to back up incomplete repression as a serious drain on a society's resources. For Spiro, the need to reinforce incomplete repression, especially in societies with elaborate initiation rites

> significantly limits the options of these societies for choosing alternative (and perhaps more productive) cultural means for the investment of emotional energy and the allocation of social and economic resources. Moreover, inasmuch as a cultural focus of this type is both a highly elaborated magical response to unconscious wishes and fears, as well as a stimulus to the arousal of still others, it may serve to reinforce the skewed ratio of magical to realistic thinking found in many of these tribal societies. If so, this would account for . . . their seeming inability to evolve an alternative cultural focus (or foci) based on realistic (alternatively, secondary-process, logical, nonanimistic) thinking. (Spiro 1982:172)

Outside of this paragraph, Spiro never directly takes up the value implications of his analysis. Nonetheless it is clear that his position is consistent with that of Freud in *The Future of an Illusion* (1961a). Essentially, Spiro, like Freud, places all other cultures on a universal path of development toward psychic maturity, with our own culture conveniently perched at the top. While it may be so, the coincidence of this scheme with our self-regard constitutes grounds for suspicion.

I do not wish to argue that judgments regarding the relative psychological health of a given culture can never be made. Whether or not such judgments should or will be possible, however, they cannot be made on the basis of our current psychological understanding. This is because a precipitous transformation of our own developmental model into a universal standard has for too long a time blinded us to the profound cultural diversity of the psyche itself. It is only after our psychological theories have been transformed by an investigation of other cultures that universal processes or standards may possibly appear.

In my view, then, Spiro's implicit judgments on the psychological health of diverse cultures reveal a flaw in his comparative method. Although often remaining unspoken, these judgments emerge in his work from time to time, only to remind us that universalism is purchased at the price of a distorted judgment of others. The very reluctance of contemporary psychoanalytic anthropologists to make these judgments tells us something as well. It suggests that the motivation behind Spiro's comparative method is not ethnocentrism as such but a desire to preclude any rethinking of his fundamental psychological framework. This, it seems to me, is the critical point at issue in my differences with Spiro. It is not enough for us to try not to be ethnocentric. What is needed is a genuine reshaping of psychoanalytic theory according to changes in the culture that is the subject of our inquiry.

Chapter 9

Toward a Cultural Reshaping of Psychoanalysis

I conclude with a broad re-presentation of the approach I have taken throughout this book. Since the critique of Spiro in the last chapter has clarified the comparative implications of the Durga complex, I make no attempt here to recapitulate this central idea. Instead, to use a Hindu metaphor, I wish to ascend the mountain by another path. Going back to square one and moving ahead in the clearest and most general terms, I want to retrace the central theoretical movement of the book. This time, however, we shall travel chiefly by way of psychoanalytic theory, making minimal reference to details of the Hindu Indian cultural situation. For comparative purposes, I draw upon an earlier analysis of psyche and culture in the Trobriand Islands of New Guinea (Kurtz 1991). As with the material on India, the details of the Trobriand ethnography will receive only the minimum necessary attention.

My purpose is to make a clear and simple case for the need to culturally reshape psychoanalytic theory. After putting forth this argument, I shall come at last, if only briefly, to America. What implications, if any, does our reshaped psychoanalysis of non-Western cultures have for an understanding of American life? By way of suggesting an answer, I shall offer some concluding thoughts on the conflicts that surround career and motherhood for women in America. For the moment, however, let us return to basics.

I take as my starting point the long-standing impasse between psychoanalysis and anthropology. Today, a generation or more since the effective collapse of the Culture and Personality school, a small and committed but relatively isolated group of psychoanalysts and anthropologists continues to strive for some sort of integration of the two fields. In the meantime, the great majority of anthropologists have developed their analyses of cultural life with scant regard for psychoanalysis and often with an active hostility toward it.

No doubt this hostility is based in part on what psychoanalysts call resistance. That is, some anthropologists react negatively to psychoanalysis itself—to the uncomfortable truths regarding the importance of sex, aggression, childhood, and emotion that psychoanalysis claims to reveal. But I doubt this is the whole story. For anthropologists and others have long complained that psychoanalysis is essentially a Western theory, based on Western norms and rooted in a particular moment of European and American history. Understandably, then, anthropologists demur when they see in the outcome of so many psychoanalyses of non-Western cultures an account of pervasive pathology. Anthropologists suspect, and I think with good reason, that the implicit Western bias in psychoanalytic theory artificially forces us to conceive of other cultures as somehow stuck along a developmental path traversed with relative ease only in the West.

It seems to me that neither the psychoanalysts nor the anthropologists have reacted well to the criticisms they have leveled at each other. Too often, anthropologists allow themselves to be satisfied with a brief allusion to the cultural biases of the psychoanalytic approach. And while it may be true that psychoanalysis was created for sexually repressed Viennese hysterics, should this not prompt us to ask how a different cultural setting might transform the impact of sexuality or child development upon cultural life? Having highlighted the cultural particularity of psychoanalytic theory, the failure of anthropologists to refine their accustomed procedure and thus to develop an anthropology of emotion, sex, and childhood does seem to confirm the feeling of psychoanalysts that some deeper sort of resistance to the subject matter lurks behind the overt culturalist arguments against applications of psychoanalysis to anthropology.

On the other hand, the psychoanalytic side has never adequately addressed the problem of the cultural bias built into the theory, and this is perhaps at the root of the failure of the Culture and Personality school. Nowadays, a number of psychoanalytic anthropologists continue to frankly speak in evolutionary terms—without hesitation assigning non-Western cultures to lower levels of psychological development. More importantly, many, perhaps most, psychoanalytic anthropologists avoid the problem altogether. That is, we commonly excise the explicit terminology of pathology from our vocabulary. Often, indeed, there is an overt plea for tolerance and assertions that different cultures support different paths to maturity. Yet the problem does not go away, and this is because it is built into psychoanalytic theory itself. The implicit Western norms within psychoanalysis determine that theory's treatment of almost any issue, and the opponents of psychoanalytic anthropology sense this bias even where it is not directly owned.

So the impasse continues, and to my way of thinking it is a tragic impasse—tragic not only because there is so much truth on both sides but also because our failure to resolve this impasse has caused something precious to be irretrievably lost. We can sense the dimensions of this loss simply by acknowledging the enormous gap in the anthropological study of sexuality between Malinowski's early work and Gilbert Herdt's recent account of the Sambia (Herdt 1981, 1987, 1990; Malinowski 1985, 1987). For a very long time now, the great majority of anthropologists have gone into the field and returned with little or no material on childhood, sexuality, or the cultural texture of emotion. Quite apart from any question of unconscious resistance, I think the absence of a culturally sensitive theory of depth psychology has made the collection of such material into a kind of embarrassment to anthropologists, for nobody knows how to treat it within the framework of a nonethnocentric theory.

My purpose, then, is to help to overcome the existing impasse between psychoanalysis and anthropology, and I think the key to this is a profound revision of psychoanalytic theory itself, particularly in its application to other cultures. I want to find a way of talking about infantile sexuality, the unconscious, and the importance of childhood that nonetheless allows us to do justice to the particularities of culture. Central to my project is the thought that we must construct numerous, culturally distinctive paths of development where before we have tended to see various cultures making either tenuous or confident advances along a single, universal path to maturation.

Before returning to the problem of what these culturally particular paths of development might look like, I want to specify the aspects of present-day psychoanalytic theory that seem to me to be distinctively Western in character, for removing or reworking these Western elements has provided the essential opening for the cultural reshaping of psychoanalytic theory outlined above. If I had to put my finger on one culprit—one locus of cultural influence within psychoanalytic theory—I would say that our villain is love. Love is everywhere in psychoanalytic theory, even if the popular knock against that theory is its obsession with sex. Indeed, the problems of love and sex are related, for bound up with a psychoanalytic account of the allegedly universal vicissitudes of sex is an unselfconsciously cultural account of love. Let me see if I can make some headway, then, toward disentangling what I view as the universal and the particular in all this.

Of course, we know that much of the originality of psychoanalysis lies in its interpretation of the fundamental physical experiences of infancy—experiences such as feeding, holding, or elimination—as the beginnings of sexual life. It is important to emphasize, however, that psychoanalysis also sees the birth of love in infancy—or perhaps I should say the birth and development of the capacity for love. For Freud love is a kind of "normal psychosis" in which the beloved is idealized out of all realistic bounds (Freud 1946:116). Love, in other words, carries at its core a recollection of the time when mother and child were connected symbiotically in a union without bounds, a union wherein the beloved was both self and universe and wherein the beloved was everything exciting and good.

In a sense, the psychoanalytic story of development traces the complex path by which this ancient, thrilling, and unrealistically idealizing core of love is both tamed and preserved. The going gets rough when the leaving starts—when the beloved disappears and you realize she was never really part of you to begin with. Now it hurts. So the tough part is the rediscovery and acceptance of the mother when she does return and the development of the conviction that she will return despite the fact that her leaving means that she is neither a part of you nor an instrument devoted solely to your pleasure. For when the mother does return, there will be pleasure again so long as that pleasure is not destroyed by the bitterness of a love that brooks no disappointment.

To put it somewhat more conventionally, the capacity for love depends on the development of object constancy in the child. The mother who occasionally disappoints must be recognized as the same as the mother who returns, and gradually the child must come to believe that, in the end, it is the mother's return that tells the deepest truth about her. Having achieved this basic trust in the presence and concern of the mother, the child has begun to learn how to love. Now the disappointments can be tolerated. Now the temporary absence of sexual pleasure at the breast can be survived. And because of the development of trust, the eventual return and offer of the breast can be savored fully, unsullied by bitterness or by fear of abandonment.

So the psychoanalytic story of development seems to be about neither infantile love nor infantile sex per se but about the path by which these two are bound together. As the capacity for love develops, so develops the capacity for mature pleasure in sex. Indeed, what is compelling about psychoanalysis is its ability to bring into relation the fundamental experiences of childhood and the intimate vicissitudes of our adult adventures in sex and love. Much of psychoanalysis is therefore about the history of the interplay of love and sex, and a central goal of psychoanalysis seems to be a bringing of sex and love into proper relation to each other.

Of course, there is a great deal more to the psychoanalytic account of childhood than the discussion of early narcissism and the development of object constancy I have alluded to here. For example, there is the classic account of the anal stage, where the issue at hand is less the development of trust in the mother's fundamental presence and benevolence than a balancing of self-will with an acknowledgment of responsibility to others. And then, of course, there is the issue of phallic sexuality and the complexities of the triangular love affair between the boy or girl child and the two parents. Throughout all of this, however, the question of love remains paramount.

For example, psychoanalysis holds that the child gives up unrestricted control over its own elimination not only at the insistence of its parents but for love of those parents. The gradual strengthening of the child's belief in the fundamental benevolence of its mother and father allows it to tolerate frustration out of the conviction that something will come in recompense. Indeed, the mere joy of parents at their child's achievements in self-control itself becomes a sort of recompense, for the relationship of love between parent and child has now become a pleasurable end in and of itself. Similarly, during the oedipal phase the boy child abandons his quest for the mother not only out of fear of retaliation from the father but also for love of the father and fear of his loss.

So it is that throughout the psychoanalytic theory of development and inextricably bound up with it we find love. At all stages of development, the pattern is essentially the same. For the sake of its growing love for its parents—at the early stages, for the mother in particular—the child is able to tolerate the interruption of pleasure engineered or demanded by those parents. Indeed, eventually, immature forms of pleasure are altogether abandoned for the sake of the loving and beloved parent. And with each such sacrifice, the growing child's ego is consolidated through an internalization of this image of the demanding but also loving and beloved parent. Thus, in time the child moves toward independence in the management of its desires—for the parental demands as well as the essential confidence in the self and in the world that the love of parents conveys have been taken in and been taken on internally by the child. And I note here that the psychoanalytic schools of ego psychology, object relations, and self-psychology, no less than traditional instinct theory, assume and incorporate a similar account of love as an essential part of their narratives of development.

If love is so important to psychoanalysis, then what exactly is it? I don't plan to offer an exhaustive or conclusive definition of the psychoanalytic notion of love here, but I do want to add another element to those I have already mentioned. First of all, recall that love has its birth in the joyous oneness experienced by the child in its earliest relationship to the mother. We then learned that maturing love requires a sense of confidence in the devotedness of an absent beloved, for this confidence permits a partial recapturing of the fundamental and irrational ecstasy of fusion despite the manifest reality of separation. But what is it that enables the mother to convey to the child a confidence in the ultimate reliability of her presence and of the sensual pleasures that this presence provides? The answer is empathy. Empathy entails the mother's ability to sense when, how, and how much her child needs her, and in this way she is able to balance the contradictory necessities of pleasing and disappointing her beloved. By her empathic attention to her child's emotional state, a mother loves her child and teaches her child how to love in return.

It is just here, however, with the question of a mother's loving empathy for her child that the psychoanalytic notion of love runs into trouble—serious trouble—in its application to the understanding of non-Western cultures. Consider, for example, some generalizations made by Robert LeVine about patterns of child rearing found in many non-Western cultures. According to LeVine, it is quite common to encounter in such diverse locations as Africa, Latin America, and much of Asia a pattern consisting of the following four elements:

1. The infant is on or near a caretaker's body at all times, day and night.
2. Crying is quickly attended to and becomes rare relative to Western infants.
3. Feeding is a very frequent response to crying.
4. There is, by Western standards, little organized concern about the infant's behavioral development and relatively little treatment of him as an emotionally responsive individual (as in eye contact, smile elicitation, or chatting).

(LeVine 1977:23)

Putting this in a slightly different way, LeVine says:

We find a certain pattern of bodily proximity, feeding, responsiveness to crying, and absence of disciplinary training that looks "indulgent" to us, but without the equally "indulgent" maternal behaviors of smiling, eye contact, face-to-face smile elicitation, chatting, cooing, and kissing, that usually supply the psychological context in which we interpret a Western mother's "indulgent" behavior. (Levine 1977:23)

I think these generalizations by LeVine are very important indeed. To me they say that something quite different from our Western notion of love is at work in the basic child-rearing setting encountered in most non-Western cultures. For what LeVine describes is the absence of a loving empathy in the sense that I defined it earlier. In this pattern of child rearing, little attention is paid to the emotional state of the child, and there is thus no opportunity to train the child in the development of mature love by a carefully adjusted program of frustration and fulfillment. In conformity with this, LeVine notes that the pattern he observes entails little overt concern for the child's development. Even considering the situation from the point of view of Kohutian self-psychology, we see that something radically different is going on. After all, the smiling and eye contact that are so basic to Kohut's conception of healthy, empathic mirroring seem to be almost entirely absent here. What we find instead is a simple, continuous physical presence—a presence focused particularly on feeding in response to crying.

Now, then, we are going to have to begin to make some difficult choices, and we will have to begin some serious rethinking as well. However compelling the psychoanalytic account of development, it will be impossible for us to retain it as a universal model without consigning most of the world to a state of relative pathology. For this is the heart of the problem the anthropologists so energetically complain about. Psychoanalysis has a developmental norm built deeply within it that is based on our own pattern of child rearing—a norm that I think has a great deal to do with our notion of love. Since few cultures outside the West raise children as we do, they are inevitably understood to push their children awkwardly or not at all along paths more smoothly and speedily traversed in the West. Specifically, I think the absence of love as the fundamental organizing factor in child rearing outside the West has made other cultures appear to be failing their children on any number of counts from the perspective of psychoanalysis. And it is here, in the situation of early mothering, where the problem has traditionally been centered.

It is, perhaps, only a slight exaggeration to say that the whole of psychoanalytic anthropology can be viewed as a fairly limited set of responses to the pattern of early mothering identified above by Professor LeVine. Most often, the persistent physical proximity of child and caretaker as well as the frequency of nursing give rise to the analytic view that mothering in a given culture is dangerously indulgent. What follows is either an assertion that a break with the mother is never properly negotiated or the related view that a break with the mother is imposed only at a late date without proper preparation and with consequent traumatic force.

LeVine implicitly calls this view into question when he argues that what seem to be physical indicators of maternal indulgence are often unaccompanied by the sort of empathic interaction one would expect from an indulgent mother in this culture. Yet this lack of empathic interplay between mother and child is occasionally recognized by analytically oriented observers, and when it is, it is understood to be just as problematic as the seemingly indulgent physical gratification so often called to our attention. Indeed, from a psychoanalytic point of view, we might say that the pattern of child care described by LeVine indicates an unfortunate separation of infantile sex and love. The child is sensually gratified, even to an extreme, but without the gentle accompaniment of a love calculated to blend with and tame the unruly forces set loose by the free offer of pleasure.

Now, as noted, I sympathize with the view of many anthropologists that this sort of approach plays out a cultural bias built deeply into psychoanalytic theory. What I argue here is that the key to that bias is love. Psychoanalytic theory is about love and about the complex ways love and sex come together or are torn apart. But neither child nor adult life in most non-Western cultures is organized around love. Yet, if this is so, what does organize the experience of childhood outside the West? If socialization in non-Western cultures is to be understood as employing neither a surfeit nor a deficiency of love, how is it to be positively conceived of? I think the answer to this question may lie in a reconsideration of yet another aspect of love. I have already noted that the empathy characteristic of love is often absent in child rearing outside the West. What then of our earlier discussion of object constancy?

Recall that the child grows in its capacity for love as it comes to trust the constancy of its beloved. Temporary absence need not mean desertion for all time, and this is a lesson that has to be learned. The one who is loved loves, and because of this, she will return. But just here a question occurs. Why do we speak of "*a* beloved?" That is, why is there but a single beloved for the infant—specifically, the mother? I think this question is much the same as the question, "Why is bigamy outlawed in the United States?" Love, for us, seems necessarily to mean the love of one for one. Why should this be so?

The very idea of a constant and reliable love seems to carry with it a notion of individualized loyalty. If the truest love were not the love of one for one, then the loss of a given lover would cause little pain nor would it even be necessary to come to trust in the reliability of the beloved. On reflection, then, the notion of one-to-one love, so vital to psychoanalysis, seems to reflect the larger presence of the individualism characteristic of Western cultures.

At first glance, this connection between love and individualism may seem suspect. After all, the purest form of love seems to involve the coming together of two people, and thus, in a sense, the phenomenon would appear to be inherently social. Nonetheless, I think that love is profoundly tied to the individualism of our culture.

The anthropologist Louis Dumont speaks of our Western attitude as a form of "normative individualism" to be distinguished from the empirical question of whether we refer at a given moment to a single person or to a number of persons (Dumont 1980:9). Normative individualism understands the individual to be the referent of meaning—as reflected, for example, in the popular political notion that the state exists for the sake of the individual rather than the individual existing for the sake of the state. We might say that the psychoanalytic counterpart of this is the notion that the family exists for the sake of the individual and not the individual for the family's sake. Thus, much of psychoanalysis is about the complex path by which an individual must eventually separate himself or herself from the family to move toward independence. But what has all this to do with the seemingly social nature of love?

I would say that in the Western notion of love, as incorporated by psychoanalysis, we have a relationship in which the individual remains the normative center. We feel loved when we feel loved for our selves—for what is individual or particular in us. And thus it is that the empathic attention we discussed earlier is so important to love, for it allows the lover to recognize and respond to the particular qualities and emotions of the beloved. Thus, it follows that true love must be a love of one for one, for to be loved for one's unique self means to be loved in preference to another. For this reason there has always been the belief in psychoanalysis that a child needs and deserves the consistent attention of a single primary caretaker for some significant portion of the beginning of its life. For this reason as well, anything that precipitously disrupts this primary, one-to-one relationship has been treated by psychoanalysis as problematic.

Once again, however, we have reached a point where the ordinary application of fundamental psychoanalytic principles—principles bound up with our Western notion of love—have the most questionable consequences for interpretations of childhood and emotional life as experienced in many non-Western cultures. This is because in many of these cultures numerous caretakers beside the mother take a major hand in the early upbringing of children.

As a rule, psychoanalysts have not made much of this fact. Generally, the presence of alternate caretakers is noted, but these caretakers are treated simply as extensions of or substitutes for the mother. Thus, if, as is often the case, a psychoanalytic observer sees in the early physical ministrations of a non-Western mother an excessive indulgence, supplementary caretakers are said to continue this indulgence, reinforcing the essential trend established by the mother herself. At other times, however, psychoanalytically oriented observers do focus more directly on the presence of alternate caretakers, and in these cases the influence of such caretakers is most often taken to be deleterious. From this perspective, multiple caretakers are thought to confuse the child, preventing it from developing a necessary sense of confidence in the reliable care of its mother. In effect, multiple caretakers make it impossible for the child to learn true love—the love of one for one.

As before, then, we are presented with a choice. If we accept the psychoanalytic account of early childhood as universal, then we are forced to understand the presence of early multiple caretakers in many non-Western cultures as pathological. Should we reject this view, however, there would seem to be nothing to put in its place. Certainly, anthropologists have hitherto offered us little that could substitute for the current psychoanalytic understanding of phenomena such as the existence of multiple caretakers. Nor have anthropologists attempted to construct an alternative understanding of the early pattern of physical indulgence combined with emotional distance identified by Professor LeVine. It is at this point, therefore, that I have attempted to introduce something new.

My suggestion is that the way out of our impasse is to take the group, rather than the individual, as our point of reference. Now by this I certainly do not mean that we should ignore the thoughts, feelings, or intimate histories of particular persons, for I find this sort of study to be most desirable and all too rarely practiced. But I do think it is possible to take such intimate material into account while still opening a place in our conceptual schemes for groups as fundamental subjects or as basic points of reference. At present, psychoanalytic theory takes the individual as its normative subject, and this individualism is manifest in the shape and importance of love in psychoanalytic theory. But what would that theory look like if all of a sudden groups were able to play a fundamental part in it? By way of answering this question, I have detailed above and name again here some ways in which an orientation to the group might shift our understanding of some of the patterns of non-Western child rearing we have been discussing.

It seems to me that the constant physical contact between mother and child as well as the frequent, almost automatic, nursing in response to crying found in so many non-Western cultures are ways in which the child is given some initial encouragement to trust in the ultimate security and benevolence of its world. Yet it is precisely the emotional distance characteristic of such mothering that prevents the child from getting hopelessly entangled in this early relationship to the mother. The lack of individualized empathy between mother and child in these cultures, the absence of smiling response, or even of a feeding experience carefully calibrated to the child's precise emotional state, all act to create a sort of opening—an opening through which the group is able to enter.

I think that much of what is interesting and important about child rearing in other cultures has to do with the varied ways in which mothers subtly push their charges away from themselves and into the life of the group at large. Similarly, groups in different cultures have developed a set of varied strategies for drawing the child toward themselves and away from the mother. These strategies generally have very little to do with what we mean by love. There is no careful dosing of gratification and frustration by a single, involved, and empathically watchful caretaker. That is our way. Nor is the emphasis on the achievement of independence through an internalization of the beloved parent. Rather, the goal is a movement away from the mother toward immersion in the group. And while I think this movement is accompanied by an internal construction of the ego, that ego is constituted differently—its ruling images and processes are constructed by the group itself rather than by the individual parent.

Now I recognize that the phrase *the group* as I employ it here may seem a bit abstract and confusing. I have some reasons for adopting the term, though. First of all, I use it because I think that in the child's internal representations of and external relationships to its numerous caretakers it is their constitution as a collectivity that is explicitly emphasized. Second, I use the abstract phrase *the group* so that I can remain inclusive of the diverse forms taken by important collectivities of alternate caretakers in different cultures.

For example, I have argued that in Hindu India the most important group of alternate caretakers in early childhood is constituted by the mother-in-law and the sisters-in-law of the mother in the joint Hindu family. These women—I have called them the in-law mothers—act as a group to help break the early tie between the natural mother and her child. In the complex rituals and mythological interrelations among the collectivity of Hindu goddesses, we catch the internalized traces of this group's activity.

In the Trobriand Islands, on the other hand, I think a more diffuse group of collective caretakers carries on the early struggle with the mother for possession of the soul of the child. The action of this group, however, is focused by the child's father, who takes a large hand even in early child care. Later, the Trobriand children's play group becomes the chief collective counterpoint to the influence of the mother (Kurtz 1991).

In the scheme I am offering here, however, cultural variety rests not merely with the diversely constituted groups of alternate care-takers but also in the principles by which those groups engineer the movement of the child away from its mother. For example, I have argued that in Hindu India the chief principle of maturation can be called renunciation. In contrast to our own situation, where a child abandons immature pleasure at the forceful insistence of but also for the love of a primary caretaker, in Hindu India the child is subtly prompted, without direct demands or force, to initiate a voluntary sacrifice of pleasure. That sacrifice, moreover, is made not so much for the sake of consolidating the relation with the beloved mother as for the opportunity to move out of the orbit of the mother and toward an immersion in the larger family group.

In the Trobriand Islands, on the other hand, I think the central principle of maturation can be called polysexualization. In polysexualization, there is neither a forceful demand for the abandonment of immature pleasure nor a subtle prompting to unforced renunciation. Rather, the child is in effect seduced out of immature pleasure by the group, which imposes upon the child stimulation at a higher level of maturity than that to which he is accustomed (Kurtz 1991).

From the standpoint of the model I am outlining here, the psychoanalytic approach appears in a new light. Traditionally, psychoanalytically oriented observers of other cultures have sought out something resembling our notion of love. They have looked for the consistent but balanced attention of a single empathic caretaker, and, not finding this, they have been forced to develop an elaborate accounting of the pathologies of love outside the West. Most often, this involves an interpretation of early, unmodified physical closeness between mother and child as indulgence and the consequent notion that seemingly precipitous demands for maturity in later childhood constitute a trauma. What is missed here, however, are the many ways in which diversely constituted groups of alternate caretakers intervene in early childhood and, acting according to culturally specific principles, draw the child out of the immature pleasures directly offered by the mother. Thus, the forceful insistence on maturity characteristic of late childhood outside the West is less an unprecedented trauma than the rapid consolidation of a movement toward maturity that has begun many years earlier. All this is missed, however, if attention is directed only to the mother and only to the presence or absence of the maturational strategy built around our Western notion of one-to-one love.

Of course, psychoanalytic anthropology has never been entirely unaware of the importance of groups in non-Western cultures. Nonetheless, the orientation of non-Western cultures to the group has traditionally been viewed as one more problematic twist along the path of love gone wrong. As a rule, the focus on group activity has been taken as evidence that the initial symbiosis with the mother is never adequately broken—due, of course, to the strains imposed by some combination of early indulgence and late, traumatic frustration. In this perspective, the orientation toward the group is understood as a kind of displacement of the unmodified early maternal symbiosis onto the collectivity—evidence of a failure to achieve independence through a loving and careful dosing out of frustration and fulfillment by the mother.

What I am suggesting here, however, is that the orientation to the group, so common to non-Western cultures, is no mere continuation of the early symbiotic attachment to mother. To see this, however, we must come to understand the multiplicity of early caretakers in non-Western contexts as something more than mere extensions of the mother. Rather, the presence of alternate caretakers in many cultures acts in complex and varied ways to break the initial attachment to the mother and to move the child along a path to maturity whose outcome is neither individual independence in the Western sense nor a simple continuation of symbiosis and dependence. Just what that mature outcome may be depends upon a detailed understanding of the varied principles of development to be found throughout the world—principles like Hindu Indian renunciation and Trobriand polysexualization.

Having pointed toward a general direction in which I think a renewed psychoanalysis of culture can proceed, I want to address a question that may have been raised by my discussion of love. Perhaps the reader wonders whether I argue here that mothers in non-Western cultures do not love their own children. After all, however harsh or radical such a statement would appear, it does seem to be an implication of the position I have taken. Well, I certainly am not asserting that mothers outside the West lack strong positive feelings for their children. On the other hand, I do think we open ourselves to many difficulties if we simply translate these feelings by the use of our word and our concept of love.

For example, Margaret Trawick has recently given us a profound and sensitive account of "love" in South Indian Tamil culture (Trawick 1990). In her discussion, she generally retains the word *anpu*, which, if translated, would have to read "love." Now one of the chief characteristics of *anpu* is that it is by nature and by right kept hidden. Thus, while a Tamil woman may freely show affection for the children of her siblings and in-laws within the joint family, her strong *anpu* for her own children must remain unseen—particularly when her in-laws are nearby.

Now, if we take this strong but hidden sense of *anpu* to be love, then I think we would have to call it a troubling or damaged kind of love. For the truest love, particularly the love between a mother and her own child, cannot be kept hidden. Thus it is that numerous psychoanalytic observers have argued that the restriction on the display of maternal affection in the presence of in-laws within the joint Hindu family creates a dangerous emotional inconsistency for the child. If, however, we think of the emotion in question as *anpu* rather than as love, we remain open to the view that a different sort of rationale for the Tamil mother's reserve in front of her in-laws is imaginable.

My own feeling is that the restraint of Tamil mothers becomes meaningful and sensible when we shift our focus from the mother as an individual to look instead at the total functioning of the family group. At the level of the joint family, the children do receive a consistent sort of affection—an affection that comes from all the adults of the family and that is kept consistent precisely by the rules of restraint on relations between children and their natural mothers. And, however simple and straightforward this point may seem, the failure to take it seriously has been at the root of deep difficulties in the traditional psychoanalytic understanding of Hindu Indian life.

It must be emphasized, however, that the form of consistent affection experienced within the Hindu joint family group is not the individualized, empathic attention that makes up much of what we call love. Thus, as noted, the entire complex is best thought of as working according to *anpu* rather than love. Much of the work of the above chapters has been directed toward making sense of this consistent but distinctive sort of affection the Hindu Indian child experiences at the level of its participation in the Hindu family group. In my own analysis, I have used the North Indian terms *prem* and *kām* rather than the Tamil *anpu*.

What, then, can we say is universal or particular in the elements of love under discussion here? As to the birth of love in the symbiotic union of mother and child, I think it can fairly be said that the essentials of this experience are to be found throughout the world. But what of the lesson concerning the constancy of the beloved? I think that the pattern of child rearing often found in non-Western cultures does impart a lesson of constancy, but one that is significantly different from its Western counterpart. Early on the child learns to rely on the presence and bounty of its mother, but in a short time this sense of constancy is experienced and learned at the level of care by the group. Yet, the very nature of constancy begins to be changed and shaped by the fact that it resides first in the relationship to the mother and later in the relationship to the group. This makes impossible the quality of individualized, empathic attention essential to what we mean by love, and it gives rise instead to a fascinating variety of cultural principles by which affection and growth are shaped and maintained. The common denominator of these principles is their task of drawing the child out of the initial tie to the mother and into participation in a form of social life in which the group is the normative center. One might call this general pattern of development *separation-integration* in contrast to our own developmental norm of *separation-individuation*.

From this point of view, then, there is a core of truth in the tendency of psychoanalysts to detect in the non-Western orientation to the group the hint of a universal, early, maternal symbiosis. I would add to this, however, that the non-Western orientation to the group is not a pathological or immature regression to symbiosis but a set of distinctive, complex, and mature transformations of it; for the non-Western child does not reach the group without first breaking with the mother, and I have been suggesting here that much of what is interesting about child rearing outside the West is to be found in the complexity and variety of cultural principles through which the break with the mother and the subsequent integration of the child into the group are achieved. Thus, just as our own notion of mature love both tames and preserves a core of the ancient unity between mother and child, so, too, does the activity oriented to the collective so often found outside the West preserve, yet also depart from, the child's early sense of merger with the mother. Heretofore, however, we have seen this only "through a glass darkly," so to speak, for our vision has been clouded by love.

In sum, I am arguing for a cultural reshaping of psychoanalytic theory. Only by the shaping of culturally varied paths of development can we avoid casting the processes of growth in non-Western cultures as misshapen approximations of our own. And the key to this process of reshaping, I suggest, is a radical reconsideration of the place of love in psychoanalytic theory along with a deeper recognition of the importance of group-oriented processes in cultures other than our own. Keeping these thoughts in mind, I hope it may be possible to make some progress toward breaking the sad and longstanding impasse between psychoanalysis and anthropology.

Mothering in India and America

We may finally ask, what, if anything, does a culturally reshaped psychoanalysis have to tell us about ourselves? For example, the reader has no doubt noticed a link between the central subject of this work—multiple Hindu mothering—and a vital problem in contemporary American society. With American mothers increasingly committed to careers, how can they devote themselves as well to the care of children? Does group child care offer a solution to the dilemma of the working mother? Or does such group care shortchange the child?

This issue has already been taken up by Roland (1988:204–206), who offers a brief and stimulating comparison of the relation between career and mothering in urban India and America. Roland notes that American women are often caught between guilt over spending too little time with their children and a countervailing anxiety over neglect of their own careers. Roland then contrasts this with the remarkable absence of such conflict among most urban career women in India. For Roland, the conclusion is that the internal woes of American mothers with careers go far beyond what the realistic difficulties of arranging child care would justify.

How, then, does Roland explain the difference between the Hindu and American cases? Drawing on his notion of the Indian "we-self," Roland stresses that Indian women undertake their careers not for self-fulfillment but for the sake of the larger family. This greatly reduces the feeling of tension between the obligations of career and child care. Roland also notes that the contextually oriented Indian self is far more able to tolerate the shift between the very different worlds of business and child care than is the American self, which strives for a consistent life perspective.

While I agree with Roland's explanation as far as it goes, there is a danger that it may mislead. Roland's implication is that the American woman's conflict between career and mothering is not entirely called for and therefore could be greatly reduced by an increased orientation toward the group. In other words, there is a subtle message in Roland's analysis that if American women could begin to see their work less as self-fulfillment and more as a contribution to the larger family group, their conflict over career and motherhood would be reduced. Indeed, Roland marks out the Jewish, Mediterranean, and black communities in America as groups that already have the Indian orientation toward the whole, at least to a degree, and that therefore might presumably point to a way out of pure individualism (1988:xv,239).

In my view, however, Roland greatly underestimates the gulf between the Indian and the American perspectives, even if we include in the American case the tendencies of various ethnic and minority communities. It is not that Roland is wrong about the importance of the group in India. He simply fails to understand how very profoundly that orientation to the whole marks out the Indian case as distinctive from our own. Indeed, the differences between the Indian and American cases are deep enough to call into question any direct lessons the Hindu situation may have to offer us. Once again, the problem centers on the importance of love as the fundamental principle of child care in the West.

The Indian career woman typically arranges to have her child cared for by in-laws or by servants of the extended family. This provokes little conflict for her because it is already close to the norm of Hindu Indian child rearing. More importantly, as I have argued extensively above, this collective child rearing works precisely because it is *not* based on the one-to-one empathic link we call love. While the Hindu natural mother does need to provide a reassuring physical presence early on, her empathic dosing out of gratification and frustration is not a part of Hindu development in infancy and early childhood. Since the group plays an early and central role in prompting the child to voluntarily renounce the mother, it is relatively easy to rely on the group to free up the mother for a career. The important point, however, as argued at length above, is that the group role in child rearing is not a diffusion or extension of the love mode but works according to the culturally distinctive process I have called renunciation.

In the American case, therefore, a mere addition of substitute caretakers cannot reproduce the effects of Indian multiple mothering. This is because our basic principle of child rearing is love, and this depends for its function on an intimate, long-term, individualized empathic relationship. That is why the American working mother's conflict is so profound. To leave her child with another caretaker is to miss the chance to share and understand the daily unfolding of that child's distinctive character, and such sharing is both the central pleasure and the operative principle of American parenting. Traditional Hindu Indian parenting, by contrast, is actually undercut by stress on a mother's empathic attention to the distinctive personality of her child. Such individualized attention would discourage the movement of the child into the orbit of the group, and it is action within or on behalf of the group that forms the locus of personal satisfaction for Hindus.

Roland is correct, then, to trace the relative ease of the Indian career woman to the feeling that her work is undertaken for the benefit of the larger group. The important point, however, is that this group perspective runs very deep—so deep that it acts as a counterpart of and substitute for our Western focus on individualized love. Without a profound and fundamental change in our orientation to love, then, Hindu multiple mothering provides us with no usable model for overcoming the conflict between child care and career. While a deep change in the role of love in American child rearing may not be unthinkable, my guess is that, given our own cultural premises, a genuine transformation of American child-rearing practices and attitudes in a Hindu direction will strike most as neither possible nor desirable.

For good or ill, therefore, our cultural reshaping of psychoanalysis yields no simple blueprint whereby we can escape the difficult dilemmas of contemporary American parenting. We have emerged, however, with a deeper understanding of the cultural roots of our own conflicts, and this may be of some use to thinkers and advocates on all sides of the parenting question. Perhaps more to the point, it is hoped that our adaptation of psychoanalysis to societies outside the West will offer something of value to those concerned to understand and protect the future of families and communities in all parts of the world.

Notes

1. Introduction: God in a Stone

1. This is the story of *Dhanā Bhagat*, not to be confused with the story of *Dhyānū Bhagat* (see below, chapter 6).

2. The name Santoshi Ma means "Mother of Satisfaction," or "Mother of Contentment." For further details on her nature and worship see Kurtz (1990).

3. Here at the outset of my investigation I encounter a seemingly minor linguistic difficulty that is in fact linked directly to the central intellectual problem of the book. I have translated the Hindi word *bhagvān* as "God." The meaning of *bhagvān*, however, is complex. On the one hand, *bhagvān* refers to the concept of an overarching deity that encompasses within itself all the multiple and concrete images of specific gods. Understood in this sense, *bhagvān* has no specific image or form but is instead a formless source of differentiation.

For this very reason, concrete forms of god, such as Krishna or Shiva, are understood to be manifestations of *bhagvān*. Therefore Krishna might be referred to as "Krishna *bhagvān*," "Lord Krishna," or, more technically, "that aspect of *bhagvān* that appears as Krishna." (For a very useful discussion of the several dimensions of *bhagvān*, see Wadley 1975:116–121.)

When *bhagvān* is used in this second, more concrete sense, I have written *god*, without capitalization. The meaning here is thus "a specific god" rather than "the overarching God that encompasses all specific or lesser gods." This distinction is too simple, however. Hindi does not capitalize words. More to the point, the distinction between the broad and narrow conception of god in Hinduism is not absolute. Indeed, the important point is that the all-encompassing notion of "God" imperceptibly passes into the more concrete notion of "a god," and vice versa.

Thus, in the story of the farmer and the stone, the meaning of *bhagvān* subtly shifts between the broader concept of an overarching God, which holds the key to the story's moral, and the notion that the farmer is worshiping "a god" and that some specific form of *bhagvān* (Shiva, Ram, Krishna, etc.) actually emerges from the stone.

My choices in translating *bhagvān* as either God or god are thus merely suggestions about the level at which the concept is being pitched. In many cases the emphasis is relatively clear, but often either the word God or god would be appropriate.

This becomes important throughout the book, where I shift between discussion of The Goddess, in the sense of the Goddess whose form encompasses all particular goddesses, and discussion of particular goddesses. The all-embracing concept of the Goddess is not quite so abstract as the notion of *bhagvān*. Nonetheless, the shift between a notion of the broader, encompassing Goddess and her many concrete manifestations essentially parallels the relationship between the unified *bhagvān* and the many specific manifestations of *bhagvān*. Again, these aspects of "Goddessness" are not sharply divided from one another. Therefore, in a given case one might as easily write Goddess as goddess. Rather than focusing on any given rendering, capitalized or not, as an absolute translation, therefore, the reader needs to be aware of the complex way in which Hindus shift between related broader and narrower conceptions of deity.

4. As with the distinction between "god" and "God," or between "a goddess" and "the Goddess" (see above, note 3), the difference between the "natural mother" and the "in-law mothers" is not absolute. In the midst of the struggle to move emotionally away from the natural mother and toward the in-law mothers, the child senses a powerful distinction between these maternal types. From the perspective of maturity, however, the natural mother is transformed in the child's eyes. She is experienced less as someone unique than as another member of the larger maternal group. Thus, the natural mother ultimately becomes another "in-law mother." The child's shift from understanding the natural mother as someone with a distinct and unique relationship to himself or herself to a more mature understanding of the natural mother as just one member of a group is the source of the underlying principle of Hindu divinity. When "my mother" becomes "all mothers," the basis for an enlightened Hindu understanding of deity has been laid. This argument will unfold throughout the book.

As a marker of this complexity in the relation of mother and child, I will sometimes place the *own* in quotes. In other words, when I speak of a child's "own" mother, I mean this in only a limited and provisional sense, since from the more mature perspective all the adults in a Hindu joint family are equally the child's "own" parents.

2. Santoshi Ma Dissolved—The Goddess Constituted

1. Film in India is not a profane medium, because our very distinction between a realm of sacred and profane is not operative in the Hindu context (Wadley 1975:54–58). As conveyed in the story of the farmer and the stone, Hindus see the divine as all-pervasive. The "sacred" is everywhere and everything, and the higher one's awareness, the more evident this truth becomes. By concretely molding pieces of reality into images of the divine, one renders the latent divinity of reality recognizable and thus calls forth worship.

It is not mysterious, therefore, that Hindus should directly worship stone images or mere human children dressed up as Krishna, Rama, or as various incarnations of the Goddess (Allen 1976; Erndl 1987:91–95; Hawley 1981:13–14,60–61; Kapur 1985). Nor is it mysterious that Hindus should prostrate themselves before the movie screen when images of their gods appear (Dharap 1983:79), thereby transforming the theater into a veritable temple. I have heard reports of flowers or money being thrown at the screen in theaters showing *Jay Santoshi Ma* (Santoshi Ma's famous film), just as would be done to images in a temple. I have even heard that a man selling lemons (a food forbidden because of its sour taste to anyone worshiping Santoshi Ma) was beaten for bringing his cart too close to a theater showing *Jay Santoshi Ma*. The makers of *Jay Santoshi Ma*, who produce, direct, and star in the most successful mythological films made in Hindi, tell me that they frequently receive gestures of worship even off-screen.

2. Mayer (1981) has carefully analyzed the Hindu idea of *sevā*, or meritorious, disinterested service. This notion penetrates formal ritual as well as various types of public service. Central to the notion of *sevā* is that it be disinterested, i.e., performed neither for financial gain nor even for praise. True *sevā* receives money or praise only fortuitously, generally as a result of the generosity of someone who becomes aware of it and wishes to support it. Just as Hindus scrutinize and judge the degree of disinterestedness in the service rendered by their political leaders, so, too, religious practitioners are scrutinized and judged.

Because the film *Jay Santoshi Ma* is a commercial venture, the purity of its *sevā* to the goddess ranks low. Thus the film is criticized, and its controversial scenes are dismissed as commercially motivated. On the other hand, as noted above, the lack of any boundary between sacred and profane in Hinduism means that the film is in no way excluded from being a legitimate vehicle of worship. Thus, the commercial nature of the mythological film provides a temporary opening out of which exciting and generally discouraged depictions of divinity can emerge without entirely sacrificing their legitimacy, or relevance, for worship.

3. A number of scholars have recently criticized Babb's classic model (Brubaker 1983:159; Erndl 1987:337–345; Gatwood 1985; Iltis 1985:22–24; Marglin 1985). All point out that various unmarried goddesses can be described as benevolent or at least as both benevolent and dangerous. Indeed, frequently, though not always, an unmarried goddess's very fierceness is deployed to defend her devotees and thus constitutes a complex form of benevolence. Many scholars thus reject Babb's characterization of unmarried goddesses as "sinister" (Babb 1970:142; Brubaker 1983:159). Gatwood also emphasizes the dangerous aspect of married goddesses.

Gatwood, in fact, has come closest to setting up an alternative model. She clearly separates between unmarried "Devis" and married "Spouse Goddesses," claiming for each a characteristic form of benevolence and malevolence. In this, her model resembles the one I develop below. However, from my point of view, the utility of Gatwood's model is seriously compromised by her retention of processes based on dichotomies such as Sanskritic/non-Sanskritic, "great" tradition/ "little" tradition, high caste religion/low caste religion.

4. It may seem awkward to add *mother* to a term that already joins *wife* and *daughter-in-law*. The complexity, however, is a necessary one. All Hindu goddesses are referred to as "mothers," whether or not they are thought to have children of their own. As noted in the text, it is the motherliness of all the goddesses, of whatever type, that unites them and makes possible the kaleidoscopic shifts of identity among them. Indeed, it is the fact that any goddess can be referred to by a Hindu as a "mother" that calls our attention to human mothering—a central focus of this book.

3. Psychoanalytic Approaches to Hindu Child Rearing: A Critique

1. Philip Spratt's psychoanalytic study of Hindu culture and personality (1977) relies in part on Carstairs' observations and theories, supplemented by Spratt's experience as a long-time resident of India. I do not discuss Spratt at length because to my way of thinking his work is fundamentally consistent with that of Carstairs, Kakar, and Roland. Nonetheless, specialists will certainly wish to consult it.

Medard Boss, a Swiss psychoanalyst, has also written an extended study of Hindu culture and personality (1965). Boss' work is based on brief visits to India in 1956 and 1958. His observations are entirely consistent with those of Carstairs (Boss 1965:67–88). While he is not referred to by Roland, he is known to Kakar and does seem to have exercised some influence, particularly in his discussion of the allegedly traumatic "crackdown" instituted around age five (Boss 1965:72–74). Nonetheless, Boss' treatment of this and other issues is essentially identical with that of Carstairs, and it is Carstairs who seems to have most clearly and directly influenced modern psychoanalytic students of Hinduism.

2. Regrettably, this and the following chapters focus on the situation of the Hindu boy. This is because psychoanalytic treatments of early Hindu childhood, which I here rework, take the boy as their main subject. This is reflected, for example, in the psychoanalytic emphasis on the father's role in the so-called crackdown around age five, the Hindu father having more control over the discipline of his son than of his daughter. Nonetheless, the theory presented in this and the following chapters has great bearing on the situation of the Hindu girl, as the basic pattern of mother-child and group-child interaction described applies to both sexes. Moreover, I do explicitly treat the situation of Hindu women and girls at two points below: the discussion of the cases of Ms. R. and Shakuntala in chapter 7 and the discussion of Ewing's work in note 5 of chapter 8. It is my hope that the general perspective and specific suggestions offered in this book will prompt research that

directly and systematically considers the situation of the Hindu girl from a reworked psychoanalytic point of view.

3. I have been examining Kakar's early and programmatic work, *The Inner World* (1978). It is important to note, however, that the theoretical position of *The Inner World*, including its unresolved tension between relativism and universalism, is maintained intact throughout Kakar's later writings (Kakar 1982a, 1985, 1990a, 1990b; Kakar and Ross 1987).

For example, in an essay published several years after *The Inner World*, Kakar again takes up the theoretical problem of psychoanalysis and culture (Kakar 1985). As in *The Inner World*, Kakar challenges the notion that the intense physical contact involved in early Hindu Indian maternal care has negative psychological consequences. Such a judgment, Kakar maintains, flows from our Western preference for autonomy and is not applicable in the Hindu context, where cultural value is placed on close relationships. As in *The Inner World*, however, this position is undermined by Kakar's attempt to preserve traditional psychoanalytic theory. Kakar wishes simply to limit or moderate the theory's implications rather than to actively reshape psychoanalysis to fit a new cultural context.

As noted, Kakar begins his essay by questioning the basis on which we judge foreign child-rearing practices to be either excessively gratifying or dangerously frustrating. Because Hindu Indian children are accustomed to great stimulation and because Indian culture explicitly values close relationships rather than autonomy, Kakar argues that the traditionally heavy physical contact between a Hindu mother and her child is neither dangerous nor excessive (1985:442). The difficulty is that in Kakar's analysis the gratification/frustration dichotomy is itself never reformulated into or replaced by a positive, alternative principle according to which Hindu development can be seen to take place. Therefore, Kakar ultimately affirms the universality of the "developmental constants" posited by psychoanalysis and defines his task as setting boundaries to these constants or moderating their importance in a given cultural setting (1985:444). Kakar quotes with approval Erikson's dictum that the physiologically based stages of development vary in timing and intensity from culture to culture, but not in their sequence (1985:444). What I suggest below, however, is that the developmental stages vary culturally not in their timing or intensity but in their fundamental structure and content. I argue that the developmental stages and the principles according to which they operate have to be radically reformulated in every culture or culture area, and this is a task Kakar explicitly elects not to undertake.

As a result, Kakar can never really explain *why* Hindu culture places more value on relationships than on autonomy. This difference in value is simply taken to act as a kind of moderating boundary on the action of universal psychoanalytic principles. In contradistinction to this position, I hope to show that the Hindu cultural preference for relationships needs to be brought deeply into our psychological theory, leading to a reformulated "cultural psychoanalysis." Because Kakar keeps psychoanalytic concepts intact within cultural "boundaries," his maternal seduction theory remains central to all his later work (see especially Kakar 1982a:161–165,

1989, 1990a, 1990b:129–140; Kakar and Ross 1986:186–190). As I have shown in the above discussion of *The Inner World*, this theory of the dangerously seductive Hindu mother surreptitiously restores the traditional psychoanalytic notion that Hindu mothering offers an experience of excessive gratification—the very notion Kakar sets out to criticize.

Despite these unresolved tensions within his thought, it is not entirely true that Kakar proposes no positive modification of traditional psychoanalytic theory. Kakar does suggest that several contemporary schools of psychoanalytic thought hold the key to a more culturally sensitive understanding of the Hindu Indian psyche. This is because the work of analysts such as Mahler, Winnicott, Kernberg, Kohut, and Erikson focuses more on relationships than on control of an individual's drives (Kakar 1985:446). Kakar argues that there is a powerful congruence between the Hindu cultural devaluation of autonomy and the work of these recent, more relationally oriented psychoanalytic theorists.

The difficulty with this view is that contemporary relational models of psychoanalysis are pervaded by precisely the value on autonomy Kakar finds to be inappropriate for understanding the Hindu Indian psyche. While modern analysts do focus more directly than classical theorists on a complex and necessary set of interactions between mother and child, the emphasis is invariably on the way in which these interactions effect a development away from symbiosis and toward autonomy. If anything, it could be argued that because of its pervasive emphasis on the process of separation and individuation, contemporary psychoanalytic theory is even more individualist than classical drive theory. Indeed, Suzanne Kirschner (1990) has presented us with just such an argument. In her elegant essay she makes the case that early European psychoanalysis has been modified by theorists like Mahler, Winnicott, Kohut, and Erikson to express the highly developed individualism characteristic of Anglo-American culture. Elsewhere she extends her argument by focusing on the work of Kernberg and Kohut (Kirschner 1991).

Whatever our final judgment on the cultural and historical roots of changes within the psychoanalytic tradition, individualism in one form or another can be found at the foundation of each psychoanalytic school of thought. However much human relations are brought into the analysis, the emphasis is always on the eventual move toward autonomy. Thus, we must look elsewhere than to contemporary schools of psychoanalytic thought for the key to theoretical changes that can successfully adapt psychoanalytic thinking to the Hindu Indian scene. (For further remarks on contemporary schools of psychoanalytic thought, see note 1, chapter 5.)

4. This brief account will become less mysterious in the chapters below, as an alternative model of Hindu child development is elaborated. While I have noted here that the child comes to desire the mother as a separate self, this should not be confused with our Western notion of individuation. The idea of individuation builds on a core recognition of separate identities, but adds to this basic notion of separation the concept of a long, complex, and—in my view—culturally specific process whereby an individual self is fully formed. Thus psychoanalysts generally speak of a process of "separation-individuation." My description of Hindu devel-

opment, however, might be characterized as a "separation-integration" model. From this perspective, primary narcissism is overcome by way of the Hindu mother's distinctive combination of physical presence and emotional distance and also by the family group's efforts to pull the child away from its mother. In the early stages of the process, the child's sense of separateness and desire is relatively strong. Toward the end of the process, the child is fully integrated into the family group, and its selfish infantile desires are consequently renounced.

5. Minturn's work was published in collaboration with John T. Hitchcock (Minturn and Hitchcock 1966). In the first part of their book, Hitchcock provides the broad ethnographic background on the village where Minturn's child observations took place. Minturn then reports her child observations in Part II. Thus, I refer only to Minturn when discussing her work in Part II of The Rajputs of Khalapur, India (Minturn and Hitchcock 1966).

6. It can be argued that the physical and emotional stance of the Hindu mother, while unlike that found in the West, is nevertheless quite similar to a pattern of mothering characteristic of many non-Western cultures. For example, Robert LeVine (1977) has described a pattern of mothering widely shared by "tropical" societies, of which the Hindu case is clearly an example. In such places

> we find a certain pattern of bodily proximity, feeding, responsiveness to crying, and absence of disciplinary training that looks "indulgent" to us, but without the equally "indulgent" maternal behaviors of smiling, eye contact, face-to-face smile elicitation, chatting, cooing, and kissing that usually supply the psychological context in which we interpret a Western mother's "indulgent" behavior.   (LeVine 1977:23)

How can we approach the comparative problem raised by this broadly dispersed pattern of mothering? I think the key lies in the fact that most "tropical" cultures—indeed, most non-Western cultures—emphasize the importance of groups as opposed to individuals. As I argue below (chapter 9) and elsewhere (Kurtz 1991), the relative emotional distance of mothers in non-Western cultures provides an opening through which groups can draw children away from immature attachments and toward mature participation in group life.

The precise composition of groups as well as the principles of behavior used by these groups to draw the child away from the natural mother vary profoundly from culture to culture or at least between larger culture areas. For example, in chapter 9 I contrast the situation of the child in the Trobriand Islands with the situation (described below) of the Hindu child. In both Hindu India and the Trobriand Islands, the group intervenes to draw the child away from too close an attachment to the mother. In Hindu India, however, that group consists mainly of female in-laws in the mother's joint family. In the Trobriand Islands, on the other hand, the group that breaks the child's attachment to the mother is made up chiefly of the father, a wide variety of adults, and various young children of the village. Moreover, in Hindu India, the group breaks the child's immature attachments by subtly inducing voluntary renunciations on the part of the child. In the Trobriands, on the other hand, the group draws the child out of immaturity through an active and very physical process of seduction.

I argue that such differences in the composition and behavioral principles of the groups that exploit the opening provided by the mother's emotional distance link up to profound cultural differences in personality and ideology. Thus, while LeVine correctly points to a widely dispersed general pattern of maternal behavior, one in which Hindu India is surely included, careful attention to specific principles of interaction within this broad pattern and to the precise group context of such interaction will reveal the distinctive nature of a given society's "mothering."

4. Renunciation on the Way to the Group: A New Approach to Early Hindu Childhood

1. Only very recently has any recognition of the gap between psychoanalytic and anthropological accounts of early Hindu childhood surfaced. In a study of South Asian sex roles, Mandelbaum notes parenthetically that Kakar's exposition does not always square well with anthropological observation (1988:58). Nonetheless, Mandelbaum bases much of his study on Kakar's analysis (1988:54–62).

Seymour, in her review of Mandelbaum's book, takes issue with his adaptation of Kakar's work. Seymour maintains, without giving her reasons, that Kakar's view of Hindu socialization is not supported by her own field research (1989:225). This chapter uses evidence provided by Seymour, among many others, to complete a systematic critique of Kakar's theory of Hindu socialization.

2. There is, however, one significant incompatibility between Trawick's data and the picture of Hindu childhood I outline here. Children in the family studied by Trawick were weaned at about one year of age. This is much earlier than the weaning time reported by any prior observer of Hindu childhood, including observers in the South. There is ambiguity, however, in Trawick's account. This is because one of the men of the family (a Tamil religious virtuoso, who joined the family after his marriage) was himself weaned at five. Indeed, Trawick reports that many Tamil men have memories of being nursed up to age five or beyond (1990:171). Clearly, then, numerous Tamil families wean at ages compatible with reports from other areas of India. It remains to be seen, therefore, how typical the early weaning age of Trawick's family is of Tamil practice generally.

3. In a brief reference and without spelling it out, Trawick seems to place her own account into relation with that of Kakar as if her work and his were variations on the theme of emotional closeness within the family (Trawick 1990:101,271). In my view, however, the actual thrust of Trawick's work, particularly her extensive documentation of distancing mechanisms between "own" parents and their children, can be seen as an almost ideal typical depiction of the processes I outline below—processes notable for the problems they point up in Kakar's outlook.

It is most interesting to note that in a recent publication, Kakar himself, while discussing a minor symbolic point, refers briefly to an early, unpublished manuscript of a crucial chapter from Trawick's work (Kakar 1990b:137,154). Yet Kakar goes on to reiterate his earlier approach to Hindu childhood, making no further reference to Trawick. Clearly, neither Trawick nor Kakar have adequately recognized the deep challenge anthropological observations of Hindu child rearing pose to current psychoanalytic treatments of Hindu culture.

4. The principles and patterns of behavior I describe here are carried out most thoroughly in the joint Hindu family. Of course, not all Hindus are raised in joint families. In Hindu nuclear families, however, the same principles are at work if somewhat attenuated in effect (Seymour 1975:49,51). Moreover, because these principles operate best in the joint family, Hindus generally view this setting as ideal (Luschinsky 1962:46; Rohner and Chaki-Sircar 1988:69). Finally, a number of observers note that Hindu nuclear families often approximate the joint family setting by moving close to relatives and/or by using neighbors as supplementary caretakers (Beals 1962:13; Luschinsky 1962:121; Rohner and Chaki-Sircar 1988:69).

5. It may be possible to develop a theory in which Hindu purity/pollution practices are seen to ratify and reproduce the developmental achievement by which infantile sexual pleasures are renounced for the sake of participation in the group. At the close of the next chapter, I show how the meaning of pollution practices in a Hindu myth turns on the principles of caretaker-child interaction described in this chapter.

6. My view of the Hindu entitlement to "impose" differs from that of Roland. Roland notes the Hindu conviction that a friend or relative can be called upon at any time of day or night, regardless of convenience (1988:196–201). He also notes the tendency to presume on a relationship through repeated requests. However, Roland interprets these behaviors as powerful forms of intimacy or emotional connectedness.

No doubt, there is an emotional content to this sense of entitlement. Nonetheless, I think terms like "intimacy" and "emotional connectedness" obscure the roots of entitlement in Hindu child-rearing practices (such as intermittent nursing and the uncomfortable bath), which are important precisely insofar as they depart from what we generally mean by emotional intimacy. Thus, Roland assumes much more emotional mirroring in early Hindu mother-child interaction than does in fact take place (Roland 1988:230–250; see also above, chapter 3).

In this regard, it is significant that Roland emphasizes that Hindu intimacy and mirroring even among adults are largely nonverbal (1988:200,230–250). I think it is precisely the nonverbal character of so-called Hindu intimacy and mirroring that suggests that these terms are inappropriate labels for Hindu modes of relating. We must be cautious about reading Western patterns of subjectivity into nonverbal behaviors since such behaviors do not readily "speak for themselves" (Surya 1969).

7. I suggest that such discrepancies between relatively cool maternal care and more affectionate nonmaternal care are to be found in many cultures. As I argue here for India, these discrepancies probably serve to draw the child away from the mother and into the orbit of various groups.

For example, Robert LeVine (1966:126–127) describes a marked contrast between aloof mothers and actively affectionate nurses and relatives among the Gusii of Kenya. However, to emphasize the primacy of the attachment to the mother, LeVine notes that a frightened Gusii child still runs to his mother and wants to follow her even when she wishes him to remain with other children. What needs to be considered, however, is the possibility that the division in caretaker attitudes is directed toward eventually drawing the child out of his primary attachment to the mother.

Parin, Morgenthaler, and Parin-Matthey (1980:132–159) report dramatic differences in affectionate behavior toward children by mothers and nonmaternal caretakers. These psychoanalytic observers understand the mother's aloof behavior as narcissistic and productive of a prolonged symbiosis with the child. Again, there is no attempt to explore possible relationships between the mother's stance and the contrasting stance of the group. Perhaps these two opposed adult attitudes are part of a consistent, if non-Western, strategy for drawing the child out of maternal symbiosis.

As above (chapter 3, note 4), I emphasize here that a widespread pattern involving cool mothers and affectionate groups does not rule out important socialization differences between the cultures employing this strategy. For example, the particular composition of the groups that draw the child away from the mother differs widely from culture to culture, and this has powerful consequences. Moreover, the precise character of interaction between the group and the child also differs from culture to culture, and this too is of great importance. In chapter 9 I make a comparison along these lines, using data from both India and the Trobriand Islands.

8. Kakar's reading of the evidence is facilitated by Dube himself, who fails to appreciate the significance of his own data on the interaction between the child and the broader family group. This is because, like the psychoanalysts, Dube puts more stock in the physical fact of prolonged nursing than in the emotional character of the nursing relationship (Dube 1955:149).

9. Bhattacharyya briefly recounts these patterns of teasing and also reports the same phenomenon of delayed response to the child's requests I discuss at length in this chapter (Bhattacharyya 1986:146). The structure of Bhattacharyya's account helps to clarify the fundamental intentions of my own work. In the body of her text, Bhattacharyya explicitly affirms the positions of Carstairs, Spratt, and Kakar on the Hindu child's "spoiling" (1986:133–135). Her account of teasing patterns and of the characteristically Hindu pattern of delayed response to requests, on the other hand, is presented in a brief, cautionary footnote.

In my own work, I seek to transform the accounts of Hindu child rearing (Carstairs et al.) that Bhattacharyya affirms. The key to this transformation is not a denial of the facts presented by the psychoanalysts. Rather, I attempt to systematically integrate into the theory of Hindu child rearing facts that, until now, have stood as anomalous afterthoughts on the periphery of our knowledge. Thus, information running counter to the current consensus, which Bhattacharyya must relegate to a brief cautionary footnote, can now be placed in the center of the analysis, thus transforming it.

10. In a subtle and impressive analysis of Tahitian childhood, Robert Levy (1973:430–469) has argued for the existence of processes very like those that seem active in the Hindu case. Levy shows how an overt indulgence is subtly modified through an interlacing of microfrustrations at the breast and elsewhere. Thus,

according to Levy, the Tahitian child is made to feel as though he gives up the breast and other forms of infantile indulgence on his own. There are, of course, differences between this and the Hindu situation. The Tahitian baby seems to be granted more individuality and also to be the subject of more direct emotional interaction in its early years than the Hindu child. Moreover, the Tahitian mother tends to move away around age three, somewhat earlier than the Hindu boy is pushed into the more demanding company of his father.

These important differences are grist for the mill of comparison. The Hindu and Tahitian cases are hardly identical. Nonetheless, Levy's work does provide important evidence of a socialization process I suspect is very widespread and of which Hindu and Tahitian child rearing are important variations. In this larger process, physical gratification, which appears as unmitigated indulgence to Western eyes, is in fact dosed out in a complex fashion designed to subtly push the child toward maturation. I think we have only begun to identify and differentiate the types of microfrustrations that underlie the alleged indulgence so often attributed to non-Western child rearing.

5. The Ek-Hi Phase

1. Clearly, the reformulation of psychoanalysis I offer here takes as its touchstone classic instinct theory. This theory of the stages of infantile sexuality—oral, anal, and phallic—has exercised a powerful influence over the most important syntheses of psychoanalysis and anthropology, and it continues to play a major role in mainstream psychoanalytic theory. Thus, by carefully situating my own approach with reference to instinct theory, I can clearly specify where I join and where I break with classic psychoanalytic anthropology.

I emphasize, however, that my reformulation of the psychosexual stages is meant to serve as a *model* for analogous changes that must also be made in the cross-cultural application of more recent psychoanalytic approaches to childhood. Thus, in my discussion of Alan Roland in chapters 3 and 4, I presented the nucleus of a critique of the use of contemporary self psychology as a tool in cross-cultural research. That critique parallels my approach to instinct theory.

Kohutian self psychology, for example, is based on the notion of a "mirror stage" of infancy, the core of which is an empathic visual interchange between a single mother and child (Kohut 1971:117). The child sees itself, so to speak, in the responsive gleam in the mother's eye. As we saw, Roland's work, based on Kohut, attempts to treat the data on Hindu mother-child interaction under the rubric of mirroring. The project becomes strained, however, because empathic visual contact between Hindu mothers and children is generally absent and even avoided. Roland attempts to circumvent the difficulty by a problematic broadening of the mirroring notion to cover interactions that to many appear positively nonempathic. Roland also attempts to distinguish various types of mirroring—mirroring of dependency needs versus mirroring of striving for independence, for example. Yet, as I show in chapters 3 and 4, a careful consideration of the available data on child rearing calls the application of mirroring theory to the Hindu Indian case radically into question.

What is of importance in India is that what we think of as mirroring is positively *avoided.* The reason for this avoidance, moreover, only becomes clear when we take into account the distinctive role of the group—its intention to pull the child away from the mother. Thus, Kohut, who shares the classic psychoanalytic emphasis on empathic interaction between a single mother and child, cannot be invoked to rectify the deficiencies of traditional instinct theory's approach to cross-cultural data. What is new in my approach—and what is lacking in *all* contemporary schools of psychoanalytic thought—is the notion that in many cultures, groups of caretakers, acting as groups, play a fundamental role—a role that has its own character and does not simply echo that of the mother.

For example, one encounters a problematic individualism in attachment theory quite analogous to that found in instinct theory and self psychology. Ainsworth, the preeminent exponent of attachment theory in cross-cultural research, clearly allows for the possibility that children do become attached to more than one caretaker. However, her central question is whether one figure can "make up for the absence of another." Or, as she also puts it, "to what extent are attachment figures interchangeable?" (Ainsworth 1977:64)

As with the instinct theorists and the self-psychologists, then, supplementary caretakers are seen as doubles of the mother. They are never given their own distinct role as primary players in the drama of infancy.

Yet, in most non-Western cultures, as I argue here and elsewhere (Kurtz 1991), the group adopts a series of culturally distinctive and heretofore unrecognized strategies for drawing the child out of early attachments. That is, the stance of these groups to the child is important precisely because it *differs* from that of the mother. The biologically based, universalist focus of attachment theory on the role of a primary caretaker is unable to grasp this complex cultural variation in caretaking roles as they diversify over more than one figure. All it can do is attempt to spread out a single, universal attachment mode over a group. For further comments on contemporary schools of psychoanalytic thought, see the conclusion of note 3, chapter 3.

2. Luschinsky (1962:184) and Minturn (1966:118–119) report that the traditional pattern of parents focusing more attention on nieces and nephews than on their own children is gradually fading although it is still regarded as ideal. According to Minturn, these traditional patterns hold more force today for the men of the family than for the women.

On the other hand, the tendency of mothers-in-law to restrain a mother's discipline of her own child (reported by Minturn, among others) shows that the principle of joint family control over "own" parent control is still powerful (Cormack 1953:21; Luschinsky 1962:184; Minturn 1966:118; Rohner and Chaki-Sircar 1987:71; Wiser and Wiser 1963:82).

3. This myth was told to me by the priest at a Goddess shrine in Ujjain, Madhya Pradesh, the same state where Babb conducted his fieldwork (Kurtz 1990).

4. The distinction I adopt in this book between the "natural mother" and the "in-law mothers" carries with it some problems of translation. Our English terms for these Indian kin statuses embody a distinction between "biological relations"

and "legal relations" which, as Inden and Nicholas have shown (1977), is not present in Hindu India, where all family members are thought to share in the same physical substance. However, the terms "natural mother" and "in-law mothers" have the advantage of comprehensibility for a broad audience of non-specialists.

In any case, the process I argue for works—indeed works even more effectively— from the standpoint of Inden and Nicholas. Inden and Nicholas note that Bengali kin terms for members of the "maximal family" are "modified" forms of kin terms for the members of the "minimal family" (1977:84). From the standpoint of Inden and Nicholas, then, our distinction between the "natural mother" and the "in-law mothers" might better be rendered as the distinction between the "mother" and the "modified mothers." According to Inden and Nicholas, the creation of terms for the maximal family through a modification of minimal family terms emphasizes the subordination of immediate kin ties to membership in the larger family group (1977:84). In other words, the structure of the kin terminology itself emphasizes that "all the mothers are one."

At the same time, while in-marrying women of the larger family are thought to come to share in the same physical substance as other family members, the fact of marriage is known and marked through distinctions as the veiling of a family's daughters-in-law (or "modified daughters") as opposed to its unmarried daughters (not to mention the emphasis in Hinduism on the marriage ceremony itself). Thus, discarding the distinction between biological and legal kin, there nonetheless emerges a connection between the symbolism of marriage and the status of the "modified mothers." And while the in-marrying "mothers and daughters" of a family may come to share its substance, the unity of the larger family is not a simple taken-for-granted "biological" fact, but an accomplishment hard-won against the dangers posed by these in-marrying women (Bennett 1983).

6. The Durga Complex

1. Hindu concern for the "identity of the cleaner" is manifest in many contexts. Caste hierarchy is indicated by which groups remove which polluting substances. Worship is conducted by taking on the polluted leavings of the deity (Babb 1975:31–69). Hindu informants often speak of early parental care by emphasizing or comparing a parent's willingness to clean up the child's excrement (Carstairs 1967:64; Mayer 1960:218).

2. The approach taken here to the ascetic-erotic paradox of Shiva mythology differs from that of Kakar. Kakar argues that the seemingly nonerotic character of Shiva's phallic worship stems from a narcissism defensively instituted in response to the trauma of the second birth (Kakar 1978:154–160). In other words, Kakar interprets the detachment underlying Shiva's erotic activity as indicative of an insecure self-preoccupation among Hindu males. These men are preoccupied with themselves because as a result of early disappointments in their relations with their mothers, they are unable to fully trust their erotic partners. In my view, however, the detachment that undergirds Shiva's phallic prowess represents the Hindu boy's self-imposed distancing from the mother, a culturally distinctive resolution of imma-

ture attachments that makes the child's mature sexuality as a long-term member of an extended family group possible.

3. At one point Kakar does offer a psychological explanation for the benevolent endings, at least of myths he sees as depicting oedipal rivalries among males (1978:152). For Kakar, the emotional distance of Hindu fathers means that they are not seen as sources of profound or lasting aggression toward their sons. This explanation, however, clearly would not apply to myths in which goddesses, rather than gods, heal symbolic castrations since Kakar sees Hindu mothers, in contrast to fathers, as intensely involved with their children.

As I am arguing here, however, the benevolent restorations common to Hindu myths (myths involving both gods and goddesses) stem from the solution that renunciation on the way to the group represents to the rivalries that flow from a too close attachment of the son to his mother. By letting go of the mother, the son avoids (and protects his mother from) the wrath of both the in-law mothers and his father.

4. According to Goldman, Hindu myths in which heroes freely submit to their fathers, thus symbolically castrating themselves, do produce rewards for sacrifice. Yet these rewards, "are generally compensatory, as major heroes of this type are commonly excluded from the pleasures and privileges of sexuality and temporal power" (1978:363). Yet Rama, whom Goldman concedes (with unspecified qualifications) to be the most important, admired, and imitated hero of this type, is clearly not excluded from either sexuality or temporal power. On the contrary, his willing sacrifice brings genuine restoration.

5. Depictions of male rivalry in Hindu epic and myth have been treated in detail by Goldman (1978) and Ramanujan (1983). Whereas Ramanujan (like Carstairs, Kakar, and Spratt) points out the predominance of negative oedipal imagery (i.e., sexual and aggressive submission of the sons to the fathers), Goldman reveals a widespread pattern of myth in which Hindu sons aggressively attack symbolic father substitutes (for example, gurus). Goldman concedes cultural priority for myths of filial submission, but he argues that it is an error to deny the existence of positive oedipal mythology in Hinduism.

It is not difficult to reconcile the positions of Goldman and Ramanujan, even from a traditional psychoanalytic standpoint. The negative oedipal stance is defensive and thus overlays but does not eliminate positive oedipal emotions. Myths of filial submission predominate and are approved of. Myths of filial rebellion are more rare, less socially emphasized, and themselves disguise filial aggression through the use of father substitutes. All this is consistent with the notion that Hindus adopt a negative oedipal stance in a defensive retreat from positive oedipal conflicts.

However, as I am arguing here, yet another view of this situation is possible. Hindu boys do experience what we call positive oedipal rivalry with their fathers. Yet this rivalry is transcended not by retreat to negative oedipal submission, but by an advance to immersion in and empowerment by a male group. I suggest that a failure to refer symbolic action to the level of the group has resulted in a mistaken reading of the Hindu son's apparent submission as a total surrender to the individual father. Rather, such a submission is a recognition that the father embodies and is embedded in the group. Thus, the empowerment of the son is not a consolation prize for cowardly self-destruction; it is a solution wherein the son shares in the power of the group to which both he and his father belong.

While further investigation of male rivalry in Hindu family life and myth may show that the notion of a post-Durgan, male-centered complex is desirable, my current thinking is that issues of Hindu male rivalry can be properly understood under the rubric of the late Durga complex.

6. In seeing Ganesh as both castrated and hyperphallic, I depart somewhat from Courtright's important and wise study of Ganesh. Courtright draws extensively on Carstairs and Kakar, and I think because of this he overemphasizes the asexual or "castrated" aspect of Ganesh (1985:105–122). For Courtright (following Kakar), Ganesh is too close to his mother and is thus turned into a "child-ascetic-eunuch." For example, Courtright sees Ganesh's elephant trunk as a caricature of Shiva's *linga*—too flaccid, large, and out of place to be of real sexual use. Yet Leach has recently seen in Ganesh a much more paradoxical melange of ascetic and erotic characteristics (1983:259–260). For example, Leach points out a sculptural representation of Ganesh—with his trunk placed provocatively on the vagina of a goddess. In this sculpture, Ganesh's penis is erect.

Obeyesekere has recently taken issue with Leach's depiction of Ganesh (Obeyesekere 1990:105–139). For example, Obeyesekere's claim is that the erotic iconography of Ganesh is culturally peripheral in South Asia. Also, occasional reports that Ganesh has wives are said by Obeyesekere to emphasize the marriage's intellectual rather than its sexual or procreative aspects (Obeyesekere 1990:134–139).

However, while Ganesh *is* frequently portrayed as an ascetic with no wives or children or as the husband of "intelligence" herself, this is certainly not the case in the very popular mythology of Santoshi Ma. Santoshi Ma is Ganesh's daughter, and this fact is stressed in both myth and conversation. In Santoshi Ma's printed story, Ganesh is said to have two wives (whose names mean roughly "wealth and prosperity"), and the film *Jay Santoshi Ma* expands this brief comment into a lengthy birth scene. In this scene, Santoshi Ma's birth takes place when Ganesh extracts a flame from the breasts of each of his wives and combines them to produce Santoshi Ma.

Hindu mythology rarely depicts divine births as resulting from ordinary sexual intercourse. Even Ganesh's own birth as son of the phallic Shiva was not by way of intercourse. Indeed, Parvati bore Ganesh on her own. The birth of Santoshi Ma is thus entirely typical in this respect, and its special circumstances in no way obviate the myth's implication that Ganesh is a prolific father. Indeed, in the film, Santoshi Ma is created to be the sister for Ganesh's two prior sons, her older brothers. Thus, Ganesh is both erotic and ascetic.

My point, then, is that the traditional psychoanalytic portrait of Hindu boys as castrated prisoners of their mothers distorts both the situation of the child and our interpretation of the mythology that grows out of that childhood setting.

7. Clinical Psychoanalysis in India: Toward a New Reading

1. When I refer to child-rearing practices, myth, or ritual, I use the phrase "more obviously cultural." This is because I do not wish to establish a fundamental dichot-

omy between, say, the text of a myth and the record of a patient's free associations. Both of these texts are cultural, the one more obviously so than the other. The shared aspects of a popular myth are clear. The social forces behind an "individual's" free associations are less clear but no less real. Thus, as I argue below, clinical material does give us a way to approach cultural phenomena. If collective texts provide more transparent access to the patterns of culture, such access is nevertheless not theirs exclusively.

2. The approach to the psychology of the Hindu Indian ascetic suggested here contrasts radically with the position taken by Masson (1976, 1980). Masson's work possesses the twin advantages of honesty and consistency. His frank reading of the Hindu family is that it imposes "pathologically excessive restrictions" on adolescent sexuality, leading to the ascetic's bitter rejection in ironically rebellious compliance of all pleasurable connection, including the connection to the family itself (Masson 1976:624–625). Furthermore, Masson sees all ascetics as victims of child abuse or of early parental death (1976:623). From his perspective, the emotional detachment of Hindu asceticism is a defensive, masochistic flight from rage against childhood pain.

Masson's negative view of Hinduism allows him to elaborate the pathologizing tendency of psychoanalytic universalism. This taste for pathology, evident in early psychoanalytic anthropology, has been overtly shunned by contemporary psychoanalytic anthropologists, but it has not been overcome in the theory itself.

From my point of view, Masson makes important connections: the link between asceticism and the loss of a close caretaker or companion in childhood, for example. Masson's universalism and cultural preferences, however, block his recognition of the ways in which Hindu ascetics overcome these traumas in a culturally distinctive manner. Masson sees the detachment of Hindu asceticism only as a regressive and defensive flight from emotion. From my point of view, however, this detachment in its mature form signals the Hindu way of moving beyond infantile attachments and into the more mature world of the group.

It is true that the relatively traumatic childhoods of the great ascetics mark them out as, in a sense, more pathological than their Hindu brothers. On the other hand, these people are distinctive for passing through pathology, rather than being engulfed by it and for solving their conflicts in a way that holds a lesson for the larger culture. This is what distinguishes McDaniel's divine madness from ordinary madness.

The analogy here is to the shaman or the psychoanalyst many of whom are stricken with conflict and disease before they find how to overcome these through their culture's characteristic path to health. Having experienced more conflict— having moved with more struggle and awareness toward health—such people have something to offer others in the way of help and example.

3. Unfortunately, Kakar does not tell us for certain whether there were relatives living in D.'s father's home, other than the father himself. If in-law mothers were present, this may have afforded D. an opportunity, albeit limited and belated, to experience the normal Hindu Indian process of distancing from the natural mother. On the other hand, even this opportunity may have backfired, given the lack of

preparation in the vital first three years. In any case, Kakar gives no indication that anyone was present in D.'s new home besides the members of the nuclear family.

8. South Asia and Beyond: Obeyesekere and Spiro

1. While I focus my critique on Obeyesekere's recent book, *The Work of Culture*, the approach I take here is both relevant to and informed by a reading of Obeyesekere's two previous psychoanalytic books, *Medusa's Hair* and *The Cult of the Goddess Pattini*. I have already made some reference to *Medusa's Hair* in my discussion of renunciation as a defensive process (see the latter part of chapter 6). Moreover, *The Work of Culture* itself is a reflection by Obeyesekere upon his two earlier works. For example, the case of Abdin and the symbolism of Pattini, each of which I discuss below, are taken up for discussion in *The Work of Culture* directly from earlier treatments in *Medusa's Hair* and *The Cult of the Goddess Pattini*, respectively.

2. It is true that Kakar (1987) has criticized Obeyesekere for paying too little attention to postclassical psychoanalytic theory. However, Kakar and Obeyesekere remain alike both in their basic reading of the Indian situation and in their fundamental strategies for adapting psychoanalysis to cultural material.

3. This theoretical strategy is very widespread in contemporary psychoanalytic anthropology and is not at all limited to Kakar or Obeyesekere. Another example of it can be found in the recent work of Desai and Collins (1986), who approach Hinduism from the standpoint of Kohutian self-psychology. Desai and Collins apply essentially unmodified Kohutian concepts to the Indian material. However, they posit the existence of a cultural process that moderates the effect of the psychological mechanisms they uncover. With this cultural concept in place, Desai and Collins freely offer what is in fact an interpretation of Hinduism's core concepts that treats the religion as pathological. However insightful and suggestive the presentation, the fascinating links made between Kohutian and Hindu concepts of the self simply cannot be accepted in this unmodified and pathologizing form.

Specifically, Desai and Collins consider the process of empathic mirroring in childhood as Kohut has described it to be universal. Cultures are said to differ only in their ways of dealing with the challenges posed by this universal problem (1986:268–269). Expected breakdowns in empathy that are normal in the West are said to be avoided in the Hindu context, either by a high degree of responsiveness in the environment or by a unique capacity of the Hindu self to adjust to the environment (1986:270–271). It is also noted that Hindu culture "idealizes merger" rather than autonomy (1986:286). Yet the precise way in which these cultural processes work, particularly in the child-rearing situation, is never spelled out. The authors seem to have in mind a variation on the traditional psychoanalytic view of Hindu childhood as an experience of unrelieved gratification.

In any case, despite the bow to culture, the body of Desai and Collins' analysis focuses on the regressive and defensive character of Hindu religious notions of the self (1986:284–287). Classical Hindu discussions of the self are certainly not treated as culturally characteristic developmental solutions to psychic conflict. On the contrary, understood in Kohutian terms, these religious notions appear to be radical exemplifications of pathology. This is only to be expected since, despite the notion of a cultural approval of merger, Kohutian theory sees an unrelieved emphasis on merger as pathogenic.

The difficulty is that the underlying Kohutian notion of empathic mirroring upon which the analysis is based is not applicable to the Hindu Indian child-rearing situation. I have already pointed this out in some detail in my discussion of Roland's Kohutian work. Thus, Desai and Collins' bow to a cultural context of "empathic response" actually forestalls an ethnographic consideration of the situation of the Hindu Indian child along with the deeper theoretical reshaping this could prompt. That is because the goal is really the application of Kohutian theory to Hinduism, and cultural difference is referred to only insofar as it makes or appears to make conventional Kohutian interpretation possible.

As I have argued above, this illustrates that contemporary schools of psychoanalytic thought (e.g., self-psychology), no less than classical theory, yield pathology oriented results when they are applied to non-Western cultures without serious reshaping.

4. While my focus here is on the final, theoretical chapter of *Oedipus in the Trobriands*, I have elsewhere offered an interpretation of some detailed Trobriand ethnographic material (Kurtz 1991). The reader is referred to that work for a concrete application of the psychoanalytic approach put forth in this book to a non-Indian culture.

5. The recent and very valuable work of Katherine Ewing (1991) raises some of the same issues I have been discussing here in my critique of Roy and Spiro. For example, Ewing notes that the Hindu mother appears to intrude into the life of her young married son even to the extent of regulating his sexual contact with his own wife. Ewing denies, however, that such seeming maternal intrusiveness indicates a failure to achieve autonomy on the part of the son. Instead, Ewing explains the mother's enforcement of distance between husband and wife in terms of "culturally patterned" and "practical" motivations based on the need to concentrate the joint family's authority in the hands of a senior figure (1991:140).

I certainly agree with Ewing about the cultural and practical motivations behind the mother-in-law's actions. However, I strongly disagree with Ewing's argument that such actions are not also fundamentally psychological in character. To my way of thinking, Ewing creates far too sharp a dichotomy between social and intrapsychic concerns, even considering the fact that she allows for some "empirical relationship" between the two realms (1991:141). The attempt to make this distinction arises from a laudable desire to rescue South Asian cultures from the charge of pathological dependency. While Hindu mothers may closely control their children for practical and culturally shared reasons, the argument goes, those children do not necessarily fail to attain a degree of *intrapsychic* autonomy. Thus, the attribution of pathology appears to be overcome.

Ewing's position does yield a vitally important insight. She correctly uncovers signs of intrapsychic separation between Hindu children and their mothers. I think she is mistaken, however, to uncritically associate such a separation with what our Western psychological theories mean by autonomy or individuation. In my model, the Hindu child does separate from the mother, but the movement which both follows and prompts this separation is not toward individuation but toward the group.

When we understand this, it is possible to see that the mother's authority over her adult son does have a psychological dimension. As I noted in my critique of Roy, the mother's tie to her grown son depends on his having intrapsychically, in childhood, successfully transformed the natural mother into a member of the group—i.e., into an in-law mother. Moreover, the "practical" and "culturally patterned" ability of the mother-in-law to distance pairs within the joint family is at the core of this early developmental movement toward the in-law mothers. From this perspective, the mother's disregard for her child in the presence of the mother-in-law parallels the later distancing enforced by the mother-in-law on her adult son and new daughter-in-law.

The early movement of the child from the natural mother toward the collective in-law mothers also has a parallel in the shift of the young wife from her natal home to the home of her new in-laws. Again, I think Ewing correctly and insightfully shows that this shift normally works because of a prior intrapsychic separation between a girl and her mother in childhood. What Ewing misses, however, is the way in which the integration of the young wife into her new family builds upon the psychic groundwork laid by the integration of the young girl child into the group of in-law mothers. Both the separation from the mother *and* the integration into the group are *psychological* processes while also being social.

It would have been impossible to formulate the Hindu developmental psychology outlined in this book had I adopted Ewing's sharp distinction between the social and intrapsychic realm. The important point is that practices like the distancing authority of the mother-in-law in the Hindu joint family have psychological causes and consequences. Of course, such practices are also culturally patterned, but that is the point. We must not wall off these cultural patterns from psychology, but use them in order to rethink and reshape our psychology along cultural lines.

References

Ainsworth, Mary D. Salter. 1977. Attachment theory and its utility in cross-cultural research. In P. H. Leiderman, S. Tulkin, and A. Rosenfeld, eds., *Culture and Infancy: Variations in the Human Experience*, pp. 49–68. New York: Academic Press.

Allen, M. R. 1976. Kumari or "virgin" worship in Kathmandu Valley. *Contributions to Indian Sociology*, 10:293–315.

Aziz, Barbra Nimri. 1985. Review of *Dangerous Wives and Sacred Sisters: Social and Symbolic Roles of High-Caste Women in Nepal* by Lynn Bennett. *Contributions to Indian Sociology*, 19:216–220.

Babb, Lawrence A. 1970. Marriage and malevolence: The uses of sexual opposition in a Hindu pantheon. *Ethnology*, 9:137–148.

——— 1975. *The Divine Hierarchy: Popular Hinduism in Central India*. New York: Columbia University Press.

Beals, Alan R. 1962. *Gopalpur: A South Indian Village*. New York: Holt, Rinehart and Winston.

Bennett, Lynn. 1983. *Dangerous Wives and Sacred Sisters: Social and Symbolic Roles of High-Caste Women in Nepal*. New York: Columbia University Press.

Bettelheim, Bruno. 1977[1975]. *The Uses of Enchantment: The Meaning and Importance of Fairy Tales*. New York: Vintage.

Bharati, Agehananda. 1975. *The Tantric Tradition*. New York: Samuel Wiser.

Bhattacharyya, Deborah P. 1986. *Pagalami: Ethnopsychiatric Knowledge in Bengal.* Syracuse: Maxwell School of Citizenship and Public Affairs.

Bhardwaj, Surinder Mohan. 1973. *Hindu Places of Pilgrimage in India: A Study in Cultural Geography.* Berkeley: University of California Press.

Bose, Girindrasekhar. 1949. The genesis and adjustment of the Oedipus wish. *Samiksa,* 3:222–240.

Boss, Medard. 1965[1958]. *A Psychiatrist Discovers India.* London: Oswald Wolff.

Brand, Michael. 1984. An introduction to Santoshi Ma: Textual origins and media transmission. Paper presented to the 75th Annual Meeting of the American Academy of Religion, Chicago.

Brubaker, Richard L. 1983. The untamed goddesses of village India. In Carl Olson, ed., *The Book of the Goddess Past and Present: An Introduction to Her Religion,* pp. 145–160. New York: Crossroad.

Carstairs, G. Morris. 1967[1957]. *The Twice Born: A Study of a Community of High-Caste Hindus.* Bloomington: Indiana University Press.

Cormack, Margaret. 1953. *The Hindu Woman.* New York: Teachers College Columbia University.

Courtright, Paul B. 1985. *Ganesa: Lord of Obstacles, Lord of Beginnings.* New York: Oxford University Press.

Daniel, E. Valentine. 1984. *Fluid Signs: Becoming a Person the Tamil Way.* Berkeley: University of California Press.

Das, Veena. 1980. The mythological film and its framework of meaning: An analysis of *Jay Santoshi Ma. India International Centre Quarterly,* 8:43–56.

Desai, Prakash, and Alfred Collins. 1986. Selfhood in context: Some Indian solutions. In Merry I. White and Susan Pollak, eds., *The Cultural Transition: Human Experience and Social Transformation in the Third World and Japan,* pp.261–290. Boston: Routledge & Kegan Paul.

Dharap, B. V. 1983. The mythological or taking fatalism for granted. In Aruna Vasudev and Philippe Lenglet, eds., *Indian Cinema Superbazaar,* pp. 79–83. New Delhi: Vikas.

Dimmitt, Cornelia, and J. A. B. van Buitenen, eds. 1978. *Classical Hindu Mythology: A Reader in the Sanskrit Puranas.* Philadelphia: Temple University Press.

Dimock, Edward C., Jr. 1982. A theology of the repulsive: The myth of the goddess Sitala. In John Stratton Hawley and Donna Marie Wulff, eds., *The Divine Consort: Radha and the Goddesses of India,* pp. 184–203. Berkeley: Berkeley Religious Studies Series.

Dube, S. C. 1955. *Indian Village.* London: Routledge and Kegan Paul.

Dumont, Louis. 1970a[1953]. A structural definition of a folk deity of Tamil Nad: Aiyanar, the Lord. *Religion/Politics and History in India: Collected Papers in Indian Sociology,* pp. 20–32. Paris/The Hague: Mouton.

—— 1970b[1967]. The individual as an impediment to sociological comparison and Indian history. *Religion/Politics and History in India: Collected Papers in Indian Sociology,* pp. 133–150. Paris/The Hague: Mouton.

—— 1980[1966]. *Homo Hierarchicus: The Caste System and its Implications.* Chicago: University of Chicago Press.

Dundes, Alan. 1972[1962]. Earth diver: Creation of the mythopoeic male. In William A. Lessa and Evon Z. Vogt, eds., *Reader in Comparative Religion: An Anthropological Approach*, pp. 278–289.

Erikson, Erik H. 1969. *Gandhi's Truth: On the Origins of Militant Nonviolence*. New York: Norton.

Erndl, Kathleen M. 1984. The absorption of Santoshi Ma into the Panjabi Goddess cult. Paper presented to the 75th Annual Meeting of the American Academy of Religion, Chicago.

———— 1987. Victory to the mother: The Goddess cult of Northwest India. Ph.D. dissertation, University of Wisconsin-Madison.

———— 1989. Rapist or bodyguard, demon or devotee? Images of Bhairo in the mythology and cult of Vaisno Devi. In Alf Hiltebeitel, ed., *Criminal Gods and Demon Devotees: Essays on the Guardians of Popular Hinduism*, pp. 239–250. Albany: State University of New York Press.

Ewing, Katherine P. 1991. Can psychoanalytic theories explain the Pakistani woman? Intrapsychic autonomy and interpersonal engagement in the extended family. *Ethos*, 19:131–160.

Fenichel, Otto. 1945. *The Psychoanalytic Theory of Neurosis*. New York: Norton.

Freed, Ruth S., and Stanley A. Freed. 1962. Two mother goddess ceremonies of Delhi State in the great and little traditions. *Southwestern Journal of Anthropology*, 18:246–277.

Freud, Sigmund. 1946[1918]. *Totem and Taboo: Resemblances Between the Psychic Lives of Savages and Neurotics*. New York: Knopf.

———— 1961a[1927]. *The Future of an Illusion*. Garden City: Doubleday.

———— 1961b[1930]. *Civilization and its Discontents*. New York: Norton.

———— 1962[1905]. *Three Essays on the Theory of Sexuality*. New York: Basic Books.

———— 1963[1914]. On narcissism: An introduction. In Philip Rieff ed., *General Psychological Theory: Papers on Metapsychology*, pp. 56–82. New York: Collier Books.

———— 1966[1917]. *Introductory Lectures on Psychoanalysis*. New York: Norton.

Friedlander, Eva. 1985. Review of *Dangerous Wives and Sacred Sisters: Social and Symbolic Roles of High-Caste Women in Nepal* by Lynn Bennett. *The Journal of Asian Studies*, 65:160–162.

Gatwood, Lynn E. 1985. *Devi and the Spouse Goddess: Women, Sexuality, and Marriages in India*. Riverdale: The Riverdale Company.

Gold, Daniel. 1987. *The Lord as Guru: Hindu Saints in North Indian Tradition*. New York: Oxford University Press.

Goldman, Robert P. 1978. Fathers, sons, and gurus: Oedipal conflict in the Sanskrit epics. *Journal of Indian Philosophy*, 6: 325–392.

Gough, E. Kathleen. 1955. Female initiation rites on the Malabar Coast. *Journal of the Royal Anthropological Institute*, 85:45–80.

Hawley, John Stratton, in association with Shrivasta Goswami. 1981. *At Play With Krishna: Pilgrimage Dramas from Brindavan*. Princeton: Princeton University Press.

———— 1983. *Krishna: The Butter Thief.* Princeton: Princeton University Press.

Hayley, Audrey. 1980. A commensal relationship with God: The nature of the offering in Assamese Vaishnavism. In M. F. C. Bourdillon and Meyer Fortes, eds., *Sacrifice*, pp. 107–125. New York: Academic Press.

Herdt, Gilbert H. 1981. *Guardians of the Flutes: Idioms of Masculinity.* New York: McGraw Hill.

———— 1987. *The Sambia: Ritual and Gender in New Guinea.* Fort Worth: Holt, Rinehart and Winston.

Herdt, Gilbert, and Robert J. Stoller. 1990. *Intimate Communications: Erotics and the Study of Culture.* New York: Columbia University Press.

Hippler, Arthur E., L. Bryce Boyer, and Ruth M. Boyer. 1975. The psychocultural significance of the Alaska Athabascan potlatch ceremony. In Warner Muensterberger, Aron Esman, and L. Bryce Boyer, eds., *The Psychoanalytic Study of Society*, Volume 6, pp. 204–234. New York: International Universities Press.

Iltis, Linda Louise. 1985. The Swasthani Vrata: Newar women and ritual in Nepal. Ph.D. dissertation, University of Wisconsin-Madison.

Inden, Ronald B. and Ralph W. Nicholas. 1977. *Kinship in Bengali Culture.* Chicago: University of Chicago Press.

Jacobson, Doranne. 1982. Purdah and the Hindu family in central India. In Hanna Papanek and Gail Minault, eds., *Separate Worlds: Studies of Purdah in South Asia*, pp. 81–109. Columbia, MO: South Asia Books.

Kakar, Sudhir. 1978. *The Inner World: A Psycho-analytic Study of Childhood and Society in India.* Delhi: Oxford University Press.

———— 1979. A case of depression. *Samiksa*, 33:61–71.

———— 1980. Observations on the "oedipal alliance" in a patient with a narcissistic personality disorder. *Samiksa*, 34:47–53.

———— 1982a. *Shaman's Mystics and Doctors: A Psychoanalytic Inquiry into India and its Healing Traditions.* New York: Knopf.

———— 1982b. Fathers and sons: An Indian experience. In Stanley H. Cath, Alan R. Gurwitt, and John Munder Ross, eds., *Father and Child: Developmental and Clinical Perspectives*, pp.417–423. Boston: Little, Brown.

———— 1985. Psychoanalysis and non-Western cultures. *International Review of Psycho-Analysis*, 12:441–448.

———— 1987. Psychoanalysis and anthropology: A renewed alliance. *Contributions to Indian Sociology*, 21:85–88.

———— 1989. The maternal-feminine in Indian psychoanalysis. *International Review of Psycho-Analysis*, 16:355–362.

———— 1990a. Stories from Indian psychoanalysis: Context and text. In James W. Stigler, Richard A. Shweder, and Gilbert Herdt, eds., *Cultural Psychology: Essays on Comparative Human Development*, pp.427–445. Cambridge: Cambridge University Press.

———— 1990b. *Intimate Relations: Exploring Indian Sexuality.* Chicago: University of Chicago Press.

Kakar, Sudhir, and John Munder Ross. 1987. *Tales of Love Sex and Danger.* New York: Basil Blackwell.

Kapur, Anuradha. 1985. Actors, pilgrims, kings, and gods: The Ramlila at Ramnagar. *Contributions to Indian Sociology*, 19:57–74.

Kardiner, Abram. 1945. *The Psychological Frontiers of Society*. New York: Columbia University Press.

Khare, R. S. 1982. From *Kanya* to *Mata*: Aspects of the cultural language of kinship in north India. In Akos Ostor, Lina Fruzzetti, and Steve Barnett, eds., *Concepts of Person: Kinship, Caste, and Marriage in India*, pp. 143–171. Cambridge, MA: Harvard University Press.

Kinsley, David R. 1975. *The Sword and the Flute: Kali and Krsna, Dark Visions of the Terrible and the Sublime in Hindu Mythology*. Berkeley: University of California Press.

——— 1977. "The death that conquers death": Dying to the world in medieval Hinduism. In Frank E. Reynolds and Earle E. Waugh, eds., *Religious Encounters with Death: Insights from the History and Anthropology of Religions*, pp. 97–108. University Park, PA: Pennsylvania State University Press.

——— 1982. *Hinduism: A Cultural Perspective*. Engelwood Cliffs: Prentice-Hall.

——— 1986. *Hindu Goddesses: Visions of the Divine Feminine in the Hindu Religious Tradition*. Berkeley: University of California Press.

——— 1989. *The Goddesses' Mirror: Visions of the Divine from East and West*. Albany: State University of New York Press.

Kirschner, Suzanne R. 1990. The assenting echo: Anglo-American values in contemporary psychoanalytic developmental psychology. *Social Research*, 57:821–857.

——— 1991. American cultural values in contemporary psychoanalytic discourse. Paper presented to the 11th Annual Meeting of the Division of Psychoanalysis (39) of the American Psychological Association, Chicago.

Klein, Melanie. 1975a[1932]. *The Psychoanalysis of Children*. New York: Dell.

——— 1975b. *Envy and Gratitude and Other Works 1946–1963*. New York: Dell.

——— 1975c. *Love, Guilt, and Reparation and Other Works 1921–1945*. New York: Dell.

Kohut, Heinz. 1971. *The Analysis of the Self: A Systematic Approach to the Psychoanalytic Treatment of Narcissistic Personality Disorders*. New York: International Universities Press.

Kolenda, Pauline. 1984. Woman as tribute, woman as flower: Images of "woman" in weddings in north and south India. *American Ethnologist*, 11:98–117.

Kondos, Vivienne. 1986. Images of the fierce goddess and portrayals of Hindu women. *Contributions to Indian Sociology*, 20:173–197.

Kurtz, Stanley N. 1984. The goddesses' dispute in *Jay Santoshi Ma*: A mythological film in its cultic context. Paper presented to the 75th Annual Meeting of the American Academy of Religion, Chicago.

——— 1990. A goddess dissolved: Toward a new psychology of Hinduism. Ph.D. dissertation, Cambridge, MA: Harvard University.

——— 1991. Polysexualization: A new approach to Oedipus in the Trobriands. *Ethos*, 19:68–101.

Laplanche, J., and J.-B. Pontalis. 1973[1967]. *The Language of Psychoanalysis*. New York: Norton.

Leach, Edmund R. 1967[1958]. Magical hair. In John Middleton, ed., *Myth and Cosmos: Readings in Mythology and Symbolism*, pp. 77–108. Austin: University of Texas Press.

——— 1983. The gatekeepers of heaven: Anthropological aspects of grandiose architecture. *Journal of Anthropological Research*, 39:243–264.

LeVine, Robert A., and Barbara B. LeVine. 1966[1963]. *Nyansongo: A Gusii Community in Kenya*. New York: John Wiley.

LeVine, Robert A. 1977. Child rearing as cultural adaptation. In P. Herbert Leiderman, Steven R. Tulkin, and Anne Rosenfeld, eds., *Culture and Infancy: Variations in the Human Experience*, pp. 15–27. New York: Academic Press.

Levi-Strauss, Claude. 1963[1955]. The structural study of myth. *Structural Anthropology*, pp. 206–231. New York: Basic Books.

Levy, Robert I. 1973. *Tahitians: Mind and Experience in the Society Islands*. Chicago: University of Chicago Press.

Long, J. Bruce. 1977. Death as a necessity and a gift in Hindu mythology. In Frank E. Reynolds and Earle E. Waugh, eds. *Religious Encounters with Death: Insights from the History and Anthropology of Religions*, pp. 73–96. University Park, PA: Pennsylvania State University Press.

Luschinsky, Mildred Stroop. 1962. The life of women in a village of north India: A study of role and status. Ph.D. dissertation, Cornell University.

Maduro, Renaldo. 1976. *Artistic Creativity in a Brahmin Painter Community*. Berkeley: Center for South and Southeast Asia Studies, University of California.

Malinowski, Bronislaw. 1985[1927]. *Sex and Repression in Savage Society*. Chicago: University of Chicago Press.

——— 1987[1929]. *The Sexual Life of Savages in North-Western Melanesia*. Boston: Beacon Press.

Mandelbaum, David G. 1970. *Society in India: Volume One, Continuity and Change*. Berkeley: University of California Press.

——— 1988. *Women's Seclusion and Men's Honor: Sex Roles in North India, Bangladesh, and Pakistan*. Tucson: University of Arizona Press.

Marglin, Frederique Apffel. 1985. Female sexuality in the Hindu world. In Clarissa W. Atkinson, Constance H. Buchanan, and Margaret R. Miles, eds., *Immaculate and Powerful: The Female in Sacred Image and Social Reality*, pp. 39–60. Boston: Beacon Press.

Masson, J. Moussaieff. 1976. The psychology of the ascetic. *Journal of Asian Studies*, 35:611–625.

——— 1980. *The Oceanic Feeling: The Origins of Religious Sentiment in Ancient India*. Dordrecht (Holland)/Boston (U.S.A.): Reidel Publishing.

Mayer, Adrian. 1960. *Caste and Kinship in Central India: A Village and its Region*. Berkeley: University of California Press.

——— 1981. Public service and individual merit in a town of central India. In Adrian Mayer, ed., *Culture and Morality: Essays in Honour of Christoph von Furer-Haimendorf*, pp. 153–173. Delhi: Oxford University Press.

McDaniel, June. 1989. *The Madness of the Saints: Ecstatic Religion in Bengal.* Chicago: University of Chicago Press.

Mencher, Joan. 1963. Growing up in South Malabar. *Human Organization,* 22:54–65.

Minturn, Leigh, and William W. Lambert. 1964. *Mothers of Six Cultures: Antecedents of Child Rearing.* New York: John Wiley.

Minturn, Leigh, and John T. Hitchcock. 1966[1963] *The Rajputs of Khalapur, India.* New York: John Wiley.

Murphy, Gardner, with Lois Barclay Murphy. 1953. *In the Minds of Men: A Study of Human Behavior and Social Tension in India.* New York: Basic Books.

Narain, Dhirendra. 1964. Growing up in India. *Family Process,* 3:127–154.

Nicholas, Ralph W. 1982. The village mother in Bengal. In James Preston, ed., *Mother Worship: Theme and Variations,* pp.192–209. Chapel Hill: University of North Carolina Press.

Nichter, Mimi, and Mark Nichter. 1987. A tale of Simeon: Reflections on raising a child while conducting fieldwork in rural south India. In Joan Cassel, ed., *Children in the Field: Anthropological Experiences,* pp. 65–89. Philadelphia: Temple University Press.

Obeyesekere, Gananath. 1981. *Medusa's Hair: An Essay on Personal Symbols and Religious Experience.* Chicago: University of Chicago Press.

——— 1984. *The Cult of the Goddess Pattini.* Chicago: University of Chicago Press.

——— 1990. *The Work of Culture: Symbolic Transformation in Psychoanalysis and Anthropology.* Chicago: University of Chicago Press.

O'Flaherty, Wendy Doniger. 1973. *Asceticism and Eroticism in the Mythology of Siva.* Delhi: Oxford University Press.

——— 1980. *Women, Androgynes, and Other Mythical Beasts.* Chicago: University of Chicago Press.

O'Flaherty, Wendy Doniger, ed. 1975. *Hindu Myths: A Sourcebook Translated from the Sanskrit.* Baltimore: Penguin Books.

Padoux, Andre. 1986. Hindu Tantrism. In Mircea Eliade, ed., *The Encyclopedia of Religion,* 14:274–280. New York: Macmillan.

Pai, Anant, T. D'Rosario, and C. M. Vitankar. 1979. *Kannappa: The Devotee Who Offered His Eyes to Lord Shiva.* Bombay: Amar Chitra Katha, India Book House Education Trust.

Parin, Paul, Fritz Morgenthaler, and Goldy Parin-Matthey. 1980[1971]. *Fear Thy Neighbor as Thyself: Psychoanalysis and Society Among the Anyi of West Africa.* Chicago: University of Chicago Press.

Partin, Harry B. 1986. Paradise. In Mircea Eliade, ed., *The Encyclopedia of Religion,* 11:184–189. New York: Macmillan.

Paul, Robert A. 1984. Review of *Dangerous Wives and Sacred Sisters: Social and Symbolic Roles of High-Caste Women in Nepal* by Lynn Bennett. *American Anthropologist,* 86:1000–1001.

Pocock, David F. 1961. Psychological approaches and judgments of reality. *Contributions to Indian Sociology,* 5:44–77.

———— 1973. *Mind, Body, and Wealth: A Study of Belief and Practice in an Indian Village*. Totowa: Rowman and Littlefield.

Poffenberger, Thomas. 1981. Child rearing and social structure in rural India: Toward a cross-cultural definition of child abuse and neglect. In Jill E. Korbin, ed., *Child Abuse and Neglect: Cross-Cultural Perspectives*, pp. 71–95. Berkeley: University of California Press.

Ramanujam, B. K. 1986. Social change and personal crisis: A view from an Indian practice. In Merry I. White and Susan Pollak, eds., *The Cultural Transition: Human Experience and Social Transformation in the Third World and Japan*, pp. 65–86. Boston: Routledge & Kegan Paul.

Ramanujan, A. K. 1983. The Indian Oedipus. In Lowell Edmunds and Alan Dundes, eds., *Oedipus: A Folklore Casebook*, pp.234–261. New York: Garland Publishing.

Rohner, Ronald P., and Manjusri Chaki-Sircar. 1987. Caste differences in perceived maternal acceptance in West Bengal, India. *Ethos*, 15:406–425.

———— 1988. *Women and Children in a Bengali Village*. Hanover: University Press of New England.

Roland, Alan. 1988. *In Search of Self in India and Japan: Toward a Cross-Cultural Psychology*. Princeton: Princeton University Press.

Roy, Manisha. 1972. *Bengali Women*. Chicago: University of Chicago Press.

———— 1975. The Oedipus complex and the Bengali family in India (a study of father-daughter relations in Bengal). In Thomas R. Williams, ed., *Psychological Anthropology*, pp. 123–134. The Hague: Mouton.

Sears, Robert R., Elanor E. Macomby, and Harry Levin. 1976[1957]. *Pattern of Child Rearing*. Stanford: Stanford University Press.

Segal, Hanna. 1964. *Introduction to the Work of Melanie Klein*. New York: Basic Books.

Seymour, Susan. 1971. Patterns of child rearing in a changing Indian town: Sources and expressions of dependence and independence. Ph.D. dissertation, Harvard University.

———— 1975. Child rearing in India: A case study in change and modernization. In T. R. Williams, ed., *Socialization and Communication in Primary Groups*, pp.1–58. The Hague: Mouton.

———— 1976. Caste/class and child rearing in a changing Indian town. *American Ethnologist*, 3:783–796.

———— 1983. Household structure and status and expressions of affect in India. *Ethos*, 11:263–277.

———— 1989. Review of *Women's Seclusion and Men's Honor: Sex Roles in North India, Bangladesh, and Pakistan* by David G. Mandelbaum. *American Anthropologist*, 91:225.

Shengold, Leonard. 1988. *Halo in the Sky: Observations on Anality and Defense*. New York: Guilford Press.

Sinha, T. C. 1966. Development of psychoanalysis in India. *International Journal of Psychoanalysis*, 47:427–439.

Spratt, Philip. 1977[1966]. *Hindu Culture and Personality: A Psychoanalytic Study*. Bombay: Manaktalas.

Spiro, Melford E. 1982. *Oedipus in the Trobriands*. Chicago: University of Chicago Press.

———— 1987[1965]. Religious systems as culturally constituted defense mechanisms. In Benjamin Kilborne and L. L. Langness, eds., *Culture and Human Nature: The Theoretical Papers of Melford Spiro*, pp. 145–160. Chicago: University of Chicago Press.

Sundararajan, K. R. 1974. The orthodox philosophical systems. In Frederik H. Holk, ed., *Death and Eastern Thought: Understanding Death in Eastern Religions and Philosophies*, pp. 97–113. Nashville: Abingdon Press.

Surya, N. C. 1969. Ego structure in the Hindu joint family: Some considerations. In William Caudill and Tsung-yi Lin, eds., *Mental Health Research in Asia and the Pacific*, pp. 381–392. Honolulu: East-West Center Press.

Tober, Lina M., and Stanley Lusby. 1986. Heaven and hell. In Mircea Eliade, ed., *The Encyclopedia of Religion*, 6:237–243. New York: Macmillan.

Trawick, Margaret. 1990. *Notes on Love in a Tamil Family*. Berkeley: University of California Press.

Vatuk, Sylvia. 1982. Purdah revisited: A comparison of Hindu and Muslim interpretations of the cultural meaning of purdah in South Asia. In Hana Papanek and Gail Minault, eds., *Separate Worlds: Studies of Purdah in South Asia*, pp. 54–78. Columbia, MO: South Asia Books.

Wadley, Susan Snow. 1975. *Shakti: Power in the Conceptual Structure of Karimpur Religion*. Chicago: The Department of Anthropology, University of Chicago.

Whiting, Beatrice B., and John W. M. Whiting. 1975. *Children of Six Cultures: A Psycho-Cultural Analysis*. Cambridge, MA: Harvard University Press.

Winnicott, Donald W. 1964. *The Child, the Family, and the Outside World*. New York: Penguin Books.

Wiser, William, and Charlotte Wiser. 1963(1930). *Behind Mud Walls: 1930–1960*. Berkeley: University of California Press.

Yalman, Nur. 1963. On the purity of women in the castes of Ceylon and Malabar. *Journal of the Royal Anthropological Institute*, 93 (part 1):25–58.

Index